ADULT
CHILDREN
OF
ALCOHOLICS
REMEMBER

ADULT CHILDREN OF ALCOHOLICS

REMEMBER

TRUE STORIES OF ABUSE AND RECOVERY BY ACOAS

E. NELSON HAYES
EDITOR

Harmony Books   New York

"Ghost of My Father" originally appeared
in slightly different form
in the *Worcester Telegram.*

Published by Harmony Books, a division of Crown Publishers, Inc.,
225 Park Avenue South, New York, New York 10003

HARMONY and colophon are trademarks of Crown Publishers, Inc.

Manufactured in the United States of America

Designed by Shari de Miskey

Library of Congress Cataloging-in-Publication Data

Adult children of alcoholics remember / edited by E. Nelson Hayes.
 1. Adult children of alcoholics—United States—Case studies.
 2. Codependence (Psychology)—United States—Case studies.
3. Adult children of alcoholics—Rehabilitation—United States—Case
studies. I. Hayes, E. Nelson (Eugene Nelson).
HU5132.A29   1989
362.2′92—dc19   89-1751
CIP

ISBN 0-517-57207-9

1 3 5 7 9 10 8 6 4 2

First Edition

FOR ALL THE CHILDREN

Contents

Contents

Contents

Preface

When concern about alcoholism was renewed in the 1930s following the fiasco of national prohibition, the focus was on the suffering alcoholics. Gradually the work of scientists in medicine and allied disciplines revealed and taught and increasingly persuaded that alcoholism is a disease and that alcoholics are sick victims of their disablement. Slowly, organizations were formed, laws were framed, and facilities were opened to offer humane sympathy and to provide medical and psychological treatment.

In that progressive era, the attention of the public and of professionals was so firmly fixed on the alcoholic that the "other victims" of the disease all but escaped notice. Were there disgraced parents? Too bad! Were there suffering wives? Too bad! Were they not sometimes causers and facilitators? Were there suffering children? Too bad! Their suffering was all too inevitable, and one could only hope they would outgrow it.

Only relatively late did it become apparent that multitudes of children of alcoholics did not in fact outgrow their unlucky childhood. In part, this recognition developed from the discovery of an extraordinary fact. Considering the deprivations and sufferings these children experienced from the alcoholism of their parents, one would expect them almost universally to shun alcohol. The opposite is the reality. The children of alcoholics tend, statistically more frequently than others, to become alcoholics!

Some of this pattern may be a genetic phenomenon. While alcoholism is not a disease that can be inherited like, say, hemophilia, there may be a certain combination of genes that renders some people more susceptible to either alcoholism itself or, more likely, to addictiveness. In any case, the recognition of the increased frequency of alcoholism among the children of alcoholics at last called attention to them as victims. Their special disadvantages, their special sufferings, and their special needs for help and treatment have now come to wider public attention.

How can this fantastic phenomenon—that the children of alcoholics should be more likely to become alcoholics than to shun alcohol—be understood?

In many laboratories, efforts have been under way during the past twenty years to discover some biological cause, but, so far, without success. I think that a specific answer will be found, not in the laboratory, but in the natural phenomena of the circumstances of childhood upbringing. I think the answer will be found in the study of cases, in the reading of the life events that mold the fate of the children.

Here, then, are seventeen different real-life stories, told from the inside, told from painful remembrances. These adult children of alcoholics give in their own words histories more revealing than the mechanical readings from countless test tubes and electroencephalograms. These are stories of how the children of alcoholics, in quite different circumstances, grow up and how many of them become alcoholics, and some addicts to other drugs. Here is how it happens.

And yet—and yet—it isn't all so one-sided. A child of alcoholics can become what one would expect, an abstainer, and even a moderate drinker, and this phenomenon too is demonstrated in these stories gathered by the editor.

Wisely, he has let his friends tell their stories in their own words. So there are seventeen different tones and feelings in this collection. Two wonderful characteristics in them that I especially enjoy are the obvious honesty and the consistent literacy. But most important and valuable in this work, to me as a student of alcoholism for more than fifty years, is the beginning of insight into the strange process of becoming a child of alcoholic parents, and surviving!

I am reminded of the dramatic series of mid-nineteenth-century sketches by the great English satirical artist George Cruikshank, titled *The Drunkard's Children*.* In eight vivid scenes those unfortunates move to their early, ill-fated ends. The verbal sketches in the present book show indeed that such children are specially endangered, but show too that now there is help and hope.

This is a book of true stories. Though they read like fiction, sometimes like fantasy, they offer a gift of understanding of a segment of real life in our time.

Mark Keller
Brookline, Massachusetts

EDITOR'S NOTE: Mark Keller has worked for more than fifty years in the field of alcoholism. He has given lectures and seminars at Yale, Columbia, Rutgers, UCLA, Brandeis, and other universities; and in Brazil, Canada, Israel, England, Japan, and other countries. He has edited the *Journal of American Studies on Alcohol* and *DATA* magazine, contributed to the *Britannica* and *Americana* encyclopedias, and coauthored several books and written more than 200 articles.

*Reproduced, with my introduction, in the *Quarterly Journal of Studies on Alcohol*, Vol. 5, No. 3, pp. 483–504, 1944.

Introduction

E. Nelson Hayes

Collected here are the stories of seventeen survivors. A folklorist, an artist, two college students, a housewife, and all the others are adult children of alcoholics. They tell of their experiences growing up in a dysfunctional family with at least one alcoholic parent, how they believe these experiences affected them, and how they have progressed toward adulthood.

The origins of the book go back some years. I had long thought of writing an account of my growing up in the home of a father addicted to both alcohol and morphine. I hoped that by doing so I might clarify for myself the effects of that experience on my adult life. Yet when I tried to write the story, I found the task impossible—the memories I brought up were much too painful to deal with.

Later, when I sensed that two of my children might be heading down the long road of alcoholism, I debated with myself whether to tell them something of my own experiences with their grandfather and of my own life as an alcoholic. But my deep reluctance to admit and express feelings and to expose intimate details of my life prevented me from speaking frankly to them.

Instead, I returned to the idea of writing my experiences. Over many months, I finally completed "Ghost of My Father." Writing it was one of the toughest experiences of my life, yet also one of the most therapeutic and rewarding. I felt I was reaching out not only to my own children, but also to the many other men and women whom I knew to be haunted by similar experiences.

In May 1987, my piece appeared in the magazine section of the Sunday *Worcester Telegram*. When I first read it in print, my reactions were strong, confusing, contradictory. I had understood that writing it had been another step toward recovery both as an alcoholic and as the son of an addict. But why had I allowed publication of such intimate details of my life, my feelings, my thoughts? And, at the insistence of the editor, signed the piece?

In time, the answer came strong and clear. Publishing did mean sharing with others, helping others as I would be helped myself. The response from readers echoed that belief. As one reader wrote me: "We have a relationship with you, if only through your byline."

I had given much thought to the issue of anonymity. I drank for years, quite publicly, and caused great harm both to others and to myself. I would not now hide my druken alter ego, deny my past guilt, and conceal my means of being helped by writing under an assumed name.

Yet anonymity is a personal choice. It permits many people to say what otherwise they would not. Most contributors to this volume are anonymous or pseudonymous. A few write under their own names.

Readers of my account, several of my friends, and others agreed to write for this book. The contributions came in slowly, over the next year. Without exception, the authors found writing their autobiographies extremely difficult and painful. One made three tries at it before settling on an approach that satisfied him. Yet all reported, once the task was completed, the same catharsis I had experienced.

In editing their texts, I was as scrupulous as possible not to influence the contributors by my own feelings and thoughts. I wanted the book to reflect many different viewpoints, not solely that of Al-Anon or the organization ACOA or a particular "school" or practice of psychologists or sociologists.

These and other groups and individuals have done much in

recent years in gaining public recognition of the so-called ACOA syndrome—a common set of character traits and defensive postures assumed by some adult children of alcoholics. They have also helped in providing the understanding and support that many ACOAs need. For these accomplishments they are to be much praised.

But merely listing traits common to many ACOAs can be limiting. The personal recollections that make up this collection do cover the gamut of recognized symptoms—guilt, fear, and low self-esteem, for example—but none represents a "typical case," for there is none. Alcoholism affects every person differently, and each account here is an individual human story.

As their stories differ, so also do their backgrounds, from wealth to poverty, from violence to passivity, from sensitivity to callousness. Their present lives are equally varied, not only in occupation but also in marital status, in attendance at self-help groups or individual therapy, and in their sense of recovering from the effects of being ACOAs.

The primary theme and purpose of this book is that the ACOA must rethink his or her past and develop new ways of thinking and feeling about the present. In recovery, ACOAs learn to accept the truth about themselves. They learn to be responsible for their own behavior, rather than continuing to blame the past behavior of others. They learn to set practical goals for themselves. They learn to forgive themselves and others. In sum, they break the destructive habits and patterns acquired during the years in the dysfunctional home of the alcoholic and acquire new ones that are life-sustaining.

That has been our road toward recovery and freedom.

GHOST OF
MY FATHER

E. Nelson Hayes

My father died when I was fifteen years old. I can remember exactly where I was at that moment: playing horseshoes next door in a small pine grove made fragrant by the heat of a July morning. My mother called softly, and I ignored her; loudly, and I ran to our cottage. She embraced me and said he had passed on.

For years I felt guilty that I had been enjoying myself when he died, an oppression compounded by all the shame and anger I held because he was addicted both to alcohol and to morphine. I believed that he could, if he chose, abstain from both; go to work; and be a man, not the helpless, fragile figure lying all day in bed, falling asleep with a lighted cigarette between yellowed fingers, who now, after three months of agony from intestinal cancer, was dead.

Only years later did I mention these feelings to my mother. Mostly we did not talk about such matters, both of us living in bondage to a Boston Brahmin tradition that forbade the expression of emotion.

"Oh, no!" she told me. "You were in your room crying when he died."

Where is the truth? Was she trying to assuage my guilt by

lying? Or perhaps did we both distort the past, each for a different reason?

For this and other confusions, I later sought professional help in order to reveal the past, layer by layer, like an archaeologist uncovering a buried life. I then believed in that help. Most psychologists taught that through hypnosis, or drugs like sodium pentothal, or psychotherapy, especially psychoanalysis, the troubled among us could recall the past exactly, and then be relieved of it.

Now they—and so we—know better. Memory is transformed by fantasy and desire. The mind erases some recollections and distorts others before they can become a safe and useful residue in the permanent memory. We hope to remember only what will not destroy us.

I remember that when I was fourteen, I asked my father to teach me to play chess. He refused, remarking that I would become obsessed with the game. That was the winter of 1934–35. Prohibition had been repealed, so my father no longer had to brew his terrible-tasting beer in the cellar. I had sipped it once, spat it out, and supposed only someone as odd as he could like it. I do not remember, perhaps because I did not see, his drinking any other alcohol in those days.

Half a mile away, a roadhouse had opened; my father was an old friend and a favored customer of the proprietor. Across the street lived the proprietor's brother, a beefy Irishman of bloated face, who was a traveling salesman for a liquor company. He agreed to teach me to play chess. I studied every chess book in the local public library and played with every opponent I could find— including the secretary at the YMCA, my one contact with religion. As my father had predicted, I became obsessed with the game. Soon the salesman and I were equals.

One hot July evening, he and I played a long, hard game while he worked away at a bottle of whiskey and I nursed a ginger ale. His wife, a lovely young woman of French background, kept calling from upstairs, "When are you coming to bed, honey?" Finally she came halfway down the steps to where I could see her, in net pajamas with nothing underneath: my first glimpse of an almost naked woman, nipples jutting and pubic hair apparent. When her husband saw her, the game came to an abrupt end as he made a stupid move.

Reality or reverie? I cannot tell even now as I call up the image of her figure. Whatever the truth, the constellation of that moment was fixed—chess, liquor, sex, books.

Books had a special meaning for they had long been for me a means of living with my parents, which I had not done for the first seven years of my life.

I was born in 1920, while my parents were living in a residential hotel in Salem, Massachusetts. At six months old I was farmed out to a family I now do not remember at all. Other foster families followed, but I remember almost nothing of those years either: a rubber-tire swing in a dirt backyard, a strange new bed under which I saw lint and reported it to Mother, a near drowning when I was tossed into the ocean and told to swim.

My mother visited me every Saturday for an hour or two, usually with a gift: the first radio on the block, a tricycle, a ball. She spanked me only once. I had rampaged through the neighborhood and tipped over every garbage can. She might have done better to ask me why I was so angry.

Every now and again I stayed overnight with my parents at the hotel; they had a sitting room, bedroom, pullman kitchen, and bath. My mother prepared dinner in a pressure cooker. As a treat, my father would sometimes take me to a nearby diner. While he talked in low voice to the other men, I gorged on pea soup and chocolate pudding—I still have a fondness for both.

I went to first grade in a brick schoolhouse a block away from the foster house where I lived. I evidently learned nothing because I failed that year and was kept back. My mother and father must have been desperate when they realized that I could read not a single word, so they rented half a house in Salem Willows, and that June I moved in with them. Real memory now begins.

They explained that I had not lived with them earlier because they believed my father had tuberculosis. However, his stay at a sanatorium had convinced the doctors he did not have TB—only a very severe case of bronchial asthma. Years later I would develop the same symptoms, aggravated by heavy smoking and probably by emotional factors. Since then I have long questioned why I did not live with them those early years. Were my father's addictions out of control? Or was he engaged in some illicit doings? My mother's brother told me many years later that my father ran booze out of Canada, but I could not imagine that frail figure engaged in such a hazardous business.

That first summer my parents taught me words, then sentences, by reading Stevenson's *Treasure Island* aloud, finger following text, while I looked on and listened. When I entered the one-room schoolhouse that fall, I was put in the second grade. Although I do not recall thinking it, I surely had learned my first great lesson with my parents: Read and I would be rewarded by living with them.

That summer was a great joy to me. My father knew every carny on the boardwalk: I had free rides on the merry-go-round, free passage on the little excursion boat to Marblehead, even free candy and ice cream. On clear evenings, after my mother returned from work as an office manager in a Peabody shoe factory, the two of us, and sometimes my father also, would walk to a small, isolated beach. There she sketched scenes in charcoal, my father read a magazine, and I would run over the sand, skim flat pebbles across the harbor water, gather seaweed and shells, build castles.

What my father did I had no idea. Other fathers went to work in the morning. Mine did not, but every few days he would take the trolley to Salem and return two or three hours later without explanation.

One afternoon during the fall of my first year with my parents, I came home from school and found turmoil. A strange odor of medicine permeated the kitchen, my mother was in tears, and soon I discovered my father was in bed, the doctor ministering to him. He had gone to the horse races at Topsfield Fair, and the wooden stand he was sitting on had collapsed. He had broken every rib on his left side and suffered other injuries. Now during the week when my mother was at work, I had to nurse him and wait on him at lunch hour and after school. He had always been fragile, but now his physical condition deteriorated, the bronchitis becoming worse, the headaches more excruciating, the constipation more in need of relief. It occurred to me something was not right, but I never asked questions. Only years later could I assign some of his symptoms to morphine.

The winter was long and cold, nor'easters bursting across the narrow peninsula, snow piling the gulleys and fields, waves pounding the beaches. Before dinner I would go into the parlor, closed off to save heat, and listen to "Jack Armstrong, All-American Boy." Why wasn't I like him?

We spent the next summer there also, then moved to a tiny house on a side street off the common in Salem, the Witch City, where my mother's folks had settled in the 1630s.

I went to a grimy neighborhood school. That winter I had the same nightmare again and again. At an intersection off the far end of the common was the statue of a pilgrim in wide-brimmed, floppy hat and long cloak. In my dream, he would leave the high stone pedestal and walk toward me at the other end of the common, growing more menacing with each step, then turning into a witch. He/she never reached me because I would begin to scream. My parents would get me on my feet, walk me, wash my face with a cold, wet towel, and gradually I would wake up.

Now the Great Depression had set in. My mother became very ill with impacted wisdom teeth and was told by the doctor that to recover she must live in the country. We moved to North Beverly, a semirural community. My parents had "bought" the customers of a kennel business run by an English couple. We had the chicken coops converted to runs and boxes, hung a sign by the road, and waited for business. I remember coming home from school one afternoon to great celebration—we had our first dog to board, at three dollars a week.

My mother and I did pretty much all the physical work, Father being too weak most of the time to help. I cleaned the kennel boxes and runs, fed the dogs, mowed the lawn, shoveled the snow, buried the dog shit and the cardboard containers of the heavy sputum my father coughed up, burned the trash.

I was ashamed of that life. I resented having to tend the dogs and their needs. I rarely had friends to the house because I feared they would see my father, in his bathrobe, unsteadily getting coffee or Bromo Seltzer in the kitchen of our small house, or suffering one of his coughing fits, which could be quite frightening. Charity comes hard to the young. Looking back, I am now ashamed of my shame.

But school was fun, and I learned well. On the way home to chores, I sometimes stopped for scrub football or baseball. There was great skating on Wenham Lake. I earned money by making Christmas wreaths, refinishing and caning chairs, selling muffins with my friend Dan. I joined the Boy Scouts and went to camp in New Hampshire several summers.

We baked beans every Friday, made doughnuts and bread, and canned vegetables I grew in a small lot. There was much work, but later I would be grateful for it—I learned the Protestant work ethic without attending church and later felt compelled to work despite the numerous benders in the long years of my second marriage.

The land meant much to me—two and a half acres, mostly pine trees, from the highway to the B & M Railroad tracks, the north boundary defined by a low stone wall marking the Beverly-Wenham line. Our first fall there, we contracted for half the wood we had from the pine trees in back. We burned the other half and half a ton of coal that winter. As the scrub replaced the trees, I looked for spring flowers, chewed new grass, and in the fall watched for deer.

Another great love was the sea. I finally learned to swim when I was about twelve, and every fine summer afternoon thereafter, when work was done, I cycled to the beach. I would dream of the sea captains, many my ancestors, who had sailed from Salem Harbor and returned with the riches of the Far East. Whatever spiritual feelings I had were bound to the sea and to the land and to the moon and stars of twilight.

Those feelings would soon be strengthened by poetry and classical music. I read as much as possible—orgies of Jules Verne, Alexandre Dumas, Sir Walter Scott, Sir Arthur Conan Doyle, both his science fiction and the Sherlock Holmes stories. Once a week my mother and I drove to the Beverly Public Library and checked out armloads of books. Through her loans I began reading anthropology, archaeology, psychology. And with a friend up the street, I read history and biography. When a sophomore in high school, I was told by my English teacher to read the poetry of Sara Teasdale. Her lyrics appealed to my morbid adolescence. I went on to Keats, Shelley, Whitman. Classical music came to me one Sunday afternoon. I had returned from skating and was so tired I simply listened to what my mother had on the radio. It was Tchaikovsky's Sixth Symphony, and I was hooked for life.

At home we rarely talked about religion. My mother read the Bible by the light of her own conscience. My father read *Billboard* and *The Saturday Evening Post*. I read everything I could get my hands on, except the Bible. We did, however, try Christian Science in the hope it would help my father's many illnesses. It didn't—my first and last disappointment with God.

We were a singularly unemotional and uncommunicative family. Feelings were seldom expressed openly. I never saw my mother and father touch except for a hello or good-bye kiss on the cheek. Not surprisingly, I could not confess my feelings to others, but within me anger and resentment boiled. Once I even tried to burn down the kennels, but immediately repented and ran to the house yelling "Fire! Fire!" The firemen quickly extinguished the grass I had torched.

Much of the time I was diffident, withdrawn, often silent. I had two or three close friends during high school. With girls I was abnormally shy. During my senior year, I went for a walk every Sunday afternoon with the pert, redheaded daughter of the secretary at the YMCA; only now and again was I bold enough to hold her hand. On a May afternoon, as we sat on high rocks overlooking a lovely valley, she told me we could no longer walk together. I was stunned. "Why not?" She then told me she was pregnant and was marrying immediately after graduation.

Sex was furtive, looking at what were the most modest of pinup magazines, skimming books for references to bosoms and hips, and of course masturbating. I felt as guilty about sex then as I would later about alcoholic drinking. And in time it would not escape me that drinking in our society is generally seen as macho, an assertion of masculine aggression and superiority, yet is also a displacement of sex itself as the alcohol breeds temporary and sometimes complete impotence.

So far as I was aware, my father drank heavily only when my mother visited her closest friend, Edith, in the Berkshires, to escape for a day or two the burdens and pressures of our life. I would learn later that he thought she had a lover. As soon as the car left the driveway, he sent me bicycling to that roadhouse for pint cartons of martinis. He was drunk most of the time she was away, but very quietly drunk. I saw little difference in his behavior from how he usually acted.

Looking back now, I realize how little a part my father's alcoholism seemed to play in my youth. Indeed, it was not until after his death that my mother labeled him an alcoholic and told me how he had begun drinking heavily soon after his father died.

But there was an explanation for my seldom seeing him drink. One day, reading whatever was at hand and thinking my father asleep in bed, I opened the bathroom door. He was standing there, a full kit laid out: Sterno, hypodermic needle, rubber tubing, a brown bottle. I shut the door quietly and never mentioned the scene until a year after his death, when my mother and I briefly talked about his addiction to morphine. He had begun taking it to cure hangovers when it could be bought openly, without prescription. After 1912, when the Pure Food and Drug Act was passed, he obtained it illegally. About 1935, two Treasury Men appeared at our house to question him about where and how he got it. He was by then near death, and my mother had to call in the doctor to force them to leave. I learned that for several years he had had an open prescription for it from the same doctor, who believed my father would die without it. For my father at least, morphine was more than an adequate substitute for alcohol.

I still have a few snapshots of him. In one he has a fox terrier on a leash. In several others he is one of several in family groupings. Those photographs show him to be frail, slightly bent, his hair already gray although he was still quite young. In the years I lived with my parents, I saw him as the coughing figure on the bed, cigarette always dangling from his mouth. Or I saw him cutting as dapper a figure as he could then command: expensive clothes and shoes, bought with the interest from the trust fund my grandmother left, even though we could barely afford to buy food from day to day.

My mother waited on him. She rolled his Bull Durhams, manicured his nails, prepared his favorite foods with little thought of what she and I might want to eat. To this day I hate tripe and cheese soufflés.

I would learn little about him. The spoiled son of a successful, energetic newspaper publisher and politician, he had at his father's death refused to go to Harvard, where he had been admitted. My mother told me almost nothing about the years that followed, although her brother informed me that my father had associated with the criminal underworld in Greater Boston. He gambled a good deal, boasted about his skill at billiards and pool, and now and again talked about poker games. By the 1930s he was reduced to occasional bets on the horse races.

My mother told me bits more about him and his family. My

grandfather had had a stroke and fallen down the stairs shortly after he was appointed to a high federal position; she hinted that he was drunk at the time. My grandmother was sufficiently realistic to leave my father only the income from a small trust fund; I was to have the principal after his death and my majority. Much of this fund disappeared in the Crash and at the hands of a dishonest executor.

I asked my mother why she had stayed with him. She said, "He was a kind and gentle man." And indeed he was, although I did not understand that until many years later.

For a very long time, I carried on an intermittent, internal debate about my parents. At first I blamed my father wholly for the pains and frustrations of my childhood. Later I understood that theirs was a marriage, a living together that demanded each play a role. My mother's part then seemed to be that of the strong, maternal manager who met the needs of an immature husband.

Two years after my father's death in 1936, my mother married a Scotsman. They had the closest relationship I have ever seen, one that excluded not only me but also his son, whom he had abandoned after the boy's birth killed his first wife. He spent years wandering this country, from job to job, returning to Scotland only occasionally and briefly to visit his son, who then lived with his grandmother.

Two months after their marriage, I entered Cornell University, tuition and some living expenses paid from the trust fund left by my grandmother. I worked for the rest, first as the most awkward and forgetful waiter in Ithaca, then as an assistant, under the National Youth Administration, to a part-time librarian from Germany. From him I learned much, not only about library work but also about the realities of Nazi Germany from which he was a grateful refugee.

At Cornell I made myself several promises: that I would never be poor again; that I would never work merely for money, but rather do what was valuable in itself; and that I would never trade on family names. I also determined that I would major in English, go on to graduate school, and become a professor. All these I managed, even as during graduate school and teaching, alcoholism gradually took over my life.

As an undergraduate I drank as income permitted, which is to say relatively little, mostly beer on Saturday evenings when the week's work was done. My first real drunk I remember. I had foolishly joined a fraternity on the urging of the new executor of my inheritance. Just before Christmas we pledges were required to put on an extremely vulgar, blasphemous play. I went through with it, then got very drunk on beer, staggered back to my rooming house, and collapsed on the bed. I remember only embarrassment that I had gotten drunk. It was too early for shame or regret. I later determined not to be initiated into the fraternity, so perhaps I felt some unconscious need to blame the incident on my fraternity brothers.

After I entered graduate school, a group of us usually played poker Saturday evenings, which meant none of us got drunk—too much was at stake on our slim budgets.

Early in my graduate years of studying and teaching English, I began sleeping twelve hours out of every twenty-four, an impossible situation. I was given a test for thyroid deficiency, found to have a basal metabolism of -29, and prescribed thyroxine. On a grain and a half a day, I tested normal but slept only four or five hours a night and was horny all the time. The doctor then prescribed phenobarbital and beer, to be taken after work every evening. Within a year, the pheno being limited, I was drinking a quart of whiskey every evening, but was still able to teach eight o'clock classes. Again, only years later would I understand that I would have taught much better had I not drunk that amount.

That test of basal metabolism was mechanical rather than chemical, and probably inaccurate; later, without thyroxine, I tested normal. I'd guess now that the heavy sleep was an escape from depression, as it would be later for my two daughters. And I also believe that the pheno and beer merely hastened the onset of alcoholism. I would have become alcoholic anyway so long as I drank socially over a few years rather than abstaining altogether. Like so many others—at least half the AA members I meet—I would seem to have a genetic predisposition to alcoholism, although that by itself does not make one an alcoholic. Other factors, emotional, mental, and social, also play a crucial role.

The years of drinking that followed were much like those told in most of the drunkalogues one hears in AA: years of denial, then partial acceptance of the illness but not of its consequences (that I could never again drink safely); repeated benders; hospitalizations before there were even detoxification centers; much psychotherapy from which I learned a good deal except how to stop drinking; then finally hitting bottom and the slow progress toward recovery, as slow as the progression into alcoholism and utter despair.

My personal life was also defective. Two marriages failed, in part because of alcoholism. In a real sense, when I first married I had almost no idea of how to be a husband, and when my wife became pregnant, I was terrified, for surely my father was no model for fatherhood. After three children, endless quarrels over booze, money, and parental responsibility and a suburban environment I detested, I abandoned my family for another woman who believed initially that alcoholism was a consequence of emotional deprivation and that adequate psychotherapy would fix everything. Meanwhile, I felt secure because of a subconscious realization that with her I could get away with drinking. My second wife would take me to detox, where I would be sobered up and of course resentful. I would then return to my house and job for a time, and then the pattern would be repeated — again and again.

That second marriage was typical for many alcoholics, I the drunk and she the enabler, each of us feeding off the sickness of the other. When I was drinking heavily, she would often bring home a bottle of vodka for me before she went to work, her rationale being that it was better for me to drink at home than at a bar. When I was drunk, my wife took over all practical matters; when I was sobering up and then sober, she would not relinquish control. We attempted marriage therapy a number of times, but it became a pointless exercise as each of us tried to justify intolerable behavior. Eventually she left to take up with another man, whom she later described as paranoid and schizoid. Despite her lovable qualities, she needed a sick mate, as both he and I did also.

Alcoholics Anonymous speaks of the drunk "hitting bottom," reaching a point where literally the only choices remaining are institutionalization, the grave, or sobriety. That moment came to me during a bender that lasted several weeks and left me quite helpless and hopeless. Fortunately, a friend in AA knew of my condition and arranged for me to enter a detox and rehab facility in New Hampshire. I stayed there for a month, learned a great deal about alcoholism, its chemistry, its effects on the mind and body, and its genetic transmission — about 50 percent of the children of an alcoholic become alcoholics themselves; if both parents are alcoholic then 75 percent. Quite as important as lectures, AA meetings, and group therapy were the informal discussions with the other patients. I think what made the most difference to all of us was renewed hope that we could achieve lasting sobriety if we would diligently work for it.

At this writing, I have been sober two years. I still rebel against much of AA—its religiosity, its rituals, its absolutes. But it is the only game in town, so I go to meetings even though I often feel like an outsider. It still surprises me that I have never gone to an AA meeting and then directly to a bar or package store.

I attend an occasional Al-Anon meeting, although like so many others in my situation, I feel as if I'm the enemy the nonalcoholics there are talking about. I have also attended two meetings of ACOA (Adult Children of Alcoholics); in Greater Boston these are loosely affiliated with Al-Anon. Members of ACOA seemed to me to be driven by an almost overwhelming anger against their parents. I hope that as ACOA matures, this unwholesome rage may soften. I see a counselor about once a month. Herself an alcoholic, ten years sober, she is enthusiastic but not rigid in her own views of AA. Together, all these help to keep me sober, although ultimately it is myself, a day at a time, who stays sober by not picking up one drink.

What effects has my being the only child of an alcoholic had on my life? It is difficult to answer that question, to separate out those effects that can singularly be assigned to the influence in my youth of that strange household of mother and father and booze and morphine and their attendant pains.

Half a dozen lists of characteristics seemingly common to adult children of alcoholics have been compiled; some are derived from the comments of ACOAs themselves, others from the observations of psychologists, sociologists, and other professionals. The lists suffer from the faults of all such compilations: most of the characteristics given are not common to the majority of ACOAs, nor are they unique to that population. As with the alcoholic, so with his or her child—some defects and deficiencies that a person may have are made worse by drinking or by witnessing alcoholic drinking.

So many causative factors are at work in the development of

all individual personalities that assigning an effect to a single cause is very hazardous indeed. However, several characteristics are so often noted as common to ACOAs that they merit some attention, so long as they are seen as the consequences of various factors.

The first is a sense of guilt: the ACOA feels in some way responsible for the parent's drinking. There are ironies here! The most common negative feeling of alcoholics in AA is guilt, and indeed—despite the assertion in that program that its members should not feel guilty, because they are sick—the feeling is in some respects quite justified. Whatever the etiology of alcoholism, whatever its medical aspect as an illness, once the drinker knows he is an alcoholic, he is fully responsible for his behavior, whether he beats his wife or steals from the boss or neglects his children. He is not excused because he is under the influence of a powerful compulsion/obsession, no more than is the mass murderer or the rapist. But contrary to the therapeutic mythology of our time, guilt is not necessarily damaging. It is the conscience saying, "Don't do it again!" And just maybe for that reason he won't.

However, it is indeed tragic when the guilt infects the drunk's children. Often after a bender the alcoholic expresses to his family great guilt and remorse. The child, who may feel that if he were good enough he could stop the parent from drinking, now mimics the guilt of the parent. The child rationalizes: "Father feels guilty, so I must be guilty also." We should never underestimate the power of example.

Accompanying that guilt is fear. The sober alcoholic fears becoming drunk again, and with good reason: he may kill himself in an automobile accident, may murder his friend, may squander all his money, may become so brain damaged from booze that he spends the rest of his life in a mental institution. It is silly to say he merely has a vague sense of doom—these and other dread possibilities are realities, as every member of AA knows.

The fear of the child is also grounded in reality. Will Daddy be drunk tonight? Will he beat Mommy and/or us? Will he lose his job? Will he make us feel ashamed in front of our friends? Will he abandon us? Too often that feeling continues into adulthood when the fears are no longer based on reality, because Daddy is sober or dead. Then indeed there is for the adult child a nameless fear, a sense of impending doom. Life becomes a tangle of confusions and uncertainties.

I am not aware of feeling guilty for my father's addictions. Yet I have again and again felt responsible for situations that in fact were beyond my influence, and when failure ensued, I have felt guilty.

My mother died of gross medical malpractice in 1959. Ten days later, my stepfather committed suicide by slashing his left arm from wrist to shoulder with a straight razor and wandering around their cottage until he dropped. For years I felt guilty about both deaths, although reason told me I could not have prevented them.

Fear seems to have been with me always. An obvious expression has been nightmares, which I remember beginning about two years after I moved in with my parents. The horror of the witch approaching me continued into late adolescence. Later there were nightmares of suffocating, drowning, being consumed, often but not always in periods of respiratory distress. The bronchial asthma was of course made worse by drinking. Today my worst nightmare, one often reported by members in AA, concerns booze: I am drinking and am devastated by the realization that I'm out there again. Waking is slow. Minutes pass before I understand it was all a dream.

Reality has involved other fears—the sudden shock of believing I will lose my job or that a loved one will leave or that an automobile will swerve and hit me. Yet these are common to everyone and merely made worse by one's own or a parent's alcoholism.

Advancing age and the consequent intimations of mortality have placed my fears in a more reasonable context, have given them a basis in reality. I do not fear death, perhaps because I was "dead" once, for twenty seconds, in an ambulance as a result of combining booze and sleeping pills. But I fear dying, and that easily becomes the focus of previously free-floating anxiety.

A prevalent, although by no means universal characteristic of ACOAs is low self-esteem, a sense of being inferior to one's peers, of being a fraud and a failure even in the face of obvious achievement. I was teaching freshman English at Cornell University when I was twenty-one; six years later I was an assistant professor at a small college for women and had already published a lengthy critical essay on Jane Austen. Yet I felt I was a fake, that I was deceiving my students even when they graded me the best teacher in the department.

For many years I was editor in chief of a division of a large and most prestigious research institution, where I worked closely with some of America's most distinguished astrophysicists and space scientists. Yet I sometimes thought I was accepted by them merely because as scientists they knew less than I did about good writing and the mechanics of publication.

Many ACOAs cannot tolerate personal success, for to do so would imply they are in fact worthy, at least to others. I have had three different careers. Quite good at each, I destroyed each. And the means of doing so was what I most hated in my father—addiction. I literally boozed away my jobs. In doing so, I rejected the values and goals of my youth and settled for less and less. Recently added to the *Diagnostic and Statistical Manual III* of the American Psychiatric Association is a new category: the self-defeating. Many alcoholics and ACOAs would seem to belong to that classification.

Finally, fear of rejection by others and fear of being abandoned by them are frequent themes in the lives of many ACOAs, certainly in mine. No one can be more rejecting than the parent who is drinking, and that rejection is a kind of abandonment. The resulting fears often inhibit the ACOA from forming deep personal attachments, from expressing love and affection. The less the emotional investment, the less may be the emotional loss. Too easily, attention substitutes for affection, sex for love.

Consequently, many ACOAs and active alcoholics experience devastating loneliness, a sense of isolation from others, perhaps even of being unique because they do not communicate easily. They do not know that these feelings are common to many others, whether affected by alcoholism or not. Both AA and Al-Anon are powerful instruments for relieving this isolation.

As I write this, it is Father's Day. I am again reminded how sobriety is reached through breaking old patterns and building new ones. And how also the children of alcoholics must do the same if they are to find some serenity and lead productive lives.

My children, three biological and two step, telephoned me in remembrance of the day. The eldest was born with a cleft palate; for her first two years, before the operation to correct it, she was unable to communicate orally with anyone except her parents and a cousin; many years later the cousin committed suicide because he could not get off drugs and alcohol. Another daughter was severely traumatized by finding the bloodied body of Grampy—my stepfather—a year after I had abandoned them. At an early age, the two stepchildren were deprived of their father.

Today most of these baby-boom children have had their share of problems with alcohol and other drugs, with sex, and with social norms. Two of them are possibly alcoholics, and three have been divorced. Several also seem to have shared at differing times a weakened or distorted sense of reality. That deficit is common among active alcoholics, and frequent among sober ones. They swing between irrational extremes of hope and despair. Those feelings are common among children who live in homes of denial and deceit. Yet this deficit, this denial of reality, seems to be characteristic of many of their generation without reference to parental alcoholism.

My children have had their successes. Two of them have very reputable careers, four make suitable livings, and three seem to have settled into stable and satisfying domestic arrangements. And they have coped with personal problems in ways acceptable to them, including psychotherapy for several.

I cannot separate out the effects of my alcoholism on these children. It is tempting, for example, to believe that much of the difficulty of two of them derives from the traumas in childhood that I have mentioned. And since I did not meet my stepchildren until they were eight and ten years old, after the unpleasant divorce of their parents and the subsequent neglect by their father, I can easily assign their problems to that domestic turmoil. But then I question whether I am seeking to avoid responsibility for the effects of my alcoholism on them—the scenes they witnessed of drunkenness, of rambling and raving speech, of hugs too tight or no hugs at all. And surely they remember how often I did not show up for parties and other celebrations, or showed up crocked. And they remember the times they needed me for counsel and comfort and I was not there.

I still identify myself more as an alcoholic than as the adult child of an alcoholic. I obsess over the fact that I have spent much of my life drinking and was repeatedly irresponsible as a consequence. As I approach seventy, I must accept that there is now no way I can truly make amends, either to others or to myself, for what I have done and what I have not done. So I must constantly fight remorse.

I remain an uncomfortable agnostic, yet I have some sense of a creative force in the universe. And I gain increasing consolation from a prayer that for me is an instruction to be responsible for my own actions and to know the past as unchangeable and the present as an unfolding of possibilities, not certainties:

Grant me the serenity to accept the things I cannot change,
Courage to change the things I can,
And the wisdom to know the difference.

And a very simple wish:

Let there be peace on Earth, and let it begin with me.

BOOTLEGGER'S SON

Avon Neal

I grew up in southern Indiana, in what was called by some "hillbilly country." The people there were mainly farm folk. They worked from sunrise to sunset and attended church on Sunday. My mother's family was respectable, descended—as she liked to remind us—from fine stock. They were known as diligent workers and good neighbors. They rarely drank hard liquor, so there was no problem of alcoholism on that side of my family.

On the other hand, my father's family lived fast and loose. The men took pride in hard drinking, gambling, and brawling. They claimed as their motto, "fast horses and loose women," and most of the males followed that precept to early graves. Their lifestyle epitomized what we now call "machismo." They pursued all things that could lead to trouble and ended up with more than their share of problems, alcoholism among them.

My paternal grandfather, however, drank very little. He was a serious man of few words, honest and direct, nobody to trifle with. He was also ambitious and determined to amount to something. In time, he became a leading contractor and built many of the roads and bridges that exist to this day in that part of the country. Because of my grandfather's efforts, my father's family enjoyed sufficient money for all their wants and needs. Unfortunately, he died a short while after I was born, fatally injured while saving the life of a friend. His chest was crushed by the fall of a huge block of limestone, but he clung to life for months afterward.

Since I was the first grandchild and his namesake, he lavished much affection on me and predicted for me success and a bright future. They say that, bedfast though he was, he used to toss me into the air and laughingly promise me all the things a boy could have, including, down the line, a college education. Had he lived, it might all have happened as he said, but the years of my youth became almost the opposite from what he envisioned.

Years later the man my grandfather had sacrificed his life for became the town drunk. When I was nine or ten years old he used to take me aside and, in the throes of a crying jag, lay a scrawny arm across my shoulders and begin telling me what a fine, upstanding man my grandfather was. "Your granddaddy," he'd start off, slobbering and breathing alcohol fumes in my face, "the man whose name you carry . . . well, he saved my life once. A finer, more decent and upright man never walked the face of the earth. Yes sir, I owe my life to your dead granddaddy." I couldn't help but wonder at the injustice of it all. I wanted to shout at him, "You let a decent man die so you could become a drunkard." But I felt sorry for him and could never bring myself to say that to him. I suppose the poor, miserable soul suffered with his guilt all those years. Even then I had serious questions about drinking.

In the mid-1920s we moved to Indianapolis, where we must have prospered for a while. My father was working for a great-uncle who owned a Cadillac car dealership. They catered to well-heeled customers and there was plenty of money floating around. But the good life didn't last long. When the stock market crashed, my parents lost everything. I remember my father was driving a shiny new sixteen-cylinder Cadillac, the pride of the line. It had come his way because the uncle told his employees one morning, "Men, we've lost everything. We're out of business. I'm taking bankruptcy. So just pick out a car, any one you want. It's all yours!" That's how my dad came to own such a luxurious automobile. That's all he came away with. He had lost his house, furniture, and everything else. Bad investments with crooked Wall Street bankers, he claimed.

Bootlegger's Son

There were absolutely no jobs to be had. Factories shut down, leaving strong, able-bodied men begging for work at any wage. We were finally forced to move back to the country, into an abandoned farmhouse offered to us by my mother's family. There were three of us children by then. I must have been about seven years old. I remember driving to that old house on a cold November evening, my mother sobbing about our disgrace and misfortune, my father comforting her with a pat on the shoulder and a few words I'll never forget: "Don't worry, Mommy, this will all blow over in a few weeks and we'll be back in the chips before you know it." Well, it didn't blow over and we were to spend eight years of sheer hell out there in the sticks.

My father had taken up city ways. He'd already had the habit of tippling but, as I recall, he didn't get totally loaded. Drinking was just something to do with the boys. But as he couldn't find employment, he began drinking and gambling and spending his time in town. Sometimes he came home with a roll of money, but more often he returned drunk and disappointed, with his pockets turned inside out.

One cold, wintry night he rolled in too far gone even to get out of his car. My mother managed to get him inside and into bed. He forgot to drain the car's radiator. The next morning when he went outside, he saw his beautiful Cadillac with icicles sticking out the sides of the motor block. It must have been the first time he realized how the cards were stacked against him. I think he virtually gave up right then. There was no money for such massive repairs and without wheels he was out of business. He was stuck, with no way of getting back into the bright lights to gamble and carouse. He brooded for weeks before he began scheming to make quick, easy money. He thought all he needed was capital. However, all his uptown friends were either too wise to invest or found themselves in the same boat. No funds were forthcoming, so he went back to brooding.

Part of the agreement with my mother's uncles was that our dad would exchange farm work as payment for rent. But he would have none of that and reneged early on. He refused to wear overalls. To him they symbolized something beneath his dignity. He swore he would not be a sharecropper for anyone. Before we knew it, he had hooked up with one of his cronies and started making bootleg whiskey. His silent partner, a well-to-do banker in town, supplied the ingredients and my father provided the work. This was in the days of Prohibition and snooping revenue agents, so he took all the risks as well.

From the very beginning, he made high-grade whiskey, some of which found its way to the Capone gang in Chicago. I remember customers boasting, "Well, if it's good enough for Al Capone, it's sure as hell good enough for us." People used to come at any and all hours to buy booze. Even the preacher sneaked through the woods to our back door for his regular pint of "snakebite medicine." Our dad pocketed the money and sent them all away with their jugs of white lightning, "to return another day," he would say with a chuckle. It appeared that everybody was happy.

It was all supposed to be kept secret, but of course the whole community soon knew what was going on. Some of the proper ladies had conniption fits, but their thirsty husbands were able to quell their objections. The effect on our family was devastating. Our mother's threats and tearful pleadings failed to dissuade our father, so she simply closed her eyes and pretended to have nothing to do with it. In time, however, when she saw that bootlegging provided a livelihood, she relented, even to the point of helping with the still sometimes. Banty, as my father's drinking buddies had begun to call him, simply said to hell with everybody and brazened it through.

For us kids, it was pure agony. I probably suffered most because I was the oldest and more acutely aware of what was going on. At school we were always the butt of jokes and criticism. I remember fighting kids who called me Bootlegger. And when the teacher once referred to me as a bootlegger's son, I slunk away, flushed with shame and embarrassment.

Sunday school was even worse. Our mother defiantly sent us there in our best clothes to keep up appearances and put our snooty neighbors in their place. We faced the ordeal with dread. At the same time we were glad to get away from the house, where Father would be nursing his usual Sunday morning hangover. When our father's name was mentioned, usually in the news for committing some outrageous act, we knew that all eyes would be upon us. As people milled about before services began we would hear their whispering and see them casting furtive glances our way. We were so self-conscious that, no matter what was being discussed, we naturally assumed it was about us. Mother had taught us to hold our heads high and to ignore what others said, but that wasn't easy. Whenever a visiting preacher gave his standard hellfire-and-brimstone sermon on the evils of drinking and gambling, all heads turned in our direction, staring until we felt like sinking through the floor. I carried with me a constant feeling of guilt and at the same time of anger—at my father, mainly, but also at all those hypocritical Christians who so smugly snubbed us. I still feel that anger, although by now I've forgiven the people their thoughtless cruelty.

Our mother, daughter of a proud family, had grown up and taught school in this community. Now she was forced to swallow her pride and to live with a shiftless husband who openly defied the law by selling moonshine. The shame of it was almost too much to bear. Her protests fell on deaf ears, and divorce, even if she had dared consider it, was out of the question. Had she left our dad, who threatened her at any mention of separation, there was no place to go. There was also the stigma of a failed marriage heaped onto the stark necessity of earning a living for herself and her children. She was determined beyond reason to keep the family together, no matter what, and although she succeeded, she paid a heavy price for her stubbornness.

There were five of us children by now. Ten years later there would be two younger children who escaped the Great Depression and the ties that bound the rest of us together.

After our father became well established as a top-notch bootlegger, he was judged by decent folk to be a disruptive influence in the community. That collective conviction caused us to live in comparative isolation. Some mothers didn't even want us children to associate with their children. Our mother was too busy caring for her family to really be concerned, however, and our father simply didn't care, so we bore the brunt of public scorn and ostracism.

Yet in spite of everything, our dad was popular with many people and always managed to have friends in high places. Finally, though, he ran afoul of the law in a big way and had to flee the area. The next thing we heard he was living with a burlesque queen in Indianapolis. From time to time he mailed our mother a little money. Despite her resentful feelings, whatever came our way was welcome. A couple of dollars could be stretched a long way during those difficult years.

Still, we nearly starved during the depths of the depression.

There seemed no way of getting anything without begging a pittance from family members. My mother refused to lower herself to accept charity. She maintained that others had families of their own to support and that it would be unfair to take food from other children's mouths.

In the meantime, we often went hungry. I can still see the image of my sister's pale face and shiny eyes, her skinny arms and legs, and bloated stomach; the signs, I later learned, that can indicate serious malnutrition. I remember my kid brother crying himself to sleep night after night because he was hungry. There were times when the gnawing in the pits of our stomachs nearly drove us wild. We would have done anything for one good square meal. Out of desperation our mother took us into the woods, where we chopped out the inner bark from slippery elm trees; chewing it temporarily relieved our hunger and eased the pain in our bellies. I chewed a lot of slippery elm bark and drank cups of steaming herb tea, sassafras mostly, because the roots were out there for the digging.

We tramped the hills and gathered anything we knew to be edible: roots, herbs, wild plums and crabapples, whatever we came across that would provide sustenance. We fished and hunted and learned to set traps and snares for small game, but the pickings were slim. Others seemed to be doing the same, or maybe we were just too inept. In the summertime we picked and canned as many wild blackberries as we possibly could because we knew that when winter came that might be all we'd have between us and starvation.

During school recesses, when other kids traded parts of their lunches, my sister, my brother, and I kept to ourselves because we were ashamed to have them see the pitiful jar of blackberries and the biscuit-and-bean-and-onion sandwich that were our fare. One school year I braved the teasings of fellow students to carry on a puppy-love romance with a chubby, not-too-attractive girl who wore flour-sack bloomers because twice a week she shared slices of angel food cake with me.

I know now that we must have resented our father terribly. Certainly we heard our mother speak out against him a great deal. In the evenings she would sit in a rocker beside the wood stove and recount his transgressions, reciting to us dolefully the same old litany: "I came from a good family. I don't deserve this kind of treatment. You children don't deserve it either. Anyone but a no-good husband and father would be right here taking care of his family instead of going around with some strumpet in the city. I know he's spending every last cent he makes having himself a good time while we sit out here in the sticks, barefoot and hungry." Then she would weep silently for a while, and we'd try to comfort her. Finally she would get up, her eyes flashing, more determined than ever, and get us ready for bed.

When my father did come back, he came back mean. He was dead broke and sour on the entire world. His mother had drawn on her influence and financial resources to bail him out from the clutches of the law. She hired shyster lawyers and, it was rumored, paid off judges to keep our dad from "going over the road," which meant going to the penitentiary. That would have been a blot on the family record and our grandmother wouldn't allow it. She wouldn't give a dime to help support her sons' families—they'd made their beds and could very well lie in them, she insisted—but the moment one of them got into trouble, she was right there with a fistful of greenbacks. Mother told us that the money she spent on lawyers to keep our dad out of jail would have supplied our table with vittles for a very long while. Our dad knew perfectly well, as we all knew, that if he got into serious trouble, his mother would be there with the bucks to bail him out, even if it meant mortgaging her house and everything in it. I'm sure his awareness of that only contributed to his orneriness.

In the clear once more, Father devoted himself full time to bootlegging. He lay around half-tanked-up most of the time and had us wait on him hand and foot while he sipped booze and read Wild West and detective stories in pulp magazines. I could see our mother's disenchantment with him. I was old enough to begin to understand a few things.

It was around then that my father decided I was up to operating the still for him. Against my mother's gallant protests, he kept me home from school to run the blasted thing. I hated every minute of it. I had to set it up, get the fire going, and attend it all day. I'd take the first few drippings for him to sample. He'd sniff it, down a stiff shot or two, then proof it with a whiskey tester. My job was to bring in the wood and water, to keep the fire going full blast, and to dip off the hot water, replacing it with fresh, cold water to keep the copper coil cool enough so the mash would distill. The whiskey tester was some sort of delicate thermometer that my dad deemed as precious as gold. Once I dropped it. He flew into a rage and beat me insensible before he'd even checked to see whether or not it was broken. I was soon able to assemble the still (a converted copper wash boiler), clamp on the lid and seal it with flour dough mix, and run off the whole barrel of mash. Before long I could do the entire run alone. I even sold the moonshine when customers came by. It had come to the point where our dad didn't even have to be on hand.

He did a lot of drinking and fighting during that time, and I remember he was always in some kind of trouble with the law. He enjoyed his reputation as bully of the town. He loved showing off and winning out over anybody he came up against. Sometimes I had to accompany him to the county seat to buy cigarettes and groceries. It was often a futile endeavor, for he usually gambled away what little money he had and got sloppy drunk in the process. When that happened he refused to leave town until everybody else had gone home. Then he would stagger out onto the street late at night, parade around the courthouse square, and sing at the top of his lungs the popular song "I'm Looking for the Bully of the Town." I was always mortified, but I had to stay with him. And indeed he was the bully of the town. The local police wisely avoided confrontations with him, letting his drunken behavior run its course until finally, with nobody to disturb or applaud him, he decided to go home. That was the time I dreaded most. I was deathly afraid of those wild midnight rides with him, fearful he'd stack the car and get us both killed.

During those years, his worry and frustration must have been eating away at him, for his temper tantrums became more frequent and more violent. He seemed more prone to rampages that wrecked the house. All of us were subjected to daily cuffings and what seemed like regular beatings. When our mother sensed he was on the verge of another rampage, she cautioned us to keep quiet and to walk softly around him. He was totally unpredictable. Sometimes nothing seemed to ruffle him. At other times the least little thing might set him off. He seemed to have no control over his temper. He would attack anything or anybody who got in his way. Guests, family, and strangers all came in for the same treatment. When someone disagreed with him or inadvertently said the wrong thing, Father would suddenly flare up, utter a string of vile curses, and flatten him. After a while, nobody would risk visiting except for a few friends or relatives who dropped by briefly for a half-pint of Banty's Best.

We lived in growing fear of his all-too-frequent outbursts. None of us knew where the boom would fall next or who might be the victim. Our dad was a big, powerful man, so we didn't stand a chance against him. He was also diabolically mean, and we were without protection. There was no use appealing to the sheriff and his men because they were either too friendly with him or, as people told us, scared to death to cross him. Besides, he kept them in booze so they weren't about to spoil his game. In fact, our dad's only real trouble with the law came from outsiders like government men or some state cop who didn't know any better. Even then he worked his charm and came off smelling like a rose. It was either because of his mother's money or because some official had a nose for superior booze and befriended him so as not to cut off the source. So our dad became almost a law unto himself while in his own territory. That left him free to bedevil us as he pleased.

Our father was a confirmed womanizer, too. In a drinking crowd there are always good-time ladies available, so he had his choice. It was no secret; he ran with women all his life. That caused him trouble at home and outside the home. In the end our mother ignored the rumors and closed her eyes to the way he carried on around other women. She was willing to tolerate almost anything in order to keep her brood together.

When our father abandoned us for the bright lights and left us without a cent it was bad enough. But it was worse when he finally came home; we preferred being hungry to being terrorized. Too many times we were whipped and sent to bed. Too many nights I lay there sobbing and vowing to get even. But the next day, as though nothing had happened, he'd be easy on us and act like a good father should. Still, we knew that at the slightest provocation —like dropping a spoon at the table—he'd react by backhanding us off our chairs. He wouldn't hesitate to throw a cup of coffee against the wall if it was too hot. I recall a holiday dinner with several people at our house when our dad got angry at something and overturned the table, dishes, food, and all, in everybody's lap.

We lived from day to day through the Depression years while it slowly dawned on us that alcohol wasn't the only cause of our dad's erratic behavior. We could see that it was alcohol that set him off, but there was something else. The roots went much deeper, but we were not equipped to realize it. Drinking was only a symptom of something none of us could understand. In fact, we had all come to believe that our father was insane.

No matter how others saw him, he was the devil incarnate in our eyes. In school one day the new teacher passed around sheets of paper and requested that we each draw a picture of what we thought our parents looked like. Without hesitation I drew a picture of the devil. I shall never forget the teacher's look of shock and consternation. She demanded to know why I had drawn that image. I told her, "That's how I see my father." All the students had begun laughing and the teacher backed off in dismay.

The worst thing, I suppose, was the anxiety caused by living in constant fear. My father spared nobody. Once he whipped my kid brother with the buckle end of a belt, and every time the leather fell it ripped off a piece of flesh. I got a lot of undeserved punishment in those days. We all did but I, being the eldest, seemed to attract the brunt of his wrath more often than did the others. Another time, for some unremembered reason—I think I had won at a game of cards—my father straight-armed me. The blow knocked me, tumbling and sprawling, the length of the dining room, where I crashed through a door and went sliding across the kitchen linoleum. The only thing that stopped me was the wall. As I came back to my senses, my dad loomed over me, kicking and flailing like a madman. I was all of twelve years old at the time. My mother was on the receiving end as often as the rest of us; she took scars from our dad's rampages to her grave. We dared not show it, but we hated the ground he walked on.

A particularly bitter memory concerns the time a neighbor knocked at our door early one Christmas morning, bearing what he thought were bad tidings. We clustered around our mother at the door. The man, hat in hand, Adam's apple bobbing up and down, could barely get the words out. "Mrs. Neal, I have terrible news for you." He swallowed several times, then went on. "I'm afraid I have to tell you that your husband got himself killed last night." "Oh, my God," Mother gasped. "How did it happen?" He went on to tell us there'd been a fight, a knifing, and a shooting at the roadhouse where our dad hung out on Saturday nights. The man continued, "I left the Blue Moon at a run, but Banty was still in the thick of it. I knew they'd called the police, and I wanted out of there. Just as I was leaving I heard somebody yell that they'd shot Banty Neal."

Mother stepped outside to talk further, pulling the door closed behind her. We children looked at each other with unsuppressed joy and immediately broke into a spontaneous dance of jubilation around the parlor. We couldn't let Mother suspect our feelings, but we kept thinking that this was the best Christmas ever. Mother couldn't believe the news; she was in tears all morning, repeating over and over again, "I knew something like this would happen." Then she'd burst into tears again. We had no telephone, so there was no way of confirming what our neighbor had told us. We had to just wait. We kept expecting the sheriff to show up to give particulars of our dad's death. By midafternoon Mother had had enough of waiting. She bundled up to go to a neighbor's to use the phone. Just as she was preparing to leave, we heard a car barreling along the country road, great clouds of snow billowing out behind it. There was the squeal of grating brakes as it approached our lane, then more fast and reckless driving as it sashayed up the lane and came skidding into the yard, where it stopped within inches of the front porch. It was our dad, loaded to the gills, with a carful of drinking buddies and a bevy of giggling, painted-up women—hussies, our mother hissed to us as they tumbled out of the car, wafting perfume and tramping snow into the house. While we stood about glum and downcast, they proceeded to have themselves a bang-up party. I don't think any of them even knew what day it was, our dad least of all. Santa Claus had passed us by, but I'll never forget that wonderful feeling Christmas morning. It had started out being so beautiful, then abruptly turned sour. We were struck dumb. There was no way of expressing our disappointment. We had simply to grin and bear it. Since then I've found very little joy in Christmas.

On days when we were left to our own devices, we figured out ways of getting even with him when we grew up. Our favorite fantasy was that when he grew old and feeble, we'd kick his cane out from under him and beat him unmercifully with it just as he had so often beaten us. There were other punishments, some too horrible to mention, that we placed in store for when we had him at our mercy. By then we had learned to recognize the sound of his car and would listen anxiously as it wound around curves and picked up speed on the straightaways. His driving would give us a clue to whether he would arrive drunk or sober. Or, as we hoped, not at all, for the hills and curves provided obstacles that just might get him killed. We waited hopefully to hear the screech of brakes, the rending crash, and then the infinite silence. At the foot of the hill across our valley where the gravel road plunged downhill to end in a sharp curve, there was a huge old tree waiting to catch the unwary. We imagined that it was our father's destiny to plow head-on into that tree and be killed. But luckily for him, and unhappily for us, that never happened.

He cracked up any number of cars during his wild and reck-less driving career but led a charmed life when it came to getting killed or injured. He loved big fancy cars and drove a different one every few months, until he wrecked it or the finance company caught up with him. He contended that a fast, powerful car was necessary in the bootlegging business, so he tinkered with each of his until he was sure it could outrun the law. He had driven race cars for a brief spell and claimed he could drive an automobile where most people couldn't walk. One of the pranks that delighted him most was luring people into his car, then driving hell-for-leather toward town, taking curves on two wheels, hitting his brakes to make the car spin out of control, and fishtailing down the road throwing dust on all sides. His frightened passengers could plead all they wanted but he wouldn't slow down. He loved to terrorize them until they begged to be let out.

Our dad's riotous escapades gained him a dubious reputation and eventually made him a legend in that neck of the woods. Even now old-timers speak of him in reverent tones as they recall his feats of strength, fast driving, and his epic fights. After all, he was the bully of the town and took on all comers. He prided himself on never having been defeated. He boasted that the man who whipped him, fair or foul, was as good as dead, because he'd shoot him the next time they met. There weren't many who didn't believe he was serious when he said that.

Somewhere along the way he had picked up some wrestling

skills, claiming to have done a stint as a professional in the bright lights of the ring. He became a regular at county fairs and carnivals, the local champion shilling for the carnies and helping them to draw crowds. He reveled in showing off for the yokels and picking up a few bucks at the same time.

It was at one of these affairs that he proved how tough he really was, and how extraordinarily lucky. It happened on the midway. Somebody shouted my father's name and the crowd simply faded away. A man stood off a short distance aiming a pistol in our direction. My dad quickly swept Mother and us kids behind him. The man said, "I'm going to kill you, Banty. I found out you've been running with my wife." My father stood stock-still while people held their breath. The man moved closer and stuck the gun into my dad's belly. I was less than six feet away. I heard my dad say through gritted teeth, "You son of a bitch, you don't have guts enough to shoot me." The man shut his eyes and squeezed the trigger. There was a sharp metallic click. At that instant Dad, in one lightning movement, grabbed the gun and clubbed the man with his fist, felling him like a poleaxed steer. Then, while the onlookers stood transfixed, my dad began firing the gun, emptying all six chambers into the ground. From then on, people concluded that our dad led a charmed existence and, like a witch or a warlock, could not be killed in an ordinary manner.

Years later I returned to the place where I grew up. A man I barely remembered gave me a bullet cast from a silver dollar with my father's initials cut into it. He told me, "I was going to use this on your father but he died first. I thought you might like it as a souvenir." I realized then that I wasn't alone in seeking revenge for wrongs inflicted by my father.

I remember customers coming to buy whiskey and staying on to play cards, tell jokes, and carry on in the amiable way men do when they get together like that. Occasionally tempers flared without warning and these men ceased being friends. They cursed loudly as they pushed and shoved and fought each other. Sometimes they swung chairs or whipped out knives to hack and hew at one another. My father would leap up and join the melee, grabbing the combatants by their collars and knocking their heads together to stop the bloody fracas. There'd be threats and more cursing as they simmered down, then whoever got slashed would have the wound doused with whiskey and stitched up with plain old sewing thread. Such violence is a terrible thing for a child to witness. Its effects either repel or attract the viewer for the rest of his life. What amazed me most was how the participants went right back to their booze and gambling. In later life I was to see violence on a much more gross scale during World War II and I've always recoiled at that kind of inhumanity.

I was convinced that booze was the real culprit and associated all such violent acts with the stuff we made and sold. I was humiliated by the very thought that I was playing a part in making and selling whiskey. When I got a little older, I was able to tell my mother about these feelings. She repeated them to my dad, trying to convince him of the untoward effect his bootlegging was having on us kids, especially among our friends at school. All he said was, "To hell with the lot of them. Their parents are some of my best customers. We're as good as they are." He turned to us kids. "You don't have to take anything from anybody. If some Bible-backed bastard gets on you, all you have to do is tell him to kiss your ass. It's none of their damned business how I earn a living." When Mother told him that I didn't like running the still and didn't approve of whiskey making in general, he blew his stack. He jumped up, fuming, grabbed me by the hair, and shoved my face into the wall. He turned angrily to her and said: "Well, I don't see the son of a bitch refusing any of the food that whiskey money puts on the table." And that ended that discussion. I continued to set the mash and run the still.

My dad must have sensed my loathing. He couldn't help but know that we all feared and despised him. With me he acted accordingly. I became his whipping post and absorbed most of his anger and brutality. I swore that if I ever got out from under the yoke of bootlegging whiskey I'd never touch the stuff myself. And throughout these many years I've kept that promise, even though the pressures toward alcohol consumption in our society are monumental. During high school I more than once came home from parties roughed up, my clothes ripped and torn from resisting my buddies who tried their damnedest to pour liquor down my throat. They never once managed it, however, because of my firm determination to keep the promise I'd made to myself never to touch booze in any form.

The effects of those wretched years remain with me as I'm sure they also do with others of my family. I have not yet shucked the excess baggage of unresolved anger and resentment. Vestiges of rejection and insecurity still linger. I take a cynical view of things and am drawn toward the underdog by an empathetic disposition. Nor have I rid myself of my youthful proneness to melancholy. But I suppose that these and other such feelings might be the direct result of anyone's turbulent upbringing, not just an ACOA's. Primarily I blame living with an alcoholic parent for most of the unhappiness I knew as a child. I believe that the formation of my character rests there. I also firmly believe that one must rise above. If a person wallows in self-pity, allows it to dominate his life, it will eventually consume him. Skid rows and prisons are full of unfortunates who blame all their woes on unhappy childhoods. One must always stay a step ahead of the past. A glance over the shoulder is enough to warn that it's always there, following like a shadow, and one must hustle to keep ahead of it. That gloomy outlook is part of my father's legacy, a sort of consolation prize for growing up with booze.

The paternal side of my family had a hard time coping with booze. Perhaps their low tolerance for alcohol was inherited. To my regret, I've seen it passed from one generation to the next. My youngest brother died in an automobile accident, probably the result of his having one drink too many at a Christmas Eve party. Sadly, the alcoholic pattern established by our father has plagued our family, even after his death.

I'm glad I was able to resist peer pressures enough to remain abstinent, even though I have been subjected to the scorn of friends and relatives. To me, life is a challenge, a struggle, a difficult journey. I prefer having the edge by facing it sober. I am too familiar with the consequences of excessive drinking. I have seen too many lives and talents ruined by alcohol.

My refusal to join my father's rowdy drinking crowd—to be a "real man" as he put it—only irritated him and incurred his wrath. He sneered and accused me of forsaking my class, of being a stuck-up prude with a headful of bookish crap taught in the schools. Actually, I'm grateful that he scorned me at every opportunity, for the more he tormented me, the more my moral fiber was strengthened. It was his will against mine, and I was winning.

By the late 1930s we'd moved from the sticks to a northern city, where our father had taken a factory job. He'd given up bootlegging, but he drank as heavily as ever, spending hard-earned cash on the stuff we used to make. It was a complete reversal of his former circumstances. Still hoping for easy money, he gambled away his weekly paychecks with sickening regularity and kept us up to our ears in debt.

When I was in high school, a car I was in with a group of friends was in a terrible accident. Two of us were thrown clear and regained consciousness while ambulance attendants sorted out the injured. Since there were only two ambulances and several people were severely injured, the police determined that I was not badly hurt and somebody took me home. I was still dazed and tottery when I stumbled into the house. My father switched on the light, took one look at me, and crowed to my mother, "See, there's your precious son. He's sloppy-assed drunk. I told you he'd come to it, like a pig to a trough." I think he was truly disappointed when he found out I wasn't intoxicated. However, he never admitted being sorry for misjudging me. Why would he? I shouldn't have expected him to. We were already locked in mortal struggle.

I knew I couldn't fight my father man to man because he was too big and too experienced in rough-and-tumble fighting. But I vowed to do him in someday. When I was seventeen, I had him arrested for beating up my mother and wrecking the furniture. At the hearing next day, I declared, "I think my father is crazy and I know he's dangerous. He's always threatening to kill us and I believe someday he'll get carried away in one of his insane rages and commit murder." I was repeating what our mother told us over and over. "If you don't put him away this time," I told the judge, "if you release him again, I want permission to carry a gun to protect our lives."

The judge removed his glasses, leaned forward, and gave me a patronizing lecture. "Well now, sonny, we don't think that'll be necessary. Who'd provide for your family if the breadwinner got sent away? Think it over. You'll put this behind you before long and things will get back to normal. You just put this business of carrying a gun out of your mind. That's the quickest and surest way of geting yourself into trouble. Now you just go home and mind your parents and everything will be all right."

My father had been sitting in the anteroom, listening to all that was said. When he entered the judge's chamber, he cast me a steely look of pure hatred, and I knew my goose was cooked. He came on contrite and apologetic—the hardworking wage earner who'd had a little too much to drink and made a mistake. The judge turned sympathetic, admonished him about Demon Rum, scolded him briefly, and dismissed him.

As we walked along the sidewalk, my mother between us, there was a long and simmering silence. Finally my dad turned to me and in a syrupy but mocking tone said, "Well, Mr. Wise Guy, I guess we won't be seeing you for a while." "That's right," I snapped, no longer feeling cowed by him. I didn't even look in his direction. "Next time you come around"—his voice turned cold and menacing—"you'd better have your hand filled. It'll be a showdown, either you or me." I nodded without speaking. "You've got exactly one hour to pack your duds and go," he said, and turned into the nearest bar. I went straight home, packed my belongings, and hit the road. I never saw my father again.

Two years later, after a rambunctious weekend with friends, my father died of a heart attack. It was quick like he always wanted and no doubt he died content. He had wrecked a barroom in a brawl and won the affections of an out-of-town chippy. Then, with a quart of whiskey under his belt, he raced his car at breakneck speeds to outrun the state troopers. He came home later than usual, got my mother out of bed, and demanded supper. While she cooked, the devil caught up with him and dispatched him on the spot.

For a fleeting moment after I'd received the news I thought maybe my mother had poisoned him and I felt a surge of pride on her behalf. It was at the start of World War II and I was in the navy at the time. I was given emergency leave and traveled to Indiana but refused to attend his funeral. I was relieved and at the same time disappointed that we'd never had our final confrontation. I felt thoroughly cheated out of my revenge. It was years before I could reconcile myself to that.

It was reported that my father's funeral was, with the possible exception of the late governor's, the biggest ever held in our county. People turned up from everywhere. It was half-jokingly suggested that most of those in attendance had come just to make sure that Banty Neal was really dead.

Dead he was, and those who knew him finally breathed sighs

of relief. Whatever troublesome secrets he may have had concerning his associates were buried with him. He had lived fast and furiously, mostly on the wrong side of the law, defying convention, indulging himself however and wherever he could, regardless of the cost to others. Essentially he was a disappointed man, frustrated at every turn, rebelling against authority and responsibility, striking out blindly at anything he thought might thwart his selfish desires or stand in the way of whatever dreams he cherished. All the power and cunning and charisma he possessed could not make up for the lack of success, could not give him the happiness he surely longed for. In the end he was no more than a spoiled child refusing to accept the responsibilities of adulthood. He never really matured. He threw away his life on booze and all that went with it.

I suppose my father should have been pitied, but I couldn't muster an ounce of pity for him. I could only think of the misery and unhappiness he had caused, the lives he had ruined. He was not deserving of anybody's pity, certainly none from me. His was a wasted life. He was slightly more than forty when he died.

I sometimes think it was a miracle that I survived.

THE CHILD WITHIN

Eliza Bellamy

These recollections are edited from a transcript of the writer's sessions with an interviewer who helped her explore her past. To suggest the feelings and style of those sessions, some free association and repetition have been retained.

I am terrified to tell you about the child I was, the child who remains within me. But I am going to do it.

Others used to say "Liz is so strong, so capable...." And I used to say, "Yes, but you don't know that inside there's a six-year-old crying." So I did talk about that little girl I could see so clearly. I always referred back to her in moments of pain, to her experiences, and had feelings about what had happened to her. Those feelings were buried deep within, for she was alone—and so she remains the lonely child within.

I feel a multiple abandonment. I feel abandoned as a child and as a human being, physically and emotionally. I was left with an abiding sense of loss and grief.

I'll tell you what happened to me when I was six.

I'm sitting in the kitchen in my child's chair next to the stove.

Mother is stirring olive oil in a little pan. I'm weeping because my long curls have been cut off. It had to be done because I was going away to school and there would be nobody to make all those curls in the morning.

Mother dips cotton into the olive oil and one by one wipes my nails with the swab. Then she pushes back my cuticles so my nails will look nice for school.

Where is the school?

Three thousand miles away, in England, which meant absolutely nothing to this six-year-old. I didn't know what England was or what it meant that I was going the next day on a ship, or even what a ship was. The next thing I remember is being alone on the boat.

No one was going with you?

No. I was going alone.

Who was to look after you?

Supposedly a stewardess, but I don't remember her.

Did you have any brothers or sisters?

No, I was an only child then. There was another little girl who was returning to the school, but I don't remember her on the ship.

I later learned that my father intended I receive all my education in England, to complete his image of his Little Princess. It was quite a grand scheme for one in his social and economic position. In fact, it was surprising that he could even support a family, given his alcoholism. He was a highly skilled worker, but failed repeatedly at managing a business of his own. As soon as each business began to do well, he started drinking and my mother was unable to carry it on her own.

I remember being terribly seasick on the ship and being abused. And I still tremble each time I recall a sailor pulling me into his cabin, holding me, and fondling me between my legs. Suddenly the door opened and I was grabbed from the cabin. Perhaps the unremembered stewardess did exist and noticed I was missing.

The Child Within

I never spoke of that incident until many years later—I didn't have anybody I could tell about it. Then I told my first husband, and some years after that my mother, but nobody really heard me, perhaps because they couldn't cope with it. Anyway, that trip to boarding school was the beginning of my developing some mechanisms for psychological survival as well as a sense of deep despair.

Now I have a much earlier memory that seems important to explain. We were living on Long Island. My parents ran a small hand laundry and my mother did all the ironing. She liked to tell how she had also hand sewed for me little bloomers out of Swiss lawn with lace trim and little dresses that had smocking across the top. Without realizing it then, I know I resented that I was supposed to be grateful to her for ironing my dresses and making me fancy underpants.

One day I was standing near the foot of a bed—I can feel myself leaning back against it. My mother was standing opposite in front of a wardrobe. She opened a drawer to show me my clothes and said, "If you ever wet your pants again, I'm going to pack up your clothes and send you away." And when I was six, she did just that.

I arrived in England and was taken by train to Marlborough School out in the countryside. My first memory of the school was of being called into the principal's office. It was a quiet, pleasant room, light and bright, with a dark wood desk, a table with a lamp, and a tray with a bottle and glasses on it. A couple of newspaper reporters were there because I had been seen coming through customs alone. I asked what was in the bottle, and Miss Headling said, "It's port wine." I asked if I could have some. She said, "Eliza, surely you don't drink wine at home, do you?" "No," I said, "I drink beer." That made the local papers! I recalled for them that my father used to take me to a speakeasy, sit me on a bar stool, and give me a sip of beer.

So that incident reminds you of your father?

Yes. My father was born in England, in Manchester. From time to time he told me stories of his boyhood, but it wasn't until I was twenty-two or so that I learned he'd had a brother. When they were very little their father deserted them. His mother wasn't able to care for both boys, so she put my father in a foster home.

He spoke with great affection of his foster mother. However, there was a lot of brutality in that home. His descriptions sounded like something from a Dickens novel—how dark and dreary it was, how he cowered under the table to escape two loutish foster brothers who used to kick him around. His foster mother beat him with a broomstick whenever he was late coming in from play.

He told how it was his job to bank the fires at night and stoke the stove in the darkness of early morning, and about the long walk to school in the bitter cold. But he was resourceful and had a strong survival instinct. He began on winter nights to throw potatoes into the hot ashes so that by morning he had hot baked potatoes to stuff into his threadbare jacket. The potatoes not only kept him warm, they also provided his breakfast and served as gifts to the other children to help make him friends. In speaking of how I felt doubly abandoned, I hear echoes of what my father suffered.

I was at boarding school for about a year and I did very well at my studies.

Did you miss home?

I was lonely, so lonely that I used to kiss my pajama buttons and my toes good-night. But I don't remember talking to anyone about being lonely. I do remember being in the little girls dormitory on the top floor. There were four or five forms (classes) and a dorm for each. A teacher slept in a corner of the dorm, partitioned off with heavy drapes. We'd go to bed and later the teachers and Matron, who was in charge of the dorm for us little ones, would come up. In the meantime there was a lot of fooling around. The other children knew very little about America—only cowboys and Indians, gangsters and gun molls. My New York accent sounded tough to them. A pattern developed of my being the mascot and whatever they dared me to do I did. I taught them about chewing candle wax. When everyone was in bed and the house was quiet, they would dare me to go downstairs and gather up the wax from the candlesticks on the dining room sideboard.

Forty years later I went back to England with my second husband. We drove all over Marlborough looking for the school, but nobody had ever heard of it. A bobby said, "It's unfortunate you're here on a Sunday, because it's the only day of the week the historical society is closed." What a shock that anything of which I had been a part might now be known only to the historical society!

Eventually, with some help, we did find what had been Marlborough School, but it was now a rooming house. The building, wall, and garden were just as I had recalled. Miss Margo, one of my former teachers, now gray and using a cane, lived there. Even after so many years she remembered my name instantly and held out her arms and we hugged.

When I came home from England, I felt like a misfit because children would scoff when I told them I had toe-danced on a stage and that I had seen Saint George slay the dragon. American kids didn't know about Saint George anyway so that was patently a fairy tale, and the idea I had danced on the stage was laughable. My British accent sounded stuck-up to them and they made fun of me for it. Coming home was so hard, I felt I'd have been better off if they'd left me there.

On the first day of school here I came home crying. When my mother asked why, I told her, "There are boys in the room!" I hardly saw a male while I was away, let alone in my classroom.

Now I was back in England, asking Miss Margo: "Did I ever see Saint George slay the dragon?" and she said, "Of course you did. We took all you girls to London and you saw it on the stage." And I asked her if I ever toe-danced. She said, "Oh yes, and you were a lovely little dancer. Your whole class was so talented that for the first time in the history of the school, we gave a public performance. We hired the local movie theater and you danced."

Eventually Miss Margo said, "Eliza, it's my turn now. Did you think we never knew who came down in the night and took the candle wax?"

I can't help thinking of how different school was for my father. He told me that all the boys in his one-room English school had to make model windmills. When they finished, the headmaster came to examine their handiwork. My father's description of this man standing with his coattails to the fire, blocking the heat from the children, and the little boys lined up holding their windmills sounded again like something out of Dickens. I pictured the headmaster looking just like Uriah Heep. One by one he patted each little boy on the head and said, "Very nice." My father, handing up his windmill, said, "Sir, I know it's not very good." The headmaster took the windmill and without looking at it tossed it into the fire. He said, "If you don't think it's good, why should I even look at it?" I'm sure my father told me this story as a lesson not to devalue myself and what I did.

Have you?

That's hard to answer. I think I have felt myself to be less than others. I cannot explain what it was like to know all my life that I was very different from others but not to know what the difference was. At some level I was aware very early that my father got drunk and that his drinking made our family different. My awareness certainly grew clearer and more painful as I grew older. Until recently alcoholism among the Jewish population seemed scarcely to exist, statistically at least. Sociologists have usually explained that Jewish people are close-knit in their family lives and very observant of religious rituals, many of which take place in the home and involve alcohol—a sip of wine at ceremonial meals, a gauze-wrapped lump of sugar dipped in wine for the infant to suck during circumcision. The consensus was that Jews used alcohol in moderation because it was so closely associated with ritual family gatherings.

I remember my mother talking about her father coming home from work on Fridays. When they heard Papa's footsteps coming up the stairs, one sister would run to get a fresh roll and put it on a plate with a little piece of gefilte fish or herring; my mother would run to get his slippers, and one of the others would pour the schnapps. Thus began the Sabbath.

This was the extent of traditional observance in my mother's family. My grandmother had died when my mother was very young, and an older sister ran the household thereafter. This little nonreligious ritual was done to please Grandpa, but there was no lighting of candles and no blessing over the wine.

My father had no religious education, nor did my mother, so there was none in our home. My father didn't see the need for it, or for attending religious services. He said he didn't need to be observant to be a good Jew. All he needed to be was a good man, and by virtue of that, he was a good Jew.

However, he did feel strongly about being a Jew. During World War I he enlisted in the British army to fight for the liberation of Palestine.

This lack of religiousness left me with unsolved problems: feelings of isolation, of apartness, a sense of not belonging anywhere. I felt this most deeply in relation to my friends. When Jewish holidays came, my Jewish friends were preoccupied with plans for buying new clothes, family gatherings, religious services, all of which were a mystery to me. Similarly, when Christian holidays approached, my Christian friends excitedly anticipated their new finery, family celebrations, visits from out-of-town relatives. For me, these were times of awkwardness, of self-consciousness, even shame. My father suggested that if I wanted to know all about these celebrations, I could read about them in the public library. He did not respond to my feelings of being apart and feeling lonely, or to my idea that Jewish religion and heritage should be learned within family life. I determined then that my children would learn about them at home.

In general, Jewish men did not go out drinking. My father drank after work, and his coming home drunk was not unusual. My mother told me that when she was young, she did not know what the word *alcoholic* meant, although she knew what a drunk was—somebody lurching down the street, looking terrible, from whom you fled to the other side.

Did he ever tell you anything about how he started drinking?

No, because there was no talking about it. It pains me at this moment to recall my own disappointment and anger and hurt. I know now that I felt abandoned when he drank, but at the time I knew only that I felt awful and frightened.

In our family there was no sharing of feelings, no empathic understanding, no sense of whether or not anyone else felt as I did, not even a sense of what others in the family felt. All that was visible and audible were our reactions to nameless emotional upsets. And since we never shared our feelings, we never knew their legitimacy. We never knew mutual support in bearing up under stress. We missed mutual consolation, so important in healthy emotional development. So how could we learn that it is all right to feel unhappy, frightened, enraged? And we never hugged each other for joy, either.

There were times I couldn't speak to my father for months, I was so angry and hurt. I don't know how I got from one school semester to the next. I even feared going out with friends on a date and encountering my father drunk on the streets.

I was faced with black and white. He loved me and yet he hurt me. So how was I to know love? I've been told there were times when I was very little when my father just disappeared. Yet I seem never to have known when he was gone. There were no spoken questions about where Daddy was and when would he be back. That silence seriously affected my ability to feel grief and to recover from loss. Nobody else was grieving, it seemed. I never learned that my feelings were important to anybody. How, then, could I value them for myself?

How did your mother handle your father's drinking?

Like a martyr, a consummate martyr. She just kept working. To her credit, she kept us fed and our clothes clean. Physically we were cared for. She had a kind of valiance; she always kept going. But there was no joy, no lighter moments, no social life, no family outings. We lived in a very narrow sphere.

When I came home from England, my mother was pregnant. This meant I would have the baby sister or brother I had always wanted. My mother told me years later that that was the reason she had another child. That's what my sister was born into—an intolerable burden for us both. I have great compassion for my sister and regret terribly that she has such a deep, hard, cold attitude toward me. We were both innocent. I know that now, but I didn't know it when it might have helped our relationship. She still does not know.

I can see my mother, pregnant, sitting at the kitchen table, depressed. I now know more about her depression because about five years ago, in a calm time, I attempted to talk with her, to get her to open up about some of the hidden things in our family. I asked her what it had been like for her, the drinking and all. She told me she had had several abortions between my birth and my sister's. I had heard years before about one that had left her lying, bleeding, at the door of a police station, but I didn't know there were more. It still angers me to think what she went through and that she allowed it.

By the time of that conversation I had completed my training in psychiatric casework, and I understood better how my sister grew into such an angry woman. Perhaps my mother had been looking at her through the ghosts of those aborted babies. Her unreasonable, unreasoning harshness toward my sister might have come from her agony over those lost children, and resentment that Joan survived.

My mother repeated a constant refrain to me: "Poor Joan, you're thin, she's fat. . . . Poor Joan, your teeth are straight, hers are crooked. . . . poor Joan, Father favors you. . . . Poor Joan." She also sometimes smacked Joan. Mother told me later that whenever she noticed Joan's teeth and knew she didn't have the money to have them straightened, she would get angry and hit her! Through this talk I developed more of a sense of how the burden was put on me: She had had Joan for me, or so she thought. I was to blame for her anger and for Joan's pain. Even now I feel I am being punished for it by their anger.

There were matters between my mother and father that were very frightening to me: threats of injury, of hurting, harsh sounds in the night. Once, when I was a teenager, I took a knife from the kitchen, intending to kill my father for whatever he was doing to my mother that made her cry out in pain. I woke up in the morning with the knife under my pillow.

Have there been times you have looked back at the boarding school experience with longing?

Yes. At school I was protected. I was disciplined, and when I transgressed, the punishment was appropriate, timely, and over with. That's very important.

Another theme of this story is retribution—endless, unforgiving holding-on and magnification of hurts and slights. I think all of it has been in the service of justifying a nameless, formless, bottomless anger. The anger—maybe hostility is a better word—was and still is almost beyond comprehension.

The only way I can begin to understand these feelings now is to look into the reservoir of experience, impressions, words, prejudices hidden in the soul's memory. There, barred from our conscious awareness of the harm they do, these lingering remains—a psychoarchaeological treasure house—form a gel that informs our attitudes and behaviors today. The remains of our happy and nurturing experiences and impressions persist and show up again in our current pleasant, nurturing relationships with ourselves and with others. The gel holds also the detritus of our unhappy, damaging experiences during childhood. The latter shows up in our current lives, ossified into defensive mechanisms and troubled, unrewarding relationships. The process of therapy, of healing, involves exploring and exposing the relics and letting go of those that are still harming us. Within myself, I see very early, even prenatal, abandonment, and the consequences for my life and character and relationships.

Looking at all these people and their lives, including mine and my children's, I see that we all have been badly affected, our relationships severely damaged by this heritage of anger, blame, and silence, and of lack of attention paid. I am reminded of that line from *Death of a Salesman*: "Attention must be paid!" I now feel so apart from my sister, parents, and children, a distancing that has come out of my despair and my understanding. I know there is no hope for me to bring about a reconciliation by myself. So I am calmer inside than I have ever been. I remain aware of love and compassion and forgiveness for myself and for them.

The ways of justifying anger in my family are crazy. I don't deny the reality of their feelings. But they don't know or will not say what they are angry about. In some twisted way I became the scapegoat. I have been blamed not only for my own deficiencies but also for Joan's and my father's.

Why do you think you are the scapegoat?

Because of my identification with my father and their identification of me with him. He and I really related to each other. We tended to think alike. My son knew my father only briefly but felt a strong affection for him. He felt that there was a straight line from Grandpa through me to him, that we shared mental and emotional characteristics.

My father talked with me. I was his little Chuck (a popular British nickname), and he let me know in many ways how much he loved me. I am panicky, frightened as I say this. Suddenly something buried is coming up in me. It's about what happens when you let yourself trust someone who lets you down, who leaves you emotionally and physically with some regularity, and then when you marry, actually goes away for years without contact. My parents divorced and my father left less than a year after I married Bill. I must have learned very early to fear and avoid intimacy in relationships. So I chose two husbands who could not be intimate, could not share feelings, and I left both of them because I couldn't stand the lack of intimacy.

My father was articulate, perceptive, rational—and because of his alcoholism, totally unreliable. We lived on the edge of a precipice with him. But he was not crazy.

What is crazy?

Crazy is irrational. Crazy is anger that is triggered by events of the moment, but is driven by underlying unconscious or semi-conscious feelings that stem from unexplained, unresolved, painful experiences in the past. Crazy is hurt that just festers, becoming more and more rotten, buried under sullen politeness and pretense, eventually leading to the belief that everything is really OK. And if one tries to dig up anything for exploration and explanation, one is perceived as a troublemaker. That's me!

I heard a TV comedian who is from an alcoholic family tell how as a child he had once asked his mother if he could have a kitten. She said, "No, you can't have a cat. Cats lick the butter." And nobody argued, nobody asked for an explanation. That's weird. That's what I call crazy, for want of a more elegant word.

I was told as a youngster and many times later by my mother, "Don't fight," not speaking about fistfighting but about standing up for one's rights. I was taught not to ask for anything because if I did, not only would I not get it, but everything I had would be taken away, too. Perhaps some of my mother's hostility toward me stemmed from the fact that I have sometimes, although belatedly, stood up for my rights.

I always thought that confrontation had only one meaning: a fight or an argument. Only in the past few years have I finally been able to state my case with the goal of negotiation and reconciliation. I still hold on to my discomfort, hurt, and anger for some time before I can speak, and the confrontation has almost always made a positive difference.

When my sister was three or four years old and enrolled in a nearby kindergarten, my mother worked and I had the job of picking up Joan right after I got home from school, taking care of her for the rest of the afternoon, then starting supper. My friend Betty also had a little sister to take care of. We used to take the children down under the George Washington Bridge, where we could walk on narrow pathways right next to the granite cliff. We would play ball with our sisters, braid their hair, and bemoan our fate.

We talked a lot about what it was like in our families. Betty complained that her mother never believed the feelings Betty expressed. If she said she didn't feel like having chocolate pudding right now, her mother would say, "Yes you do," rather than, "Have it anyway or you'll have to eat it later." Her mother was really saying, "You don't feel the way you say you feel." We both got a lot of that, in different ways.

We were full of resentment, which we focused on our having to take care of our kid sisters. We both must have read *Antony and Cleopatra*, for we made a suicide pact: We would each be a Cleopatra and ride on separate barges down Fifth Avenue, each of us with an asp. We would put the asps to our breasts and die—on Fifth Avenue!

You mentioned before having lost all hope. Are you still in that mood?

Yes!

Usually people who say they have lost all hope are suicidal. Hope is the last thing they lose before they go out, but you say that's when you calmed down.

I don't agree that most suicidal people have lost all hope. Usually suicide is essentially a vengeful act. "I'll kill myself and then they'll be sorry they didn't treat me better!' The suicidal person, childlike, keeps hoping, wishing that someone or something will change, will give him what he feels he needs—love, respect, a job. His life seems to depend on whatever that someone or something is. But this hoped-for change either will not materialize or, if it does, will not fulfill the inner need that can be satisfied only by healing the child within.

Hope is not only directed outward, it subordinates the present to the future. The suicidal person suspends living fully in the present by wishing, "If only this or that would happen, I'd be OK." We become OK only after giving up the hope that the answer will come from outside ourselves. Healing begins when we accept the truth of the past—and forgive. For me this process was more painful than any other. I truly felt I could die from it.

My healing began when I was able finally to acknowledge and accept with forgiveness and without blame the impact of my early environment and say, "Yes, I was an innocent arrival in this scene and I have had to pay the price for that." Then I reached a stage of hopelessness that emptied me of the belief that if other people would stop treating me badly, I would be OK. I also had to recognize that my family was treating me the only way they knew, given what they had absorbed and were holding on to. The experience of emptying oneself is then relieving, clarifying, calming. The people in my life are who they are. I cannot change them; I can change only myself.

Right now having said this, I can look at that little child I used to be and not cry. The tears are there, but they aren't overflowing. Because I can say to my mother, and at the same time to my children, and my sister, "You poor kids, I feel so badly we all got what we got—blame, demands for perfection, lack of intelligent, nurturing guidance, avoidance of the truth, and excuses to cover up or explain away the truth." Like that poster of Vietnam days: "War is not good for children and other living things." Shit is not good for us either.

I can remember only a few truthful talks with my children, and virtually none with my mother. I was uneasy and thus unskilled at sharing feelings. It's only recently that I have understood what a truthful talk is: communicating my state of being to another who has the ability to recognize my experience as different from his own but valid by virtue of my saying so. One need not prove his state of being. He need only be aware of it and willing to communicate with others about it.

I have only lately come to know why I could not handle conflict constructively. Intense rage generated by certain situations made me unable to stay quiet long enough to really hear the other person. Not only did I not hear it, I was unaware there could be another point of view that might be valid even though different from my own.

Although not alcoholic, my first husband's family was difficult. His father was a physician and Bill was an only child. When we got serious about each other, there was real craziness on the part of his parents. For example, they announced one evening that they were going to pay a visit to me and my family to put a stop to our planned marriage. We were totally unprepared. My father wasn't home when they arrived, and I was in terror not knowing if he'd come home, and if he did, whether he'd be drunk or sober. Luckily, he came home sober.

Bill's parents put on an extraordinary performance, saying Bill couldn't marry now because he had to study in Vienna (I later learned Vienna had not been a center for the study of medicine for fifty years), and how Bill couldn't marry until his uncle returned from the war to attend the wedding, and how Bill's mother had scrubbed her own floors, and how "Every dollar we have if you tore it in four parts, every part would drip blood! That's how hard we worked for our money." To me it sounded like "Cats lick the butter," only I wasn't enlightened enough then to know the danger in that. To them I guess it all seemed relevant to their stake in their son's future, which they saw as threatened by our marriage. Our reaction was to become even more determined to marry.

On their way home, they had to stop the car to let Bill out to vomit. I felt sorry for him when he told me that. I also thought my parents were equally appalled by those carryings-on but never told me. And looking back, I can see that Bill was only acting out his upset and whatever he felt about caving in. He never worked it out and never discussed the issues with me. I was the same way. What a pair!

Later, when Bill and I were sitting in a theater lobby, I desperately needed to talk with him. I said, "There are things I have to tell you about my family, all the divorces, all the upsets." I knew I came from a different type of family from his, meaning not just my father but also my mother's extended family. I felt I was not a good marriage risk. He listened for a while and then asked, "Where did you get those big brown eyes?" We went into the movie.

I look back on scenes like that—and there were many—and I am shocked that I wasn't able to do what part of me cried out to do: get out of it, know that this was not a place for me! But I was powerless to take hold of that.

The place being marriage?

No, this person who could respond to me that way.

Then all of a sudden I had two little kids, and I am standing at the kitchen sink cleaning a chicken and screaming in my head, "Get me out of here!" and then, 'No, no, you can't go anywhere."

In the meantime, my father and mother had separated and he had disappeared. Over the next fifteen years I saw him only twice and spoke to him only twice. Once he called because he needed money—two or three hundred dollars, I think. My husband refused to give it to him. I did nothing. Again, I am shocked. I wonder who that person was who couldn't insist that something be done for her father.

There were good times during that marriage, especially when the children were young. But even then I was sometimes terribly unhappy, in part because of his awkward ways with the children, but mostly, I realize now, because there was no real communication in our marriage. I have to say that I made my contribution to the lack because I didn't know what clear and effective communication was, especially in terms of an intimate relationship. I had no experience of shared feelings. I am aware that I tried to point out problems to him, but I was not effective. Yet we remained married for twenty-two years!

In the early seventies, after I had divorced Bill and married Arnold, my adult children and I reminisced while sitting around the dining table. By then my father had died and my daughter had married. We talked about what their early life had been like and how they knew that something was very wrong and wondered why I had not done something about it sooner.

I explained what had been going on with me, that I had no money and no place to go and didn't know how I would be able to take care of them. I told them I hadn't been totally unaware of trouble in our home. Although I knew nothing at the time about the helping professions, there was a family service agency in the neighborhood and I did go there. I know now I was on automatic pilot and not accessible to treatment. I had no other resources. Furthermore, I followed my mother's line of reasoning and added up the benefits: He doesn't drink, he doesn't go after women, we have a home, there is food in the house. What's the problem? I had no language for sharing, for complaining about the atmosphere at home. I decided that the way to live was not to look for what might make me happy, but rather to look at what I had and make that make me happy.

The children and I agreed that the atmosphere had been something like that of the movie *Gaslight*, in which the wife sees the lights dim every night. The husband convinces her it's her sick imagination, when all the while he is causing the lights to dim.

There was an impenetrable fog around us. In any relationship —marriage or friendship or even a business meeting—at least one person has to be conscious of what's really happening if there is to be any fruitful result. All the years of my growing up and all the years of being married, there wasn't anybody who knew what was really going on. We were all groping in the dark, each thinking: I'm the only one who sees things as they are.

When my children were young teenagers, I took a job as administrator of a research project in child development at the psychiatry department of a teaching hospital.

Did it strike you as ironic that you were dealing with child development when you had such a traumatic childhood of your own?

No, that was still buried. During the seven years I worked in this unit, our little family was racked with problems. I learned much later that our children's behavior and development were the result of the painfully damaging atmosphere in which we lived. The uncompromising, tense relationship with my husband led us to divorce. Even that was carried through with none of the collaborative, considerate behavior I have observed in some divorcing couples.

A year later I married Arnold, who was considerably older than I, had been widowed, and had loved me for a long time. And I entered a graduate program in psychiatric casework to learn about the field of mental health so that I could become a more skilled administrator. I found the study of human development and of psychotherapy both painful and compelling.

Have you counseled others professionally?

Yes. I have held several full- and part-time positions as a therapist. Although my major work today is quite different, I still do have a part-time practice. I have used my skills in several ways. I have been a professional planner directing a major project for social services, a training and development specialist in business and government, a developer and leader of a stress-management training program, and executive producer of an award-winning training film.

The Child Within

In your counseling, do you tend to identify your client's problems with your own? How do you react to the problems of others?

The answer needs another chapter. There's my relationship to the mental health field as a professional; my attempt to develop a clear philosophy of helping, of caring; how my struggles and mistakes have led to the choices I have made. I have learned total surrender to the forces in others that I cannot control and must accept in sorrow and grief.

I have not reacted badly to clients going through their own storm and stress. I've had considerable psychotherapy myself, and for the most part it has been wonderfully helpful. I am an intellectualizer, tending to explain what the client does when terrified of his or her emotions. I've been a good psychotherapist specializing in helping people who are highly functioning, neurotic achievers—intellectualizers like myself.

Psychotherapy is also about the therapist's ability to listen with "the third ear" and to evaluate, if not dispassionately, then at least without being flooded by anxiety. The therapist must rather create responses that will help the patient.

I can now find a quiet place within myself where hearing can happen and thought can grow. Since my second divorce ten years ago I've lived alone. I suffer a lot of anxieties by myself, but now I have several dear friends to whom I can pour out what I'm feeling instead of letting it overwhelm me. I can now pretty well control my emotional thunderstorms. I let myself experience them, then let them abate, and plan how to handle them constructively. I can then feel the gratification of success, not only from the outcome, but also from the fact that I can discuss problems with myself, all alone.

However, I was not integrated as a human being until just a few years ago, when I first began to see myself as an adult child of an alcoholic. I knew about the alcoholism of my father, but did not understand what happens to the development of children in an alcoholic family. The minute I got into Adult Children of Alcoholics, I felt a validation of myself. I could be understood by other people. I went to workshops, lectures, weekend retreats, the whole bit. The empty feeling inside often went away. I felt whole.

After I had made this discovery I wanted to share it with my sister, with whom I had had no contact for some time. With considerable trepidation, I invited her to meet me for coffee, intending to invite her to a lecture on the psychology of adult children of alcoholics. After introducing the subject as tactfully as possible, I asked her how it had been for her growing up, particularly with Daddy's drinking. She said, "My childhood was fine. I knew that Daddy loved me. Daddy didn't have much to give, but whatever he had, I got the best of it. And sometime during my childhood I decided that this was not my life I was living, and that I would live my life when I grew up." I was aghast! It was a stream of thoughts with a total reversal in the middle. During the rest of the conversation, she scolded me for always looking into the past, while she always looked to the future. She was angry and scornful of me and of my telling her that I loved her.

I have learned so much from so many people, even from the angry and hostile ones I love the most. Now I feel I am really catching on to the way undamaged people live; I'm learning how it is for people who have had stability and continuity and true relatedness in their lives. And I am beginning to participate in the normal give and take of everyday conversation without undue impatience or anxiety.

I work full time, attend to my self, walk a couple of miles in the early morning whenever possible, watch my diet, and try to listen—to others, to myself, and now more often to the sonarlike reflections of my reality bouncing back from others. I can now begin to experience how others may be experiencing me. I really exist! It's a wonderful surprise to know that. I never knew I had any impact on anyone, only the impact of others on me. That was always painful, or at least it provoked anxiety in me, for the only communication channel I had developed carried almost exclusively negative signals.

I feel myself now to be a more developed human being, more calmly conscious. More often than not, I am fully present in relationships, more aware of myself. I am therefore more in control of myself interacting with my environment, making conscious choices as to how I will respond to people and situations.

Still, every morning when I awake, I need to re-create myself. For I still feel the pains of the past, the anger, lack of control, separation, embittered and shattering relationships, and the contribution I made to it all.

At times, I still can see that sad little six-year-old girl within me—and I feel again her aloneness when she was suddenly adrift far from anything familiar for so long.

I forgive myself once again, forgive others, reaffirm love for them and for myself, and stand up to the truth of how it was and how it is now. That is, after all, the only place we live and the only time we can do something. Yet the past keeps rippling through the present, like those proverbial pebbles dropped in a pool. The ripples, both happy and sad, kind and cruel, will pass. They always do.

A GOOD GIRL

Barbara Robinson

My story is not much different in most ways from that of many adult children of alcoholic parents. Being an only child perhaps added to my sense of isolation, of being different from others. However, since I experienced neither physical violence nor financial hardship, I always believed that I was not an abused child.

I was born in 1930, the only child of an alcoholic father who was himself an only child. My mother usually had a small business of one sort or another that provided her with an excuse for never being at home. She is an alcoholic, too, but I didn't know that until one of my daughters pointed it out to me about ten years ago.

My parents divorced in the first decade of my life, and although my mother remarried twice before I went away to college, she was all I had for family most of the time. We moved constantly. I was raised by a succession of boarding schools and a procession of housekeepers.

As a child I was put on trains, and later airplanes, alone. I went to wherever it said on the ticket: to school, to camp, to whoever was to care for me or wherever my mother needed me to be. Sometimes a cab would be sent to pick me up, deliver me to a restaurant where a meal had been ordered for me, wait for me to clean my plate, pay the bill, and take me home. Someone else took me to Saturday swimming lessons and ballet class. I was alone a lot.

At school I was always the new girl. I never wanted anyone there to know the circumstances of my life that made me feel so painfully different from everyone else. I was small for my age, thin, shy, sick a lot of the time. Because reading came easily to me, no one seemed to notice that everything else at school did not. I was a "good" child. At any given time I believe each of my parents would have known what grade I was in, but I doubt either would have known the name of my teacher. I went to twenty-two schools altogether.

Boarding school was a good thing for me. It provided the only stable environment I knew. The continuity and regularity of institutional life were something I really needed.

A gregarious, volatile, impulsive lady, my mother was usually in the center of some unpleasant situation, all of which was always someone else's fault. In our household the focus was on the "bad" alcoholic—my second stepfather, a violent, abusive, ugly drunk. There was never any sense that either my mother or I contributed to the chaos and unhappiness of those years.

I always understood that my mother needed me to be a daughter who would be a credit to her. In my era, the ideal was Shirley Temple. But I was not the outgoing type. I didn't sing and dance and have dimples. I didn't even speak if I could avoid it. I stayed in my room a lot, reading books and playing by myself.

Life at home was not fun. The explicit messages from my mother were clear: don't speak, don't cry, don't have an opinion, don't disagree, don't be unhappy. The implicit message was equally clear: *don't be*! So I didn't *be* until I was thirty-something and began to see what I had done to myself.

Since my mother and I moved from coast to coast several times, communication with relatives has been minimal. There is only one person from my childhood years whom I still know, a housekeeper from long ago. I loved her dearly. She may have been the only person who ever really paid attention to me. We sang and played and laughed. When I see her now, we still sing and play and laugh.

What held me together as a little person was the absolute conviction that when I grew up, I would make a family and do it right. Yet I know I still search for a parent. Today, alcoholism has not entered the scene so far, and the family I have made looks a lot better to me than many others I see. I know that I wanted children so desperately because they would have to love me—they wouldn't know any better.

When I was twenty-three, I married a lovely man nine years my senior, intelligent, witty, interesting, kind, and unable to express his feelings with any degree of ease. For some years I thought I needed him to be more expressive. Now I know exactly what happened: with no insight into what I was doing, I made absolutely sure I would never be yelled at again. There was that wisdom within me.

During all the years our two daughters were at home, my plan worked. Those years were everything I needed them to be. As each girl finished college and left home, I grieved. But when we are together, we enjoy each other as people, released from the roles of child and parent. I hate it when they leave again.

Several years ago a large boxed ad in the newspaper gave a telephone number for adult children of alcoholic parents to call. I don't know why I was impelled to call, but I did. As I listened to the two-sentence explanation given to all callers, tears were running down my face. I didn't know why.

I went to a meeting in a church in a nearby town. For the first time in my life, I wasn't alone. For the first time in my life, everyone else in the room told some variation of my story. That was mind-blowing! I had been wary at first. I thought I didn't have the time or energy to spend on someone else's problem. After all, my experience as the child of an alcoholic had been years ago. Self-pity wouldn't be a useful way to be spending my time. And why pick scabs? Two wonderful women helped me to realize that the problem is mine, and it isn't over because I've not let go of it.

Today I am a recovering "good girl" who sometimes still tries to be invisible, inaudible, and inconspicuous, to mind my manners, to behave myself, and to clean my plate. Of the famous fight or flight mechanism, I seem to have only the flight.

Probably I have an eating disorder, perhaps because of the many power struggles over food (which I always lost) in my childhood. I sometimes get too thin. Because I grew up in a milieu of chronic disarray, I have no tolerance for chaos and am rendered practically dysfunctional when there is too much confusion, disorder, noise, or too many people in my immediate environment. Since I lived in too many houses and went to too many schools, I have an inordinate attachment to the familiar.

I don't often initiate. In a disagreement I usually feel I must be wrong. I retreat instead of trying to work out interpersonal difficulties. I am a dedicated quitter. I have migraines. Sometimes I cry, but quietly and in private. I smoke. I like to be alone, and I read a lot.

There have been periods of depression in my adult life. I think I understand where they come from and can wait them out. I may be a workaholic. (With what else can I fill that large gaping hole left by my grown-and-gone-away children?) As a librarian in a school and a public library, I find endless opportunities to fill my emptiness with work. Authority figures have always terrified me, and I am still surprised to find that I have become one. Oddly, my heart does not go out to the occasional shy, frightened little child I encounter. I find I really dislike people with these qualities. Then I dislike myself for disliking them.

I don't remember many dreams these days, but those I do remember are without exception about homelessness: I am lost and can't find my way home. There is no transportation to wherever it is that I live. Whoever was supposed to meet me and take me home didn't arrive. I am house hunting because I have no home. Apparently that is a wound that never heals.

A little gray cloud has traveled over my head since I can remember. If I live long enough I may get rid of it. When I was a child, there was no recourse. If you went to a minister, a school counselor, or a law enforcement person, you were told to go home and behave yourself and mind your parents. Children had no advocates.

The negative emotion I have been aware of most of my life is fear. Fear paralyzed me as a child. Now it emerges as anger— pure, cold, hateful, and ugly. Words have come out of my mouth that I wasn't aware of having said, horrifying everyone, especially me. I have several times heard an outburst coming from a mouth that turned out to be mine.

My father died at forty-four. Both stepfathers are dead. My

mother, if she is alive, is eighty-one. Unhappily, about five years ago I found that I could not deal with her and still retain my own emotional equilibrium. We are estranged and that is how I need it to be. It feels bad to have abandoned an old, sick lady. I don't know where she is. Even now she can't stay in one place. When I see her handwriting, my stomach churns, my ears ring, my heart pounds, and I feel sick. After all these years it's still there.

The good news is that I'm getting better. Sometimes I can see the sick patterns I have incorporated over the years, and occasionally I can do something about them. My adult life is planned so that I don't have to meet many threatening situations. I am no longer ashamed to tell people about my background. (If my parents were still in my daily world, I would have major compunctions about violating their privacy.) Now I tell anyone who is interested, and many who are not, all about the resources that exist for adult children of alcoholics. I have a sense of mission about it. The difference it made in my life is immense.

Several times I tried different Al-Anon groups but felt little in common with people living and dealing with alcoholism on a daily basis. It seems that I need to be working on getting rid of leftover coping mechanisms that served me well as a child but are now maladaptive. Therapy groups and weekend workshops have been very helpful to me. Books and tapes are helping me to change some attitudes. But it's a slow process.

My family is unfailingly close and supportive. They are trying to teach me to play. There are warm and loving women friends also. Some of these people care enough about me to set me straight when that is called for. I cherish them for that.

Life might have been easier for me had I not believed the Louisa May Alcott version of family life. If I live long enough, I may finally learn to pretend I'm OK. In the meantime, there is no one else I'd rather be. There are some people who love me, and perhaps one day I will too.

BOTTLE FED

Emma Hart

The deep steps led straight up into the night sky. I cracked open one eye to catch a glimpse of a frozen star as my father carried me up to our house. The house seemed far away, and I pretended to sleep in order to relish the warmth and safety of my father's arms.

This moment stands alone in my childhood, and indeed in my whole life, as the time I felt the most secure. It is my only recollection of my father, and sometimes I think I have conjured it so that I could have a memory to cherish. According to my family history, this image of a gentle, warm father that I desperately held for so long was a fantasy. In reality, he was not often home, and when he was I would climb over his snoring body on the living room floor to get my morning cereal before going off to school. My father was a drunk. He was the kind of drunk who never should have had a sip of alcohol, yet persisted in drinking for decades until most of his life was in decay. In time, my mother demanded that he leave our family, and I did not see him again for eighteen years.

I am only just now coming to understand the impact losing him has had on my life and the role that alcoholism has played in my family. Although the words of my history are familiar to me, the tune seems to have changed. I started somewhere around my fortieth birthday to try to comprehend how much the pain of my adult life springs directly from deprivation during my childhood and how much of that pain and deprivation is accountable to a family history of alcoholism. Until recently I simply lived with the facts of my childhood; I accepted them. I cannot change the hurt. I can only deny its relevance to my current daily life, and I have done that successfully all this time. Now, however, the skeletons rattle their bones louder to let me know that these wounds continue to bleed.

My parents were beautiful-looking people. They were from privileged stock and led lives that glittered with fashionable clothes, cocktail parties, and football games. Although neither of them came from great wealth, they lived on the cusp of it and adopted all the necessary accoutrements and mannerisms. They were both tall, slender, and handsome, and still sometimes they appear before my memory's eye or in my dreams looking like Zelda and Scott Fitzgerald. This is how I think of them: socially expert, silk aviator scarf on my father, hat and gloves on my mother, cocktails in hand.

Their marriage was a love match and produced two healthy and beautiful children: my brother and me. I believe they were happy for a period of time, until my father's drinking went out of control and he became abusive. My mother spared us the details of my father's abuse, but there were hushed references to it—pursed lips, closed eyes, and a shaking of her head. I am still unable to get the straight story from her, but I understand that he used to hit her when he was drunk and that perhaps that was what finally pushed her to ask him to leave. I still have many questions about the details of that year when I was four and my brother was six and we lived in the house high above the steps.

I have never accepted the loss of my father. It hurts me now more than ever. Perhaps I am stronger now and more able to look deeply into how this loss and rejection has torn me apart and how it has shaped many of the boundaries of my adult world.

Alcohol killed my uncle Bill in his forties after two decades of destructive living. Horror stories would be relayed throughout the family, and as a child I would think they sounded like something in a book, not like a *real* family. He had three daughters. Their mother died in an institution, killed by alcohol and abuse. My mother always called her "poor Kathy." One daughter was both physically and emotionally impaired by neglect. She is partially deaf and unable to communicate coherently. Another daughter could not hold on to her sanity throughout the years of being left alone with her sisters, frightened and unfed. She now lives in a house she will not leave. The windows are covered up with newspapers and she roams the inside with her cats, talking to herself and them. The third sister gives the appearance of leading a normal life, looks good, eyes alert, has an intact marriage and a couple of children. I marvel at her strength and think of her as almost a miracle.

I remember my mother would occasionally rescue my cousins—go to their tiny cottage and pick them up and bring them to our house for baths and food. They often had head lice and unattended sores, and sometimes they were literally frightened into speechlessness. My uncle Bill and Aunt Kathy were simply too drunk to even know where to find a can opener to open a can of peas to feed their young children. One cousin used to run into the house, all skinny arms and legs, in a filthy dress, and plunge directly under the bed in the guest room. There she would stay for hours, despite all coaxing, until something inside of her had quieted enough. Then she would tentatively creep out and into my mother's arms.

My maternal grandparents also led lives distorted by alcohol. I think of the word *bastard* when I think of my mother's father. In actuality, I did not know him very well. He died when I was in my early twenties, but he had long since ceased being real to me. He was dapper and slim and quite cruel, I think. He left my grandmother for a younger woman.

My grandmother Emily played an extremely important part in my childhood and in my life. I loved her beyond words. I bestowed upon her all the misgivings, the hurt, and the questions of my growing-up years. She was my special family of one, the closest to my heart. She was also drunk much of the time. She went in and out of "farms" up-country to dry out, but in time she always went back to her drinking. She was never able to recover from the blow delivered by her husband and the dissolution of her marriage. She was broken and remained so until her death. I do not know why my grandfather left her; perhaps it was because of her problems with alcohol. My grandmother became a tremendously heavy and poignant burden for my mother.

I am still unsure of where my father went or what sort of life he led, in the years immediately after he left us. Not too long ago he told me a story that astonished me because it comes directly from a recurring dream of mine. Did my mother perhaps tell me this story long ago and I kept pieces of it with which to dream? My father is on a bus. He is a broken man, with no family, not much money, and a brown bag with a bottle of whiskey clutched in his fist—a midnight cowboy taking the first bus ride away from his children, making a move that would be regretted for the rest of our lives. The guilt and pain he felt at this loss were likely only a shapeless thing then, with a crust just forming at the edges. Later it was to become rock hard and impenetrable—a lump directly in the middle of his life that prevented him from being whole.

My father went to Utah, which became the site of many of my dreams. In one dream I go to visit with him and he is living with a busty bleached-blond woman who is dressed like a whore. He is lying on a couch, in a plumber's T-shirt, unshaven, surrounded by beer bottles. I have come to see him, to reclaim my daddy. He is not surprised to see me and not interested in my presence.

While in Utah he got married again, to a woman who had been a friend of both my parents. My father communicated with me only sporadically while he was in Utah, perhaps once or twice every couple of years. He sent me a silver ring with a long-horned cow with turquoise eyes on it, and he sent me a suede pouch with beadwork. Because I received little from my father, I still have those treasures; the pouch later held my stash of marijuana. Ultimately, his new wife worked miracles with my father. He joined AA and became a nondrinker. Like his mother, his second wife held the reins, and when she died he did not have the strength of character to take on the task of maintaining his own sobriety. He fell into drinking again and as quickly married again—a marriage that lasted about six months. Then again marriage, this time to a woman who is southern, tiny, strong-willed, and a Christian Scientist. She has him once again pretty much on the wagon, although from what I gather he falls off with some frequency.

Throughout these years, I am forced to accept that I had no father, that because he drank he also had to forcibly push me from his life. At the age of twenty-two, I went to look for him. By now he was living in Virginia, and my brother had already made this pilgrimage. The visit went exactly as I feared: it was polite, forced, pointless. It was simply a young woman talking with an older man —no knowledge, no reaching out, no love, no trespassing, no pain. I hardened against him and we did not communicate again for years.

The kind of alcoholism that destroyed my uncle and my father is not quite the same beast that is now dragging my mother down toward her death. I have read that there are as many kinds of alcoholics as there are people, and I can see drinking patterns in my family that need to be identified. My father should never have raised a bottle to his lips, not even once. It was a mistake from the first burning taste. Like my brother. Like my brother's oldest son. My mother, on the other hand, was slow to come into the destructive phase of drinking. Her drinking, like mine, was moderate and in control for decades.

During this time, my mother had plenty of male admirers. She held out, waiting for the right father for her children, the one who would love them, who could handle the difficulties with her mother, who could rescue her from her daily struggles to keep everything afloat. There was a parade of men. Some sailed big boats, some were tennis pros; all were starry-eyed over my mother. My brother and I would cast our votes and talk about the pros and cons of each one, imagining which would become our new father, for even then we knew what the dance was all about. My mother would come into my room late at night, returning from a date. She would kiss me and a breeze of her silky scarves and perfume would soften my face. To me she was the most beautiful woman in the world.

My mother married the man with the big boat. In Peter she saw her salvation. She saw a kind man who was deeply in love with her and who could, with his power and money, release her from her struggles. We moved to more posh surroundings and rented a house on a farm. My grandmother went into one more drying-out establishment. My brother edged closer toward adolescence, and I followed more quietly behind. The social whirlwind my mother had known in her earlier days picked up speed and started back around the same tracks, this time with different players: cocktail parties, beautiful clothes, perfume, and bourbon.

Soon my grandmother was released from the latest cure, and she came to New England to live near us. Once again she was my comfort, my mentor, the only one who understood me, and she remained so throughout my adolescent years.

One night when I was about thirteen, my stepfather—loud, ponderous, drunk—came into my room. He groped for my newly formed breasts, my genitals. It took me a time to understand why he was there, why he acted so strangely, what he wanted from me. The words he said that night have haunted me all these years. I was able finally to repulse him, and he lurched back down the stairs to bed. When my mother was confronted by her sobbing, hysterical young daughter, she pronounced the whole story a dream, and we have lived with that lie ever since. The part that alcohol played in this tragedy is clear. Something gentle and precious was taken from me that night, and I will always bear the scar. As I write this, there are no tears—only something hard and cold inside, stating the facts.

Around the same time my brother became a teenager, and along with hormones came cars and booze. When my brother drank, he became someone else. Quite literally he lost his mind. Alcohol was responsible for the fatal accident of his best friend and for his early and painful marriage, made, he hoped, to compensate for the loving and nurturance he lost during childhood.

One day while we were living in yet another house, my parents received a telephone call and left hurriedly on a Sunday afternoon. I remember I had tremendous anxiety about them as they left. When I heard the car turn up the driveway, I raced down the stairs to greet them. My mother walked in the door and her face took my breath away. She did not look like my mother. Her face had completely changed, and she never looked the same again.

They had been told by a neighbor that my grandmother had not been seen for a while. They went to investigate and found her body. She had been dead for several days. There was a smell. There was liquor. As hard as we tried, we had not been able to keep her from alcohol. She drowned, drunk, in the bathtub. My best friend. Her poor thin body, her damaged liver, her tired brain cells just gave up. I still have in my mind a picture of myself as a young girl walking through the rooms of Grandmother's apartment looking for bottles, looking for glasses of brown liquid, finding one, sniffing it, chastising her, begging her, and throwing it away. The loss of my grandmother left a hole in my life that has never healed. The loss of her mother to alcohol ravaged my mother's face and laid wrinkles and gray hairs where there had been none.

College came for me eventually, and it was there that I learned how to have a good time. I began drinking, partying, dating—and not studying. My college career was brief, but it marks the beginning of my persona as a party girl. I spent a month in Europe after it was clear there was no more money for college and met my first husband on a street corner in Copenhagen. It was, in true fact, love at first sight. It took me five years to understand that my overwhelming attraction to him was deeply rooted in my desperate search for male dominance. Without a father, I had never had the chance to live through the process of loving a daddy, understanding him, rejecting/accepting him, and all the other pieces of experience that are at the heart of a relationship between a father and his daughter. I chose to do this with a man who was handsome and powerful, on whom I could lean, and who would make all decisions for me. Some of those decisions damaged me. I became a fairly heavy drug user and was totally immersed in the hippie culture for years. My addictive bent had taken another road, starting with marijuana, hashish, and then finally graduating to psychedelics. I was one of the lucky ones—I survived intact. Many of my friends from that time did not.

My marriage came to an end when it became more and more clear that I was the strong one and that he was merely manipulative and, beneath that, frightened.

I have since married again, and my marriage, although at times arduous like all of life's commitments, is a solid and loving one. I have two children, who light up my every day and night. Along with their father, they worry about my drinking. I am what is called a social drinker, but even I see a sinister pattern in my background. I see alcoholism as a dark grasping force—one false step and I will fall into the abyss, just like my family members before me. During my worst moments, I fear that it is only a matter of time until alcohol becomes a problem for me. Perhaps it is already? Who can truly define the term *alcoholic*? I like to drink and if I am honest, I can see that I drink more steadily now than I did five years ago.

My mother's demise through alcohol has picked up momentum in the last decade. She has begun living out her mother's tragic story. She has lost her health and looks and feels like a thin ragged leaf with only a slender hold on the tree of life. She is seventy years old, but alcohol and cigarettes have wasted her body and face. We all grow old and wrinkled, but must we also be so without spirit, so determinedly hopeless and self-destructive? I have tried and cannot find the key with which to save her. The pain of my powerlessness goes on and on, and I am unable to come to any peace about my mother's life. It is not only that the alcohol has stolen her spirit, but all the ugly and monstrous demons that accompany it. She has lost respect for herself through countless alcoholic episodes in public; she has embarrassed her children and her grandchildren; she has undermined her own power by staying in a destructive marriage. And she has failed in her attempts to take control of her life and her alcoholism. I have flown to see her, taken her with me to AA meetings, but AA served as only a temporary solution. Often her telephone calls are sad and incoherent. I cannot bear to see her die this way, and I remain constantly vigilant for an answer.

My brother's solution to the threat of alcoholism has been to stop drinking. He tried stopping several times and stayed dry for months, even years. Now he has a record amount of dry time under his belt, and it looks like this time it has staying power. His oldest son battles an alcohol and drug dependency. My brother is about to be married to someone who has no attachment to alcohol and who will serve as a healthy partner in all regards.

For myself, I see the same path that my brother has chosen. My husband grew up in a nondrinking family and is still basically a nondrinker. He never saw the glittering cocktail parties and the drunken adults who surrounded my entire childhood.

Drinking to him is an occasional beer or glass of wine. My children are growing old enough to understand that the flames of alcoholism have seared my history; they know their grandmother is often drunk, and they worry that I will "catch" it, too. This writing has helped define my relationship with alcohol, and my path toward abstinence seems shorter and shorter. My determination is to strangle the demon before it renders my hands too weak for battle.

MANAGING MY LIFE

Mark Roberts

I wandered out of a church this morning after attending the funeral for the teenage son of a friend and colleague. He had been killed in a car accident a few days before. As I drove the fifty miles back to Boston, a cold January rain pelted my car. It was the kind of day when you might reflect on the past and try to understand the meaning of life. If I had been that young man, what would my first twenty years have amounted to? That may seem an odd question for a forty-one-year-old man who seemingly has everything.

Driving those miles led me on two journeys into my past. One reached the depths of despair; the other was a more positive one. It was like two lifetimes relived. Many ACOAs have gone through the same rough times, and many of them have been fortunate enough to salvage some of their experiences and to learn from them.

I am the second son of parents whose families had immigrated from northern Canada just after the turn of the century. My grandparents brought skills that had been appropriate for their part of the world. Unfortunately, there wasn't much need for seal hunters around Boston, so they took up trades like construction and blacksmithing. Life was hard for them, particularly during the Great

Depression. My father, an only child, was a decent man, not able to show much affection but caring just the same. I never knew his father, but I got the sense that he was very cold and authoritarian, which left my father feeling disfranchised. That just didn't seem fair to him. He became a nationally known research scientist, while Grandfather labored over an open hearth in a blacksmith shop. My paternal grandmother was never able to adjust to living in the United States and led a reclusive life.

My mother's family was an interesting mix of personalities. Her father was a simple man, proud of his job as a heavy-equipment operator. Her mother was a deeply religious woman with a very self-righteous outlook on life. She was an alcoholic hypochondriac who seemed to resent other people's happiness or success. She was also deeply dogmatic and a strict disciplinarian. Her frugality was legendary. I recall her berating my brother and me for discarding pieces of Kleenex after only one use. I still find myself sometimes tearing paper towels in half to avoid wasting a whole one.

Her brothers and sisters remained in Canada and operated successful businesses. Yet all of them had the same negative outlook on life as my grandmother. Life always seemed to them like a series of hardships. I remember their visiting us every year, their suitcases so filled with Johnnie Walker Red Label and Players cigarettes that I could never figure out where they had packed their clothes.

My parents met in college and married once they had obtained my maternal grandmother's consent. My father had to convert to her religion before she'd agree. On the surface, the marriage was relatively happy. To be sure there were some domestic problems when they moved into the bottom floor of a two-family house owned by my maternal grandparents, who lived upstairs. My father never really got a chance to be master of his own ship. He resented my grandmother for trying to dictate how he should run his life. She resented him because he was educated, successful, and respected in his field. He seemed to have defied her philosophy that life had to be hardship.

My older brother and I seemed superficially to have a normal childhood. My father's mother became a widow and moved in with us. That pretty much pulled the extended family together—father, mother, two sons, and a grandmother in one apartment, and up-stairs the other two grandparents. It was a perfect formula for both harmony and craziness. I grew up feeling that my mother and father had relinquished parenthood to my alcoholic grandmother. She wielded so much power that nobody dared to question her authority. It seemed as if my parents were nothing more than my grandmother's children. That made it hard being a kid. I never knew whom to obey. My father allowed Grandmother to retain control over everyone. That control was very important to my grandmother; it gave her the only sense of safety and continuity she ever had. My mother was pretty much caught in the middle.

Only as an adult can I now see the damage that was imminent in assembling this strange assortment of people, all related yet with so little in common, under one roof. Everyone had an agenda, yet everyone was under the subtle control of one person who had a distorted sense of reality. There was no consistency in anything. It must have made my father feel impotent, always acceding to my grandmother's role of head of the family.

My brother Bill and I were also exposed to this odd variety of pressures and roles. He became a classic overachiever, and I complemented his role by becoming an underachiever. Bill's overachieving eventually reached an almost pathological level. He had to be the best in everything he did or he'd feel a total failure. He carried this into later life and repeated many of our parents' mistakes with his own children.

I plodded along, never much of a student and always reflecting my father's disdain for education. In a sense I was pressured to compete with my brother, who was always three years taller, stronger, and smarter. The messages I got from my father were always contradictory. He wanted me to grow up to be a successful person yet bragged to me that he had been a poor student and a rebellious kid, and that he understood why I had a bad attitude toward school. He was, in a sense, encouraging me to become a failure in school. He felt generally alienated and saw this as a way of winning my love and approval, giving him validation that he was a worthwhile father. This attitude later caused him to become an irresponsibly lax parent.

My mother seemed to be a woman with two distinct sides to her personality: one was so overprotective that we feared she'd suffocate us, the other so aloof that she appeared to avoid anything serious. She is a very caring woman but has never been able to confront anything straight on. She always seemed to dance around problems and issues, never admitting what was really going on but usually finding a reason why you should do what she wanted. More often than not, it was "What would the neighbors think?" rather than "I don't like it!" It must have been very difficult for her, growing up with a domineering mother who made sense only about half of the time. The remainder of the time my grandmother was bitter and emotionally abusive. Now the woman not only lived in the same house, she owned it, and she forced her child-rearing philosophy on my mother. That left my mother caught in the middle between a husband who was not as strong as she perhaps would have liked and a mother who terrified her.

Most of the early dynamics of the family have escaped my memory, but the emotional scars remain. As an adult, I'm trying to put my memories together and they have now begun to make sense. I have only three real memories of early childhood. When two or three years old, I broke away from the grasp of my mother's hand and ran through the tulips in the Boston Public Garden.

The next memory involved a period of extended medical treatments. They were very painful and I'm still rather afraid of doctors. Anesthesia wasn't used during the procedures as it was inappropriate for children. The treatments were so painful and scary that I had to try very hard not to wet my pants. Whenever I started to cry, I heard from my mother a very clear message. "Take it like a man. After all, you're four years old, not a baby."

The third and final memory of that early era is of the worst physical pain I can remember. My mother was cooking the evening meal on the gas stove, my older brother and I standing beside her. Bill took a carving knife and decided to see if he could heat it to red-hot in the gas flame. He did, then accidentally dropped it. As it fell, it cut through my pant leg and into the flesh all the way to the bone. The wound was cauterized by the heat from the knife. I still feel self-conscious about the scar from my knee to my ankle. That incident showed how lack of attention can cause major injury: to this day, I wonder how my mother could have let that happen. When I try to pass it off as an oversight or lack of parenting experience, I am reminded of similar occurrences later.

Life started to crumble for my parents when I was about seven. My father had grown tired of living in Boston and commuting to his office in Manhattan every Monday. He decided to take a big risk and open his own business locally. After five years it went into bankruptcy. Both of my parents worked at it full time. That left my brother and me in the care of our resident grandmother, who thought she was still in Canada, and our alcoholic grandmother upstairs. One grandmother sat around wondering why President Kennedy was on television and not King George VI. The other sat around watching "The Secret Storm" and drinking highballs. When Bill and I came home from school, we'd go upstairs to be minded by an obviously drunken grandmother who by that hour of the day could be pretty difficult to deal with.

In those years life was pretty hard. My parents fought constantly. My father developed a drinking problem and began to act like a man who was angry and bitter at the world. It was not the same kind of gloomy, defeated anger that my grandmother had, but rather aggressive, overt. Whenever he came home drunk, my mother made sure we kids were sent to bed so that we didn't see what was really going on. I saw him drunk only once. I said something that he didn't like, and he hit me so hard that I lost consciousness. Next day my fourth-grade teacher called me aside and questioned me about the bruise on my face. I told her that I had fallen off my sled in the park. I was afraid if I told the truth I'd be in real trouble.

The air at home was always thick with tension, and few words were spoken. I've come to realize what a strong weapon silence can be. As the business foundered, my father got worse. He was finally detoxed after he threatened suicide. I remember going with my mother to pick him up at the detox center of a state hospital. I was too little to go inside, but I looked up at the building and saw wire cages around the windows to keep the patients in. It was an asylum. It was a place of shame, a place where bad people were sent to keep them away from the good people. I saw my father come out in a bathrobe. He wanted out so badly that he didn't bother to get dressed. He looked like a man robbed of everything, including his dignity. That was the first time I ever felt truly ashamed of my father.

He never resumed drinking, but he did get involved with barbiturates and amphetamines. We were so strapped for money that we were forced to rely on my maternal grandparents for financial support. That must have been a terrible blow to what little self-esteem my father had left. He had always felt something of a failure for not being king of his own castle. His business and lifetime dream had failed. He had wound up in a mental institution. He had to rely on his alcoholic mother-in-law for food and support. He eventually got another job in his original profession, but lost it when that company failed. Then there were more hard times. In those days, there were no laws against age discrimination, so that at age forty-six he was assumed to be too old to hire.

After doing some part-time work, he found a job in a hospital, the perfect place for a person with a drug problem. Eventually, he was busted for selling barbiturates he stole from the hospital. He was found not guilty because of entrapment, but the family never forgave him.

He died several years later. I remember my mother and brother coming into my bedroom one morning and telling me my father had died of a heart attack in his sleep. I was a very young teenager, but I was not too young to read the label on a bottle of strychnine at his bedside. Twenty-five years later I told my brother that I had seen it. I then learned about previous attempts my father had made on his own life. They had all been hidden from me. I had always wondered why my father had been rushed to the hospital so many times for unspecified ailments.

At first I didn't experience real grief after my father died. Our family doctor put us all on heavy doses of tranquilizers, and we floated through the funeral. The reality didn't hit me until several months later. Only then did I suddenly realize that he was gone. When other kids talked about their fathers, I couldn't. He may have been a poor role model, but he was the only one I had.

The next few years were very hard. My brother had left home to pursue his pot of gold. Both grandmothers had died. My grandfather became an embittered man. He was never able to accept or comprehend his wife's death. He had spent most of his life catering to her hypochondria. When she died of a stroke, she was in the midst of delivering a verbal tirade to my brother and me over something of little importance. I think my grandfather blamed us for the death of his saintly wife. I don't fault him. He was a simple man; not stupid, but he often operated on gut feelings alone. My mother and I tried to include him more closely in our family to help him through his loneliness and depression. The relationship was tense. Strangely, though, he took out his hostility by bad-mouthing my dead father. It was as if he couldn't confront my brother and me directly, and this was his way of stepping sideways into his hostile feelings.

Then one night at dinner, my grandmother's name came up in a positive light. My grandfather began blaming my father for her death: if he hadn't made such a mess of everyone's lives, she wouldn't have had the stroke. Months of hearing my father blamed for everything that had ever happened to the family had taken its toll on me. I told him to shut his mouth or I'd shut it for him. He responded by telling me what a no-good loser I was and how I had brought shame to the family just like my father. In a rare display of aggression, I threw my dinner in his face. It wasn't a bright thing for a scrawny kid to do to a large, muscular, angry construction worker. He overpowered me quickly and began smashing my head against the kitchen door. He didn't stop until my head actually smashed through one of the door panels. He then threw me down the adjoining stairway headfirst.

I stayed away from him for a long time after that. There was no way I wanted to deal with that kind of anger again. He remarried and moved away. His new wife was a carbon copy of my grandmother. I finally made peace with him and was the only family member who ever visited him on a regular basis. He died some years later, alone, in a nursing home.

My mother worked full time to make ends meet. I worked as a dishwasher part time and went to high school. School wasn't a challenge. I was rebellious and bored and never earned a legitimate high school diploma. I was given a piece of paper with my name on it, but the credits did not add up to the minimum requirements.

A couple of years in a dead-end job and a brief stint in the navy convinced me that I needed more formal education. After two years of night school with straight A's, I enrolled full time, graduated at the top of my class, then got a scholarship to graduate school. That success was viewed by my family as proof I was a "late bloomer." There was a bit of truth to that, but only a bit. I spent far less emotional energy being a shining star in college than I had just trying to hold myself together as a kid.

In college I moved into my own apartment and that gave me a feeling of independence that I had never had before. I felt as if I had been catapulted into adulthood and finally was responsible for myself. I did all the right things. My career was well launched after graduate school, and I had all of the things most people consider marks of success. Yet there was something missing. The feeling of emptiness that I remembered from childhood had returned. I had thought such feelings would go away for good once I grew up. But although I had been able to avoid them with the busyness of college, they came back once I settled down.

I used to live on if only's—if only I were on my own, if only I had money, if only I had an education. The if onlys didn't work anymore. I looked for happiness in personal relationships, but that didn't work either. Over a twenty-year period, I had probably been involved in a hundred different relationships. I wondered why they all failed or why I had lost interest in the other person. I wondered if I was somehow engineering the failures.

Eventually, I married a woman I had been with for several years and thought I had finally become a respectable married man of thirty-seven. A few months later that relationship was failing. Somehow I had sabotaged the marriage. I couldn't understand how. Neither of us had been unfaithful or had any really bad habits. We just seemed to be in separate corners of a boxing ring, never really communicating. Fortunately, we sought professional help. It was then that I began to understand what an ACOA was and the extraordinary damage parental dysfunction, whether alcoholism or some other deficiency, can do to oneself and to one's relationships. Now my second journey into the past began. It was the first opportunity I had to take a self-assessing tour and to understand and accept the person I am. The odyssey I took back into my childhood was painful. The unfulfilled expectation that my father be a strong man, the kind of man a boy could look up to, and the need for a safe, sane environment— these became real to me for the first time.

I realized during the next year or two that I had no idea what a healthy relationship was. It is hard to build a solid relationship without ever having known one. I began to understand my adult dysfunction for the first time. I never realized that most of my relationships had gone awry for the same reason: poor or inadequate communication. There was never much communication in my childhood. What little there was came in the form of commands from my alcoholic grandmother. My parents seemed too busy to talk to Bill and me. They were away all day. An occasional threat or push to act like an adult was all we really got. That made both of us feel isolated.

My parents seemed to communicate with each other either by fighting or by total silence. So I never learned to have a healthy conversation when a serious issue came up. I had learned a side-stepping technique from my mother. That is a guaranteed formula for disaster in a personal relationship.

In my late twenties I went to a movie with a woman I had been dating for a few weeks. We had a minor argument in the theater. When we left, she walked off in one direction and I in the other. We never spoke again. She was as unable to communicate as I was. People raised in families with a normal amount of healthy communication would probably have left the theater, gone to a restaurant or bar, and confronted the issues head-on. They would trust their own feelings and respect those of the other person. Only with that kind of trust can two people work toward a fair resolution of a problem. Given the family dynamics most ACOAs have grown up with—tension, denial, mistrust, silence, and a distorted sense of responsibility—it's understandable why we have difficulty communicating our feelings.

As I was guided further into my own childhood experiences, a whole labyrinth of adult dysfunctions became evident. I began to understand my need to control everything around me. As a child, I had controlled nothing. My environment was chaotic, unpredictable, never safe, never sane. My need to control as an adult grew out of a family that was always out of control. When there is no control, life can be a frightening experience, with no understandable boundaries. Some things are OK and safe; others are not because they can hurt physically and emotionally. Boundaries and controls allow you to recognize the difference. They provide you with safety zones in which you can go about the business of being a child and enjoying growing up.

The incident with the red-hot knife opening my leg from knee to ankle was just one of the experiences that had caused me to question my own feelings of safety and to develop an elaborate system of defense mechanisms. The need to feel able to protect myself escalated as I approached adolescence. When I was ten or eleven years old, a neighbor, who was a pedophile, began bothering several of us kids who hung around together. I'm not aware that he succeeded in any of his intentions with any of the kids, but he was always out there. He was about six foot three, while we were about eighty pounds each, so we had to do some serious evading of his physical advances. He'd lie in wait for us as we came home from school, offer to show us pornographic pictures, then try to grab us. At one point I threatened to tell my father about his harassment, but the man just laughed and told me that my father had asked him to introduce us to "adulthood." I didn't believe him. We always managed to keep him at a safe distance.

I was afraid to tell my parents about it. I felt that I had done something wrong; otherwise, the man wouldn't be bothering us. I remember thinking how unsafe our home felt and how out of control it was. Now the outside was equally unsafe. I had to maintain a kind of vigilance everywhere. There was no real place to escape in that kind of circumstance, at least within the creative limitations of eleven-year-olds. You can escape into the mental if onlys, but all that does is trap you into a kind of double conflict. You can't make the if onlys happen, and you can't accept that they won't happen. That causes a feeling of being powerless and trapped.

The pedophile eventually moved away, and we kids all breathed a sigh of relief. But I think some of us actually missed him. At least his harassment was something we could count on. We also knew that we could keep him at bay. I have a mental image of three or four boys on top of a steep hill and a big, bad wolf trying to climb up to get them. Each time the wolf climbs halfway up, the kids pour oil down the slope and the big, bad wolf goes sliding down to the sound of the triumphant laughter of the kids.

A year or so later we had another instance of our family being out of control. I had asked my father to buy me a .22 rifle. He knew little of such things, but he did buy one over my mother's strong objections. With no place to use it in the city and no concept of firearm safety, my older brother and I built a secret shooting range in the basement of our house. It was well-concealed by pine boards that were easily removed. At the time both of my parents worked and my resident grandmother had been placed in a nursing home. The only adult at home was my alcoholic grandmother. She'd often go out visiting or shopping and we'd be left unsupervised.

It was foolish of my father to let us have access to a rifle and ammunition with no place to use them and no responsible adult present. But that matched his behavior of telling me it was all right to do poorly in school. He was again trying to win over our affection and approval at the cost of our well-being.

As soon as we were alone, out came the rifle and ammunition, down came the pine board hiding the target, and we would have a great time for an hour or so. We continued these shooting sessions for several months, until a bullet my brother had shot hit the target and caused a ricochet that creased my scalp. The very next day another ricochet cut my left arm. We ended our basement shooting, afraid that one of us would really be hurt. I don't remember what excuse I gave my mother about the scalp and arm wounds, but I know it wasn't the truth. We were afraid she'd make us give up the rifle.

Although our shooting in the basement may have been irresponsible from an adult perspective, it was not inappropriate for kids who are given a new grown-up toy. At least we took control of our actions once we realized how dangerous they were.

People sometimes refer to guns as equalizers, and they really are. For the first time I could compete against my older, stronger, taller brother and not lose automatically because of his greater maturity. Guns can also make an eleven- or twelve-year-old boy feel as though he can protect himself against harm from others.

My interest in shooting grew into a competitive hobby in high school. I developed the necessary self-discipline, similar to that of yoga, to control my own heart rate and other physiological factors. That gave me a sense of control over my own person and pulled me out of my shell. I reached the level of statewide pistol competition and then lost interest. On a lark I took up pistol shooting again twenty years later, only to find that the two decades from the mid-1960s to the mid-1980s had taken their toll, leaving me with high blood pressure among other ailments —a little too much hard living, I suppose. I still take my wife out to plink a few tin cans once in a while, but I'll never compete again. I no longer feel that need to protect myself from all the unknown events of the future.

I am beginning to feel more normal than I ever did in the past, although I'm not sure that I ever knew what normal was. I always thought it was acting like a man when you were only four years old and did not cry when you were hurt. Now I find that I've had to go back to being that four-year-old for a while before I learn what it is like to be a somewhat normal, healthy man. I have had to experience many of the fears and pains of a child, confront them, then learn to live with them.

Not long ago I finished a series of painful weekly medical treatments not unlike the ones during which I was told to "act like a man. After all, you're four years old!" I had far more trouble and fear than most people would. The treatments bothered me to the point that I would be nauseated for a full day before each treatment. That was an extreme overreaction to a minor, routine procedure. But with some professional help, I came to understand that I was reliving all the fears, pain, loss of control, and horror of being alone and unprotected that I had been carrying with me since childhood.

I've been growing more comfortable with myself ever since then. I no longer feel the need for so much control. It was very hard to accept the fact that I didn't need complete control over everything for fear that I'd have no control over anything. Letting go of old habits and fears is like losing a part of oneself. For the first time I began to feel that I was vulnerable, but that was OK. Letting go of the excess control allows me to let my hair down for the first time and not feel responsible for the things that happened to me as a child.

The alternative is to silently carry into adulthood all of the guilt for parental dysfunction, the terror of being in an environment often unsafe, the fear of being ignored or abandoned, and to spend one's life suffocated by those feelings. It would mean never being able to separate the feelings that truly belong to me and those that belong to someone else. It would mean accepting someone else's opinion of me regardless of its accuracy, because in childhood I had never been allowed to form a positive opinion of myself. It would mean spending the rest of my life trying to please everyone else because only through their approval could I have any sense of self-worth. Then everything good about myself would come from the outside, nothing from the inside.

I once described that alternative to a therapist as a bit like an expensive suit of clothes walking around with no person inside. The emotional structure was missing.

But there is another side to consider. In these pages I have painted a rather bleak picture of growing up in a family that was out of control. However, it's important to realize that nothing is ever all bad or all good. We ACOAs may have had some rough times growing up, but for the most part we learn to survive. To be sure we may learn to sidestep or ignore problems, but ignoring and sidestepping can be valuable survival mechanisms that allow us to grow into fairly sane adults. The excessive control, mistrust, guilt, and fear of abandonment need not be mortal wounds. They are dysfunctions, certainly, but they generally do not kill; rather, they provide a painful road to adulthood. And the adult can, through the right kind of help, learn to overcome these dysfunctions. The survival techniques we learned have made us strong individuals. That strength, when channeled in a proper, healthy direction, can assist us in our quest for happiness and fulfillment.

We ACOAs tend to ignore or underestimate the value of this strength. It is a positive by-product of all the pain we endured in our journey into adulthood. We paid a heavy price for it, but I'm starting to understand what Friedrich Nietzsche meant when he wrote that "anything that doesn't kill you makes you stronger."

Not long ago my job required that I attend a meeting held in the old state hospital that originally housed the detox center my father had entered. I couldn't find a parking space near the building in which the meeting was held, so I drove around to the back of a vacant, decaying building. The parking lot hadn't been used for years. I hedged at driving a new car over the broken tar surface, but I did. Once I had parked, I looked through the windshield at the building. Not only was it the same building I saw my father come out of in his bathrobe, but I had parked in the exact same space my mother had thirty years before. When I got out of the car, I looked up at that building. The same cages still surrounded the windows and balconies. It had been vacant for years, but I still had a mental image of my father looking out at the world from inside that cage.

I tried to hold my emotions in. I leaned against the hood of my car, unable to swallow, took four or five hits off a cigarette, and turned to walk toward my destination. For a moment I felt as if the blood had stopped running through my body.

Inside me a knife sliced through my most intimate emotions. Something else told me to get on with my life. I turned my back on that building, went to my business meeting, did what I had to do, went back to my car, took one last look up at those caged-in windows, cried for a while, then continued managing my life, feeling wounded but able to continue just the same.

MISSING
LOVE

Gary Knight

I think I can remember when I first felt the loss of my father's love for me.

I grew up in a very loving home. My parents, Lydia and Mike, were Polish immigrants who met in Boston after being liberated from the wasteland that was postwar Europe. Soon thereafter, my mother's parents, Olga and John, came to live with us. At first we all lived in a small flat in a low-income area of the city. We were not rich, but we never wanted for food or clothing. My father was able to ply his trade as a skilled photographer—not the kind that goes out and sells his work to the local rag or to *Life* magazine, but the kind that is a humble genius in the darkroom with other people's work. Gradually, our economic condition improved, and I can still remember the summer day when my dad brought home a brand-new 1956 Chevy and how warm the hood felt when they sat me on it. I was two years old at the time.

In this tightly knit extended family, with parents, grandparents, family friends, and neighbors, I never wanted for love, either. I was an only child at the time, and still am, though in an entirely different way (more on that later). I would often overhear people telling my parents that I was spoiled, and I suppose they were right. Personally, I didn't see anything wrong with being spoiled.

Missing Love

Only once did my father hit me as a child, and I deserved it. Somehow, I had broken his electric shaver. I guess he didn't believe that I was as upset about it as he was, and he got in a few good whacks with his belt across my backside as I ran crying from the shelter of my mother's arms across the room to my grandmother.

There came a time when our neighborhood was scheduled to be demolished, ostensibly in the name of urban renewal; fortunately my family was, by then, well enough off to move to a more middle-class area of the city. True, it was more ethnically Irish than Polish, and some of our new neighbors looked askance at the fact that we maintained our allegiance to a Polish church across town rather than to the local parish church—all the more so because my parents intended to enroll me in a public rather than a parochial school!

Even before I was of school age, my parents encouraged me to learn and to think. They patiently taught me the alphabet before I was even admitted to kindergarten, and this put me far ahead of most of the children my age. Soon the recognition of my teachers and the good marks on my report card were all the reinforcement I needed to keep up the pace. Years later even that became unnecessary as I fell in love with reading for the sheer joy of it.

Being a teacher's pet does not endear one to his fellow classmates. I didn't have many friends at the time, and no siblings, so I became something of a loner. I spent a lot of time in the library. Science was my first love, and when I was finally able to coax my parents into buying me a small telescope, my joy was complete.

Unlike most kids my age, I enjoyed school. Like most of them, I also loved the summers. Vacations were always the same. My father's brother in Ottawa owned a small summer cottage alongside a river in rural Ontario. For many years, my mother, father, and I would drive north for three or four weeks of life in the country. There we would wake to the sound of crickets chirping and frogs croaking and roosters crowing, to seemingly endless days of long walks along dirt roads that led nowhere, to the excitement of county fairs and rodeos, to skies at night that would take your breath away. My father taught me how to fish in a river where it was impossible not to do astonishingly well. But most of all I liked getting in my uncle's rowboat, alone, and rowing for miles and hours far up and down the slow-moving river, always drawn by what might be beyond the next bend.

It was during one of those summers that I felt I lost my father's love.

My father had never been a strong or domineering figure, certainly not one out always to get his way in the family. In fact, more often than not it was my mother who made the decisions on where we would go and what we would do, and my father would usually go along, without argument and seemingly without resentment. The two of them appeared to have worked out a consensus mode of decision making, one that, I suppose, would be the ideal in any marriage.

This easygoing attitude extended to me as well. I had learned to look at both my parents not as sources of strength but as sources of support. What criticism of me they offered was usually positive and encouraging. I realize now how proud of me they had been when, for example, I was winning prize after prize in city and state science fairs.

Through all of this, my father had been a friend: always supportive, always illuminating, always there with a joke. Until that summer, that is.

The summer of 1967 was anything but a summer of love for me. There were probably a number of reasons why things changed between us then. I was thirteen, just entering my adolescence, with all the biological, social, and emotional confusion attendant upon that rite of passage. Furthermore, my mother had just become pregnant with her second child—a fact I didn't realize at the time and whose consequences I wouldn't understand for longer still. But most crucial of all was the fact that my father started drinking.

I don't remember when I first saw my father drunk; certainly, I had seen him drink for years with his card-playing buddies and on social occasions. Somehow, it had never seemed to be a problem; it had never affected his social life, his marriage, or his relationship with me.

But during that summer things changed. He began to drink by himself. He began to enjoy alcohol as an end in itself, as if being drunk were a desirable goal. He began to argue with my mother. And when he wasn't drinking, he seemed to spend a lot of time . . . well, "within himself" might be the best way I can put it.

And his relationship to me changed, as well. Not only did his support for me melt away, but it was replaced with open criticism. He would pounce on me over the slightest detail, no longer with the aim of teaching me the correct way to do something, but rather to vent his anger and contempt.

Suddenly, without warning or explanation, I had lost my father as a friend. We never went back to Canada.

After that summer life was never the same for me again. Back in Boston, my father began to have vicious arguments, not only with my mother, but with my grandparents as well. These were not quarrels that could possibly be construed as due to differences of opinion or explained away as being due to normal tension. They were not even arguments about my father's drinking, for his dependency had not yet advanced so far that alcohol could be blamed for his changed personality. (Besides, everyone drinks!) For the most part, the quarrels were senseless.

It was into this chaotic environment that my brother Jeff was born. Of course, I had mixed feelings about that. I had been an only child for thirteen years; now there was someone else who was getting more attention than I was, not only from my father, but from my mother and grandparents as well. Recall that I didn't have many friends my own age. And I had lost my father as a friend.

I tried to adjust to all of this as best I could, but inevitably I became even more of a loner. I learned to hide my feelings deep inside, to retreat into my own little world of books and fantasies. My father's drinking continued on a more or less even keel. I simply learned to duck and cover.

Our family life might have gone on like this forever, but two years later Jeff died of cancer. He had been suffering for a long time. A year earlier, he had been diagnosed with stomach cancer. A lengthy regimen of horrifying radiation treatments had been prescribed, and for a while he seemed to get better. But a short time later an inoperable tumor was found in his brain. Chemotherapy merely bought time. Cruelly, soon after he had learned to walk, he became paralyzed from the waist down. One Saturday evening, while I was watching television in my own room, he died in my mother's arms.

Within days my grandfather died, ostensibly of a heart attack. My grandmother passed on several years later.

But it was Jeff's death that was to provide all the excuse my father needed to drink. He lapsed into a pattern that he has maintained for over twenty years now. He can sustain long periods of sobriety, for months drinking in a responsible fashion or not at all. At those times he is a good, caring husband to my mother and, minor differences aside, a good father to me. Until recently he has held a responsible job, the same one he'd had since coming to this country thirty-six years ago. (During the arguments that would ensue with my mother over his drinking, he used to claim, falsely, that he had never missed a day of work because of alcohol.)

His binges, however, were terrifying. He would often put away two quarts of vodka a day for days on end. He rarely went out to drink. He'd usually buy the juice, disappear into his bedroom, and proceed to drink himself unconscious. When he woke up the swearing and cussing would begin, always directed at my mother. Always senseless. Always cruel.

Usually he would be asleep during the day and come out into the kitchen at night, as the alcohol began to wear off. He'd swear and curse at my mother, verbally torturing her and preventing her from getting any sleep or relief. He never beat her, but in some ways the psychological cruelty was far worse.

Somehow, he would manage to find, buy, or steal more booze, and the cycle would begin anew. His face might be bloody from falling or crashing into some furniture. Occasionally, he would manage to stumble, or more often crawl, to the bathroom; sometimes he didn't bother.

Eventually, something inside him would tell him to stop. As the booze wore off, his whole body would shake violently for hours. Once we took him to a detox center; they cleaned him out, but couldn't clean out whatever it is that makes him repeat the pattern again and again.

The most overpowering feeling I would have is one of helplessness. When my father was bingeing, all I could do was cower in my room. There was nothing I could do to stop him from drinking. There was nothing I could do to help my mother. I didn't fear for my physical safety; I didn't believe my father would deliberately try to hurt me. But the rage—the sheer animal anger coming out of him—was not something I could confront.

Then there was the shame. My father was dreadfully afraid

that other people—friends, neighbors, fellow workers—would find out about his drinking. But since his bouts were unpredictable, it would often happen that company would drop by while he was blind drunk. My mother and I would have to lie about his mysterious absence. The lie was always politely accepted. He always believed he could conceal his drinking, but of course they all knew about it. More to the point, I knew that they knew, and I've had to carry the guilt and shame of it around to this day.

Now, after many years, I've gained a little more insight into my father's sickness and the effect it had upon me. I've read some of the literature and listened to some of the buzzwords the shrinks use, such as *coalcoholism*, which refers to what Mother and I did and said that might have actually reinforced my father's behavior. I learned how to live with different versions of reality inside and outside the family. Even now, when a sensitive subject is broached, a little program gets triggered inside my head and forces me to ask, "Which version of the truth should I use here?" I do not like myself when I think that way.

Truth was not the only casualty of growing up in a home like mine. And my father's love—important though it was—may not have been the greatest loss in this tragedy, either. What worries me more than anything else is the real possibility that I myself have somehow lost the capacity for love. Will I ever find the love I lost on that long-ago summer?

Love cannot exist without trust. When you grow up in a home where you have to bury your feelings deep, deep, down lest they surface and make you vulnerable, there can be no trust. You dare not love.

As an adult, I've had trouble forming long-lasting, trusting relationships. Ironically, it is my father himself who pushes me to get involved. "When are you going to get a girlfriend?" he asks. "When are you going to get married? Why don't you bring your lady friend over for dinner?"

The one time I did bring a female companion over to his house for dinner, my father was lying in his bedroom in a pool of vomit. The next time I talked to him, he asked me the same question.

Growing up as a child of an alcoholic has given me some strengths—or at least given me a chance to turn some weaknesses into strengths. Perhaps because my father became so critical of me, perhaps because I wanted to impress him, perhaps because I wanted to show him what will-power can do, I began to drive myself harder. I became a chronic overachiever, getting admitted to the best schools and taking on the toughest challenges just to show that I could do it. I became involved in running and in mountaineering; two years ago, I trekked in the Himalayas and climbed eighteen thousand feet up Mount Everest. I was determined to prove that I would not become like him.

I moved out of my parents' house sixteen years ago. I have my own apartment in another part of town, a good job with a bright future, and some wonderful friends. I still visit my mother and father every month or so. They would like to see me more often, but I haven't got that kind of emotional strength. There are too many ghosts, too many bad memories, too much anger in that house. Often when I visit, I can feel the anger rising in my throat, the same rage I felt when I used to lie under the covers in my bedroom and hear my father's drunken cursing.

In one very real sense I am like my father. Like many children of alcoholics, I myself have a drinking problem. Certainly it is not as severe as his. I do not consider myself an alcoholic. But I do find that drinking damages motivation, and I have too many things going on in my life that require a clear head and a lot of ambition. When I drink, I don't run. When I drink, I don't climb. When I drink, I find it difficult to stop. I realize that I have to be careful because the odds are against me.

I am, however, taking steps to understand and repair some of the damage in my life.

For the past six months I have been in therapy, trying to work out some problems I have with self-confidence and self-esteem, such as a crippling fear of public speaking. I have a hunch that these phobias are somehow related to my growing up as a child of an alcoholic, although I am not yet far enough along in the treatment either to understand the dynamics or to have arrived at a satisfactory resolution of the problem.

I have only recently become aware of the entire children-of-alcoholics phenomenon. I now realize that I am not alone in my pain. I am ready to reach out and to make contact with other children of alcoholics.

At this point in my life, I feel that I have begun a journey that I must make. The path seems to be making some unexpected twists and turns. Where it leads, I cannot yet know; consequently, everything I say now must be regarded as provisional, a product of an understanding that is not yet complete. Others around me seem to be making a similar trek, yet their experiences can convey no more than an intellectual "map of the territory." I have a feeling that I need to laugh and cry a lot more before I can say that I have walked the path.

TO KNOW THE DIFFERENCE

Joe C.

My name is Joe C. I am an "adult child" and a grateful member of Al-Anon.

I came into Al-Anon about five years ago when my second marriage was falling apart, along with the rest of my life. A friend in the Al-Anon program had told me that I was probably an adult child of an alcoholic ("adult child" means just that, a child who has achieved adult status but because of the circumstances of living in a home dominated by alcoholism does not mature) and that there was an organization for people whose lives had been affected by such an environment. I thought that I would hear something that would provide a quick fix for my failing marriage, so I attended a meeting with my friend.

Even though I was forty years old and came from a family where alcoholism was rampant—my father, his father, my maternal grandfather, and many other relatives and family friends—it had never occurred to me that those things could have had any effect on me or the way I dealt with my life.

For as long as I could remember I had been angry—that seemed to be the only emotion I could get in touch with—and in the last five or six years before I discovered Al-Anon, the anger had grown to barely controllable rage. All situations received the same disproportionate amount of anger. I looked for any excuse I could find to dump my anger on someone else. Sometimes I felt that the only thing that would make my anger go away would be to kill someone, and maybe even that wouldn't be enough.

My thinking was obsessive; I was either in the past wondering what I might have done to change things, or in the future trying to figure out what was going to happen. I rarely lived in the present. I really believed that one could see into the future and control the outcome of events. I thought that the people who were successful had that ability and that's why they took chances. I could never figure out what was going to happen, so I never tried anything.

I felt responsible for everything: the way other people drove, the weather, the way people acted and thought. My judgmentalism was constant and unforgiving. I wanted the world and everything in it to behave perfectly, as perfectly as I wanted myself to behave. That was yet another reason I couldn't take chances. If I couldn't do something perfectly, I wouldn't do it. Not doing anything kept me from failing. No one could point at anything that I had done and find fault with it—there was nothing there to look at.

In Al-Anon I heard that:

1.   I was not the only one who had ever felt the way I did.

2.   Much of the frustration I had been experiencing as an adult child was the result of trying to use the tools I had developed as a child to defend myself in a household where rules were constantly changing along with personalities.

3.   I could learn a whole new way of dealing with the world— apparently the way that millions and millions of people dealt with it every day. This was news to me because everybody I had ever made friends with or had been attracted to had either been an adult child or an alcoholic or both. They all more or less saw the world the same way I did.

Al-Anon practices the Twelve Steps of Alcoholics Anonymous. One of the very first things I heard there was that Al-Anon was a spiritual program. This bothered me because my family had always thought that people who were religious were both odd and weak. Normal people like us didn't need to lean on a god. We could go it alone. The answers to life's problems could be figured out if you just thought about them long enough!

I have since come to embrace the Twelve Steps. They are the spiritual foundation of the Al-Anon program and now of my life. This is how they work for me.

Step One: We admitted we were powerless over alcohol—that our lives had become unmanageable.

When I first came into Al-Anon I was willing to admit that my life was unmanageable, but because I had not lived with active alcoholism for many years, I mentally skipped the first part of the step. It took me a while to see that, while the step says "powerless over alcohol," I was also powerless over much of what happened in my life, and one of the reasons that it was unmanageable was because I wouldn't accept being powerless. I have since learned that power comes from knowing when I don't have it and accepting that fact. If I know I don't have power over the way people drive or act or think, I don't have to waste time wondering why people don't behave as I want them to. That time can now be used for more constructive purposes, such as working on the things I can change—that is, changing myself.

Step Two: Came to believe that a Power greater than ourselves could restore us to sanity.

I found it extremely difficult to accept the fact that I might not be sane, and especially hard to realize that as an adult child, I had never been sane. Trusting that a Power greater than me would give me sanity seemed, on the face of it, a little crazy. Lack of trust was one of those childhood tools that I mentioned earlier. Trust was a setup. Only dumb people trusted. Trust brought disappointment and pain.

I did, however, start to change. I went to six Al-Anon meetings a week. There I heard people speak of how their lives had changed by applying the Al-Anon principles and ideas. So I guess for me, without thinking about it, I accepted the group as a power greater than myself. I began to trust in the Al-Anon groups because the people there had had my pain, felt my guilt, lived my confusion and anger. Their stories were my story, not stories about what happened to innocent children at the hands of child abusers at some day-care center or some creep hanging around a schoolyard, but nevertheless stories about emotional, physical, and sexual abuse. They told of families where concepts of love were skewed, where when the parents said "I love you" it meant they could do, say, and behave as they pleased. Words and actions did not coincide. We had a common bond—alcoholism and the devastation and ruined lives it leaves in its wake. We also had a desire to better our lives. This step opened the door for me to a different way of thinking.

Step Three: Made a decision to turn our will and our lives over to the care of God *as we understood Him*.

It was one thing to trust in the group as a source of spiritual guidance. It was quite another to decide to trust that something or someone I could not see would take care of me in a loving and gentle manner. I had, however, heard the old-timers in Al-Anon talk about their Higher Powers. Some of them lived with active alcoholism, yet they had something I had never had: serenity. I wanted to have that, too. I had no idea how one turned over his will and life to the care of a Higher Power, but as an old-timer explained to me, all I had to do was make the decision. The rest would follow. It was pointed out to me that surrender was not an act of will, but rather the absence of it. In other words, I couldn't will my life to God, but maybe if I stopped being willful I would have a chance to see what God could do if I let Him.

Step Four: Made a searching and fearless moral inventory of ourselves.

This step scared the hell out of me, and I refused to look at it for about two years. I thought that the step meant to look only at the negative aspects of myself (something I was very good at). But it was also, I learned, a way of discovering some of the good points about myself. I had never liked myself. The message that I received at home was that I had no good points, or if I did, there was something wrong with me because I failed to live up to them. I was an underachiever, a follower; I had an inferiority complex. It seemed to me that my faults were overwhelming.

Another survival tool in an alcoholic home is to be whatever you think someone wants you to be in order to avoid conflict. In contrast, Step Four allowed me to be myself. It is a step that I take often because it enables me to get to know myself, to get in touch with the "self" in myself.

Step Five: Admitted to God, to ourselves, and to another human being the exact nature of our wrongs.

This step sort of lays the cards on the table. To me it has to do with honesty. It doesn't do much good to take an inventory and then sit on it. Once you admit your defects to God and another human being, they diminish almost immediately. Now that things are out in the open, they can be dealt with. There are no dark secrets to carry around and beat yourself up with anymore.

Step Six: Were entirely ready to have God remove all these defects of character.

This step goes back to Step Three, where I made the decision to turn my will and life over to the care of God. I had been trying to use my will all my life to get things to turn out the way I wanted them to. If I could have willed away my defects, and of course the ones that I saw in everyone else, I would have done so long ago. I had to allow God to remove my defects of character because I simply didn't know how to do it myself.

Step Seven: Humbly asked Him to remove our shortcomings.

Humility was an entirely new concept to me. The word had always implied humiliation or humiliating. Now, to me, the word means simply that I can admit that I don't know. It is the ability to be able to ask for help or to accept help when it is offered. I was never able to do either. I thought that I was expected to go it alone and have all the answers. There were times when I couldn't have possibly known or been expected to know what to do in a given situation, yet it never occurred to me to ask for help. In my family, asking for help was a way of setting yourself up for ridicule.

Step Eight: Made a list of all persons we had harmed, and became willing to make amends to them all.

It had never occurred to me that I had perhaps hurt people over the years before I joined Al-Anon. As I began to see the role that I played in my life emerging, however, I realized that although I saw myself as a victim, I had also used a lot of people. For many years I worked in a bar, and it was my forum for working off anger and rage. I also lied to people. I lied to build up my ego, to protect myself, to get what I wanted. Telling the truth and lying carried the same weight, and I rarely differentiated between them. They were both tools to get me by. The list of people I had harmed was very long, and many of the people on that list were now nameless to me. I didn't know how I was going to make amends.

Someone reminded me at a meeting one night to include myself on that list of persons I had harmed. It was difficult to admit that I had done a lot of things to harm myself, but doing so helped me to start reassessing my role as a victim.

Step Nine: Made direct amends to such people whenever possible, except when to do so would injure them or others.

There were obviously many people to make amends to as I had observed in Step Eight. But I did not know how to go about doing that. Some people I could not make amends to; for instance, women I had had relationships with who were now married or with someone else.

Many of the people that I had verbally and physically abused were unknown to me as individuals. They had been patrons of the bar I worked in or individuals who broke my rules of good driving. The only way in which I could begin to make amends for my actions toward those people was by changing myself. I began to learn to act instead of react, to realize that I am not responsible for the way other people drive, only the way I drive. I don't tend bar anymore. As an adult child, I have found I cannot maintain my sense of serenity at a bar. I couldn't say I was sorry to all the people I hurt through rage and anger, but I could stop the list from growing.

I also found that many times the situation for making amends would present itself in conversation with old coworkers and friends. My apology didn't have to be elaborate, only an admission that I wasn't always in control and that I realized it and was working on changing. Most people accepted my amends. Some said they had noticed a change in me, and that did a lot for my self-esteem. I can't do anything about the people who did not accept my amends. I can only make my apologies to them; I cannot force acceptance. This step put me on the road to taking responsibility for my actions and letting go of responsibility for the actions of others.

Step Ten: Continued to take personal inventory and when we were wrong promptly admitted it.

I saw that one of the immediate values of this step was that it could prevent me from having to go back and take Steps Eight and Nine again. But more than that—and I did not see this immediately—this step also had to do with humility. I had to admit when I was wrong, and, as in the Ninth Step, take responsibility for my actions. This step also helps to keep me focused on today, so I don't feel the necessity to dwell in the past in order to try to correct the present.

Step Eleven: Sought through prayer and meditation to improve our conscious contact with God *as we understood Him*, praying only for knowledge of His will for us and the power to carry that out.

This step is not easy, because I have been used to living my life by my will. The Al-Anon literature says that if, after turning your will over to the care of God, you wish to take it back, you can have it. I know this to be true because I have done so on many occasions. And because I have done so, I can see the difference between what is accomplished by my will and what is accomplished by God's. I am no match. In no way have I ever come close to giving myself the gifts that I have received from my Higher Power, which I choose to call God.

I take my will back because I am human and definitely not perfect. Each time I do so it is a vast learning experience for me, and a painful reminder of where a lot of my feelings of being a victim come from. I victimize myself by trying to take what I call "the myths of life" I learned from growing up in an alcoholic home and applying them to a world where they have no place or use.

One of the myths I grew up with was that I was responsible for the way people felt and thought. I lay no blame on my family here. My mother and father are both adult children of alcoholics, as were their parents. I feel bad that they have not chosen to accept Al-Anon. They feel that my participation in Al-Anon is a way of holding them responsible for bad parenting. I, however, know that my family loves me, and I know that they did the very best they could in raising me. It's not their fault that their best efforts weren't very good. Alcoholism is a family disease and my family has it. We didn't ask for it any more than we would ask for cancer, but we have it all the same. It is a disease of denial. People seek treatment for cancer more readily.

In spite of everything, my relationship with my family has changed because I have changed. I don't talk to them about the Al-Anon program; I just try to live by it when I am around them.

There is a saying in the Al-Anon program and it goes something like this, "Don't ask your Higher Power for what you want because you just might get it." Since I have asked for God's will for me, I also have to be ready to accept things that happen when they are not what I want to happen. I have to remind myself continually that I have a Higher Power and his name is not Joe.

Step Twelve: Having had a spiritual awakening as a result of these steps, we tried to carry this message to others, and to practice these principles in all our affairs.

Spirituality was an alien concept to me until I began Al-Anon. It seemed to have its place with monks, Gregorian chants, Tibetan prayer wheels, mystics, and the like. It was religion, going to church, believing in a God who punished the wicked—of course with my low self-esteem I knew I was on His hit list. He rewarded the good and hardworking, and I was never good enough or worked hard enough. One thing was for sure: spirituality definitely did not have anything to do with me. I was alone in the world, and it was bad enough having myself for a critic, let alone some God looking over my shoulder and zapping me every time I did something wrong.

As a result of being in the Al-Anon program and working on

these steps, I now have a God in my life, a God who loves me even when I don't love myself, even when I don't love Him. My God is a friend who has my best interests always in mind and who never lets me down when I ask for help.

I have learned also that spirituality means that many situations turn out exactly the way they are going to in spite of my efforts. Spirituality means I don't have to force solutions to problems, especially when I often don't know what the solutions should be anyway. I have learned that other people have a Higher Power also, and that the name of their Higher Power, as mine, is not Joe.

Mostly, however, spirituality to me means faith. I have faith that I was put on earth for a purpose, and that my Higher Power will help me achieve that purpose. By being able to focus on myself and not always on people, places, and things over which I have no control, I have begun to know myself and my own talents and limitations. I have a sense of self, of who I am. Today my opinions are mine and not what I think someone else wants to hear. I have begun to be able to say no to unacceptable behavior in others, to set limits and boundaries.

I have begun to like myself and accept the fact that others like me and care about me. For years I believed that if someone liked me there must be something wrong with him or her. I would seek out their faults, focus on them, and thus prove to myself that there was really no basis for friendship.

These steps are not a simple matter of twelve weeks and "Eureka, I'm cured!" It took me forty years to become as sick as I was when I entered Al-Anon. I go back to these steps often. I go back to Step One after I have taken back my will, because I have to admit once again that I am powerless and that I have made my life unmanageable.

Gaining self-knowledge in the Al-Anon program has been compared to peeling away the skin of an onion—it is slow and there are a lot of layers. I once thought that if I had to take a good hard look at myself, I would disappear in a puff of smoke or melt like the Wicked Witch of the West. I didn't. Instead I grew. I remembered things from my childhood that I had forgotten, and that was painful. I remembered things that I had done to others, and that was painful. And what I had done to myself, which was perhaps the most painful of all. I hated myself and I was merciless in my self-condemnation.

I have cried a lot because I have hurt a lot. But I embrace the pain because through it I change. I think the only pain that would be too great for me to bear would be to go back to the way I was before I discovered Al-Anon, because now I can see the difference and the difference is truly a miracle.

THE LEGACY

Jeffrey Laign

My mother was a dancer. My mother was a drunk. Atop the cluttered chest of drawers in her shadowy tomb of a bedroom sat a cracked and yellowed snapshot of a winsome child bedecked in tights and tails, one hand tipping a top hat, the other twirling a silver-handled cane as she shuffled off to Buffalo. It was a gilt-framed reminder of a bitter woman's hopes and dreams, dashed, she railed, by circumstance and resurrected only on hopeless, dreamless nights, and then only with the help of Cutty Sark. "Get a load of this," she'd slur, bounding to her feet uncertainly and cranking up the monophonic record player. As "Swanee River" flooded the battlefield of our living room, she'd launch into the tap routine that had captivated any number of doting adults four decades earlier. My younger sister and I, perpetually on guard against our mother's unpredictable wrath, were somewhat less than beguiled, though captive nonetheless. Eventually our mother would collapse, exhausted, muttering curses for her broken life as we dragged her off to bed. For a long time thereafter, I would listen at my mother's door, grateful for the sound of her breathing. Would this be the night? I wondered.

Ten years would pass before my mother succeeded in ending her life. By that time I had nearly drowned in the disease of alcoholism, bloated by my own brand of bitterness. Today in recovery I have come to forgive my mother and myself. Today I am able to view the war that was my childhood as a legacy, a gift.

Alcoholism is a cunning creature, a fanged cat that purrs. My mother was well into her forties before the predator attacked, and there was nothing that any of us could do to stop it. Had we not been blind to the sickness, we might have noticed the symptoms of addiction, which illuminated even her sober years like phosphorescent river rocks. A chain-smoker fueled by endless cups of strong black coffee, a woman beset by a child's nagging doubts and fears, my mother had been waiting all her life for a chance to explode. "High-strung," she would say, just like all the women in her family.

And what a family that was, an Irish bunch much given to maudlin reunions at which weepy poems would be composed and read again and again. If alcoholism wrecked any of their lives, the collisions were never reported. In the time-honored tradition of southern families, secrets were kept inside, like house pets. But certainly the spoiling fruits of family dysfunction were evident for all to see.

My mother's mother was a poker-playing political activist, a gadabout friend of presidents, once arrested for assaulting an officer of the law. She loved nothing better than to publicly hammer home the merits of Democrats, except perhaps to engage her grandchildren in high-speed adventures or to regale them with far-fetched, wonderfully entertaining stories of murder and mayhem.

My grandfather was a baseball player-turned-actor who went on to make his fortune as a technical director of some of Broadway's biggest hits, but whose face his daughter saw more often splashed across the pages of magazines than in the flesh.

My grandparents were as compatible as fire and ice, and about the time my mother was learning to dance, they divorced, an act of shocking proportions in the depression-era South. Despite the shameful split, my grandmother nonchalantly moved in with her ex-husband's family and remained a true daughter of that clan until the day she died. Preoccupied by politics more often than not, she left the rearing of her child largely to her husband's maiden sisters. Those two aristocratic daughters of Dixie, who traced their lineage wistfully to the throne of England, ran their humble home with unspoken and easily breakable rules, like benevolent dictators. "We spoiled that child to death," my great-aunts later would concede. This, we all knew, was no exaggeration.

A woman who entered the autumn of her life drunkenly dancing in the shadows of the past, my mother was possessed by the spirit of a hungry child who would do anything for applause, anything to command center stage. In groups my mother came alive, and her need to be noticed caused her undoing. On parent-teacher nights, mine was the mother who shot up her hand to criticize curriculum, to cast out witty, condescending asides, to lecture on progressive child-rearing techniques, and, invariably, to suffer the disdainful, withering glances of those she lumped together as inferiors. By no means a beautiful woman, she was fascinating in spite of her flaws, a diamond in the rough, fool's gold. Men were attracted by her unorthodox charms, and women distrusted her because of them. "At least I'm not boring," she would parry when her children complained that she'd embarrassed them. And that was the truth, we had to admit. To live a life of mediocrity, we children were taught, was to suffer the cruelest of fates. Far better, she implied, to fail nobly like some classical Greek protagonist than to slump through life unnoticed.

My mother's tragic fate was sealed on a balmy April Saturday, and nothing about the simple ceremony foreshadowed hell. Following the example of her own mother, she chose a man who resembled her in no way: a reclusive, introspective scholar from a sober, God-fearing, and otherwise undistinguished breed of Huguenots who cared not a whit for politics or plays.

Opposites attract, the axiom goes. My parents were living proof. Despite their glaring differences, they bonded like eagles, magnifying the single quality they had in common: both were emotional cripples who could not stand alone. With the desperation of drowning children, they clung to each other, building a life raft of dependency. "They were like Siamese twins," my sister later said. Such ties are not severed easily.

From my earliest recollections, my father was a grand enigma, on the order of ball lightning and other natural anomalies. Never would I understand him, no matter how hard I tried. A thoughtful, well-read man of seemingly unlimited potential, he never aspired to greatness, as men ought to do according to the rules my mother had laid down for me. Yet my father was not without passion. It was his dream, indeed, that changed our lives forever, unleashing a whirlpool that would engulf our family—and destroy it.

My father was a solitary man who required little, least of all the assistance or companionship of others. And in solitude he pursued his all-consuming interests: tracking deer on godforsaken mountain paths or fishing icy streams for rainbow trout. Never far from reach was the camera with which he captured miracles: dogwoods bursting into bloom in a sun-dappled forest glen; amanita mushrooms, splendid and deadly, pushing through a loamy woodland floor; raccoons startled in the midst of furtive undertakings. These dances with creation my father performed alone, self-sufficiently, in the spirit of his forebears, who had helped settle the Shenandoah Valley of Virginia when nature was all it had to offer.

We lived in Winchester, a small city at the valley's northern entrance, unremarkable but for producing novelist Willa Cather, singer Patsy Cline, and little thereafter but apples, albeit the finest in the world. Though only an hour's drive from the fast-laned nation's capital, Winchester was as cosmopolitan in those days as it had been when the young George Washington made it his home before the French and Indian War. But even Winchester's small slice of commerce was too much for my father to stomach.

My sister and I were not yet in school when our father packed us up and forged west toward the mountains, where we settled on two hundred acres of limestone and loblolly pines, in a rough-hewn structure that had sheltered some farmer's livestock shortly after the surrender at Appomattox. Years later, when I was floundering in the inescapable eddies of adolescence, I would smirk when smarmy schoolteachers chastised: "Where are your manners? Were you raised in a barn?"

For a shy and lonely boy the forest was a paradise, a haven from a silent, angry, and often incomprehensible home. I came to know the ways of wild things. I memorized the ancient sagas of plants and trees, many of which had towered over the forest floor when Columbus was a boy and the world was flat. I learned to gossip with birds and to be led, gullible, by twisting brooks. I translated the signatures of sharp-clawed bears, treading lightly on the graves of long-dead Shawnee. And as the years went by, I began to appreciate the solitude that had shaped my father.

But solitude is a seductive drug—and one that kills. Perched on the edge of wilderness, with few neighbors and little social contact, we children were forced to imagine the boundaries of normal behavior. Our parents were our only role models and, although we did not realize it then, they both were very sick.

It was my father's peculiar sickness that troubled me most as a boy. From the time I could walk, it seemed, there was nothing I could do that pleased him. And to please him was all that I wanted out of life. We weighed our words in carats. We watched each other from opposing banks, like two wild creatures separated by a swift and treacherous current. And rarely could we bring ourselves to cross the gulf. On holidays, at church, when forced by social convention, we embraced with utter and complete embarrassment.

And the river we would not ford branched out to touch and separate us all. In my benighted family, love was veiled like a nervous bride, but expectations soared high above the clouds. We were required somehow to read each other's mind, and if one of us failed to do so, he was punished with deeper silence, or worse, with wounding criticism. Emotions were disdained, my father told me by his actions, especially the emotions of men. Men did not reveal their dreams, if they had any at all, and they kept what fondness they had for others locked tight inside their hearts. Once I confronted him. "Do you love me?" I demanded, angry, hopeful, and terrified of his response. My father stared at me and nodded. And then he turned away.

"You've got to understand," my mother whispered later. "That's just the way he was brought up."

My father spoke the untranslatable language of stones. But in his wordless way he managed sometimes to break through to me. One night I was awakened by the touch of his strong, sinewy hand to the light of the moon that poured through my bedroom window. Wordlessly we stepped out into the frosty night and watched as the moon was devoured slowly by some larger, more powerful creature of the sky, until finally the light was gone and our shadows faded from the meadow. And in that single silent moment I knew that my father loved me.

From time to time the quietude unnerved my mother, who was brought up around lots of people, and my father reluctantly submitted to her social needs. One of those times stands out in my memory. It was my summer of extremes, when I learned to think in black and white. My grandfather was working on two of the hottest hits of that decade, *The Odd Couple* and *Barefoot in the Park*, and he delighted in sharing the glamour of his world with us. From the dusty wings of cavernous theaters we watched breathlessly as award-winning performers teased roaring audiences with the skill of lion tamers: Robert Redford. Elizabeth Ashley. Art Carney. Walter Matthau. Between acts they chatted with us cordially. I stood there smiling awkwardly, like some alien from Alpha Centauri. After a week or so of such nearly unbearable excitement, we returned home to the wilderness and resumed our lives of solitude. This, then, I told myself, is the way that life will be for me, a series of violent swings from one end of the spectrum to the other. And in this lopsided worldview I would remain imprisoned for years to come.

But it was another summer that turned my world upside down. Shortly after my sixteenth birthday, my father came down with a cold that would not go away. A single visit to the family doctor confirmed the diagnosis: lung cancer. We reeled as if we had been struck by lightning. Unlike my mother, who smoked like a chimney, my father never had put a cigarette to his lips. The day he was handed his death sentence was the day I started smoking.

After an unsuccessful operation, my father's condition deteriorated rapidly. Life ebbed from him daily like the light of the moon whose eclipse we had witnessed together years before. But our family was highly skilled at denying reality. None of us would admit that he was dying, not even when it became impossible for him to walk and he was forced to remain downstairs in a sickbed.

All day long he was dying alone. My mother taught school to supplement our income, and often I was first to arrive home in the afternoons. I would make my father a glass of instant iced tea and then I would bound upstairs to my room and lock the door behind me. My father was dying on one floor and I was dying on another, and neither of us could talk about it. During that summer, which shimmers in my memory with a terrible radiance, I began to write in earnest, and in a few short weeks filled seventeen loose-leaf notebooks with stories and poems, most of which, not unnaturally, were elegiac. At night I would hear my parents whispering. I did not want to know what they were saying.

Finally, on Halloween weekend, we no longer could ignore the fact that my father would not survive. My mother called an ambulance, and I watched in silence as it carted him off to die. That autumn night, as death embraced my father, my mother took me by the hand. "Do you want to go to the hospital with me and say good-bye?" I shook my head, refusing to acknowledge that anything was happening. I buried deep within me the staggering notion that somehow it was my fault: if only I had been a better son . . . if only I had behaved as he had wished . . .

I did not tell my father good-bye that night. I went out, with a girl who was lithe and lovely and full of life. It was my first formal date, and I was alive. We went to dinner and not once during the meal did I let on that my family was being ripped apart, that I wanted to die myself. Later, we walked in misty rain, hand in hand, and I kissed her, my first real kiss. It was sweet and bitter and I will never know another like it.

When I got home, my father was dead.

It was a night of firsts, and in the grip of a nightmare, I did something I never had done: I walked in my sleep. When I reached the head of the stairway, ready to plunge, I woke up screaming: "I dreamed a train ran over me!" "Go to sleep," my mother said. "Go back to sleep."

During that awful summer of death when I came to love words, my father, too, had taken up writing. At the funeral the minister read the words my father set aside for his family during his waning lucid moments. In plain, simple prose, my father told us what he never had been able to say: that he loved us. He asked our forgiveness for his shortcomings, and I hated him all the more. I hated myself for being like him, a silent coward. "Do not be bitter," my father begged us. "My death is for a reason. God must have a plan." But I would have none of that. I despised God for the punishment that He had meted out, and I vowed to ignore Him the rest of my days.

Throughout this whole ordeal, my mother was a fortress. She did not break down at the funeral. She held her dignity before her like a shield, and the mourners at the ceremony praised her courage.

But a few weeks later my mother was overtaken by her own destiny, and our lives never were the same. My sister was the first to find her sprawled on the floor of the bedroom she had shared with her husband. I never had seen anyone drunk, and I did not know that this was why my mother sobbed and groaned. But somehow, instinctively, I must always have known that my mother was inherently self-destructive. My first thought was that she had tried to kill herself by overdosing on the tranquilizers the doctor had told her to take. That night I sat up and watched my mother and prayed that she would live to see the morning.

She did, and none of us mentioned what had happened. But the drinking did not end there. It got worse, much worse. My mother had waited forty years to fall apart, and now she did so with a vengeance. Drinking became an all-day affair, beginning when her feet hit the floor in the morning and ending only when she passed out late at night. Within weeks, my mother changed dramatically. She became emaciated; her hair turned gray, seemingly overnight; she suffered violent, unpredictable mood swings; torrents of bitterness and rage flooded to the surface. She needed a target. I gave her one.

At that time I knew nothing about dysfunctional family systems, but somehow I realized that only a martyr could hold our fragile unit together. It was natural that I should assume responsibility for my mother's disease. Since childhood I had been practicing to be the Son of God. I remember one morning when I was three years old, before we moved to the woods, some bigger neighborhood boys had roughed me up. My mother was nearly hysterical and I tried to calm her by repeating what I had heard in Sunday school that day: "Father forgive them, for they know not what they do." Needless to say, my mother was pleased, and for years she told that story to anyone who would listen. If that was what it took to win the love of my mother, I was more than willing to be crucified.

And so I allowed my mother to abuse me, again and again. According to her drunken reasoning, everything that had happened to our family was my fault. I was a drain on her, a jinx. She was, she said, sorry that she had ever given birth to me. Although I made straight A's in school and had taught myself to play the guitar and piano and to speak four languages, I would never amount to anything because I was evil, a bad seed. After a few years of these daily diatribes, I began to believe her.

The more my mother drank, the more irrational she became. She got it into her head that she was running out of money, so she began to hoard things. She hid the groceries so that her greedy children could not squander food. My sister and I would have to wait until she passed out, then rummage through her bedroom for canned goods.

Once my mother pointed a rifle at my head and told me to get out of her life before she killed me. Somehow, in my own sickness, I convinced myself that this was normal family life. Years later, when I shared that experience in a recovery meeting, I was astounded to hear myself say: "I never really considered it abuse, I guess, because I was fairly certain that the gun wasn't loaded."

The house went to hell along with its inhabitants, as if it reflected the plague that had befallen us. The place might as well have been hit by a hydrogen bomb: empty whiskey bottles peppered the floors, newspapers and magazines lay in heaps where they had been dropped, tables overturned during drunken fights rarely were set upright, obscenities had been etched with a nail on one wall and in another gaped a hole where the telephone had been ripped out at least a dozen times. My sister and I had become so demoralized by our mother's insanity that we felt powerless to change our surroundings. We may even have derived some sort of perverse pleasure in the hovel that mirrored us.

One summer a man knocked on our door. He was, he said, an aerial photographer, and for a modest sum he would take to the sky and capture our homestead on film. Then, he said, an artist colleague would paint from the snapshot a masterpiece, an heirloom to be treasured for generations. My mother, of course, was delighted, assuming no doubt that such a thing would somehow validate our family worth. But the canvas he delivered was not what she expected. Instead of an idealized rendering of a romantic country home, we got a colored-over photograph that spared no details: beer cans littered the lawn, garbage overflowed the cans, and on the roof outside my bedroom window were plastic bags that had held the marijuana I'd begun to smoke.

By now my sister and I had lost all hope. Like a dutiful son I continued to take responsibility for our family problems. If only I would try harder, I told myself, I could help my mother. And I did try to help her, again and again. I telephoned relatives and begged for help. Usually my pleas were met with embarrassed silence. They could not bring themselves to believe what had happened to her. Periodically her drinking exploded in fits of madness. Then I would haul her, kicking and screaming, to a hospital, where she would convulse with delirium tremens, stay sober for a couple of weeks, and then return to drinking more heavily than before. I tried my damnedest to control my mother. I did not realize then that she never would get well until she really wanted to.

I tried to control my sister as well, who by now was as wild as Queen Anne's lace. But I could not be her parent. I was only a child myself, although I felt as old as Methuselah. To ease the pain, to escape responsibility, I began to drink and take drugs, and from the start I did so alcoholically, suicidally. I remember one drunken escapade early in my addiction. A friend and I staggered into a gas station rest room to splash our faces with water. "You know," he said, "sooner or later one of us is going to wind up an alcoholic." I stared at him and said with certainty, "It'll be me."

I smoked marijuana. I became addicted to amphetamines and tranquilizers. I devoted entire weekends to LSD and mescaline. And always I drank. Alcohol magically blotted out my feelings of guilt and shame. When I was drinking, I could forget the world, forget how terrible my life had become. Never once did it occur to me to confide in friends. And never once did I invite friends to my house. I never could be sure what my mother would do. Would she humiliate me? Would she trot out the rifle and try to kill me? Would it be loaded this time?

The Vietnam War was at its zenith, flower children were blossoming, and rebellion was in the air. It was a perfect time to go wild and I did. I marched on May Day. I thumbed my nose at the Establishment. I reveled in revolution. I wanted to die.

And more than once I tried. On high school graduation night, I didn't bother to pick up my diploma. I stayed home instead, barricaded in my bedroom, smoking pot and playing my guitar. That seemed preferable to having classmates stare at my wrists, which were bandaged after a botched suicide attempt.

I think that sooner or later I would have succeeded in ending my life had it not been for the woman I eventually married. We had known one another since childhood, and always there had been a special bond between us. She also was the child of an alcoholic and had been abused both physically and emotionally. I did not realize that children of alcoholics seek out one another. It did not matter at the time. We were hurting. We needed comfort. We moved in together and set about rescuing one another from the horrors of the past.

Any dreams I might have had about attending college long ago had been shattered by the breakup of my family. So I began playing my guitar in coffee shops. Before long I was spotted by a disc jockey, who offered to manage my career and eventually signed me with a small recording company. In the next few years I released a couple of forgettable recordings and enjoyed working in the studio. But the pressures of the industry were enormous. To ease my fear of performing before crowds, I began to consume even greater quantities of drugs, especially amphetamines. Somehow, even in my worsening illness, I was able to realize that this sort of life-style could not continue. So I decided to quit the music business and pursue a college degree in journalism.

My mother, meanwhile, was growing sicker and sicker; by now she barely resembled the woman I had known. I realized that if I was to make it through the university, I would have to concentrate on my studies. Hard as it was for me to do, I broke off my relationship with her. For the next three years—the last of my mother's life—we remained estranged. From time to time she would call, usually to berate me drunkenly, and I would hang up the phone. If she came to the door I refused to answer it. It was, at the time, the only way I knew to survive.

After graduating at the top of my class, I landed a job as a beat reporter at a midsize metropolitan daily. It was an exciting job and, for once, I felt important. I succeeded as a journalist and treasured my success. My job became my life; I became the occupation. My sickness was overwhelming me.

My mother never knew of my success. A few months after I began the job—the day after Christmas—she collapsed and was rushed to a hospital. Doctors managed to revive her and to keep her alive on machines, but not for long.

Guilt, confusion, panic wrapped me up and squeezed. Already I felt that somehow I had killed my father. I was devastated to think of my mother meeting such an ignominious end—alone. But still I could not let my feelings show. I buried them deep inside me, allowing them to surface only in the fiction I had begun writing.

The Legacy

My drinking continued to escalate as the pressures of my newspaper career mounted. To escape feelings of anxiety, I moved from job to job. But the bitter pain that I had suppressed for years would not leave me. Finally, one Christmas Eve when I thought I might die, I sought treatment for my disease, and my life began again.

How comforting the feeling of peace, the sense of family that greeted me at my first recovery meeting. A young woman, a stranger, embraced me and assured me, "You're going to be all right now." For the first time in my life I had found a home where love was unconditional and abundant.

It was during treatment that I learned about adult children of alcoholics. When I read the list of characteristics compiled by therapist Janet Woititz, I felt, as do many ACOAs, that it was written with me in mind. Finally there was an explanation for that vague sense of craziness, that feeling that I did not belong on this planet.

Today I relish my lifelong process of recovery from alcoholism, and my wife and I continue to deal with our issues of codependency. I work as an editor for a publishing company that specializes in books and periodicals on recovery, and I devote much of my writing to the subject of addictions. I truly believe that my Higher Power has placed me here so that I may use not only my language skills, but also my pain, to help others who are suffering.

In the letter that my father wrote us from his deathbed, he underscored his faith in a higher plan. Today I believe that my father was right. We are all of us part of a grander scheme. I am certain that everything that happened to my family was supposed to happen—had to happen—and I am grateful that it did.

DAUGHTERS

Regina Gray

You were very drunk
At the end of the table,
Head nodding over your mashed potatoes.
I stared at you,
Secretly, pleading,
The tension and sickness in my stomach
Willing that your head not fall.

Watching, too ashamed to hate you,
Nana's face appeared on yours—
Vivid, slight of features.
I never saw it before,
Her behind you,
The slackness and sagging, face and body,
Into a bottle.

When Nana died,
I came home, your least favorite daughter,
Your eldest child,
The one that made you a mother,
And found you crying at the kitchen table.
In my arms you felt small, shaking,

Turning to me you said,
"Now I'll never be able to make Mum love me."

I held on to you
And on to myself,
Stunned by the words that could have been my own despairing
Requiem, my unrequited love for you,
Wrung by the grief of the daughters in my family.

When I was asked to contribute a chapter to this book, I felt very excited, glad for the opportunity to share my experiences with others. But when it came to writing, a leadenness filled me, part fear, part anxiety. I have often, in self-pity or self-righteousness, told strangers about my family—that Mom is an active alcoholic. I spent years in therapy working through feelings. I have wept with friends. I have shared a great deal about my mother and my family. But this new and scary task is much more about revealing me and the child that lives within me still.

For many years I struggled for some sense of understanding and detachment, some beginning of forgiveness. I thought that I had done much of my work by learning about alcoholism and by healing, as much as possible, my relationship with my mother. But three years ago, in graduate school, I heard the term "adult child of an alcoholic" for the first time and discovered that I—my entire self—had been affected by my mother's alcoholism. It wasn't just a matter of dealing with Mom, but of looking into and dealing with myself. Listening to that teacher, I could feel everything she said sink in. It was kind of like thinking that you had to paint your house and then discovering that all the wood had been destroyed by termites and needed to be replaced—the task felt huge. It was too deep. I felt as if I just wanted to chuck the whole process and move somewhere else.

However, it was comforting to discover that many of my personal quirks were common to ACOAs. That made me feel much less screwed-up somehow, because there was a reason for the way I felt about myself and the world. I had learned to be a certain way, and there was hope that I could unlearn it. This meant going back into the craziness of my family again, opening up wounds I thought I was finished with. But the hope of changing, of finding out that there was another way to be, was irresistible. I could do more than make peace with my life. I could learn another way to live.

So, the process began again: therapy, reading, workshops to discover what I had taken in as a child, to investigate the alcoholic distortion I'd known as reality. I have been expanding my world, learning new choices, new meanings. I don't believe that anyone ever heals completely, but I am a lot better.

This, then, is not only about what it was like, but also who I am. I am writing it under a pseudonym, a contradiction I suppose, but I am unwilling to unmask the family that still lives so much in denial, a model family in a model community. This comes less from a desire to protect them than from my unwillingness to take on the role of family savior. I don't want to try to fix my family anymore. So I step out, love them, hope they will find their own paths to healing while I get on with my life.

I hope that I may touch the memories of others who grew up as I did, not knowing that there was anything else. We may not be able to save our families, but we can help and support each other. That is almost enough.

The first memory, always, is that of coming home, tense and scared, furtively looking for someone to ask, "How is she?" All six of us did it, and I remember it clearly back to first grade.

If the answer was OK, my shoulders came down, my throat opened, I could breathe. Those were moments of safety, of being able to look forward to some happiness, some fun. If the answer was bad, my body stayed tense, stomach lurching with nausea, and I'd tiptoe into the house and head upstairs, avoiding any noise that might catch her attention.

Frequently, there were terrifying rides home from grammar school. Once a week or so Mom would arrive there late, very drunk, and drive us home at ten miles an hour, through stop signs and red lights. The six of us would sit rigidly in the back seats, not looking at each other. We made no sound of fear, afraid of increasing her anger. I knew clearly that we could have been killed. We never had an accident, and my mother has never been arrested for drunk driving. I used to pray on those rides, promising novenas, promising perfection, if only we would make it home safely. Once there we would sit in our rooms, listening to her noises, the crashing of pots in the kitchen, the loud muttering in her thickened voice. And I would dread her call. As the oldest and a daughter, I knew I would eventually have to go down into the kitchen to set the table. It was better to go voluntarily rather than to wait to be called. But sometimes I would hide, unable to force myself downstairs. I always entered that kitchen hoping that if I did it right and fast and quietly, maybe she wouldn't notice me, wouldn't attack. She rarely hit me, but I felt as though I was always waiting for a blow.

As children, we didn't know we were dealing with alcohol, but thought it was some mysterious, unpredictable mood. My family was ruled by these "moods." We all developed finely tuned antennae that were sensitive not to our own thoughts, feelings, and needs, but to hers. If we could read her, we might be able to figure out what she wanted and avoid an outburst. I don't remember that it ever worked, but we kept on trying.

We went through these dreadful experiences together and yet we never talked about them among ourselves. However, we would warn each other when Mom needed to be avoided. And there was an unspoken agreement to protect each other from being too much the focus of her abuse. If she was on one of us for too long, someone would do something like spill a glass of milk to draw her fire. As the oldest I was most frequently the buffer, but I remember being rescued often myself. The strangest part is that it was not even conscious. We have only become aware of it as we have begun to talk together in the last year. We agreed that we shared some sense of trying to take care of each other by parceling Mom's anger out among us, and that we knew when she was going too far and needed to be redirected.

Most confusing for us kids was that my mother was like two persons. One was an all-loving, playful, perfect Mom who baked her own cakes, gave wonderful parties and hugs, and told us how much she loved us. She was never angry or impatient, and she taught us that anger was bad. She told us how much she loved having us and recounted long romantic stories about how she and Dad had met. The other person was someone filled with hatred who told us she wished we'd never been born to ruin her life. She screamed at us and hit us. She said that Dad had forced her to have sex with him, and we were all unwanted and resented pregnancies. So we thought of her as two people and were always wary about which one was home on any given day. It was bewildering and terrifying.

I remember how silent we all were with each other. Maybe we were afraid to stir up trouble, but I think also it was because we'd been robbed of the capacity to name our experience. We did not have the permission, the courage, or the words to do so. We were focused on my mother's responses, not our own. As children we were allowed to be happy, even rambunctious when Mom was okay. Dad is a reserved, rational, nonexpressive man, and he would show irritation or bemusement, but was most often impassive behind a book. Anger, and to a lesser extent sadness, belonged to my mother.

Of course we fought as kids, sometimes bitterly, but always quietly, so as not to draw Mom's attention. We did not ask for help or intervention from our parents. We were both isolated from each other and bonded to each other. We protected one another, lied for one another, but did not know one another.

As I got older I continued to try to put the two mothers together, but I was never very successful. When she was in a warm and loving mood, I rushed to be with her, to tell her my adolescent secrets. Later, she would spill them out viciously to my family or friends, her contempt for me apparent. And always beneath my rage and humiliation there was a feeling of surprise, as though I'd forgotten that one Mom would know what I'd confided to the other. It took me years to learn finally to shut her out and look for intimacy elsewhere. Still, those brief moments of closeness were, somehow, worth the later betrayal.

Sometimes I think that my mother's dislike of me comes partially from my refusal to leave her alone, my persistent expectations of love, my demands that she give me what I now know she could not give. I tried to make her love me in a way that my siblings never did. I was a drain on her energies and a reminder of her inadequacies and self-doubts. I wanted her to give to me what she had never received for herself.

One time in my early adolescence, I heard a strange sound in the bathroom. I went to investigate and found my mother dazed, sitting on the toilet, vomiting down her chin and onto her chest. Cleaning up the vomit, wiping her, dragging and pushing her upstairs to her bedroom, I choked with wanting to cry out to someone to stop it—this was my mother! Seeing her that way was more than I could bear. The sense of something gone terribly wrong was overwhelming. Her degradation became my most secret shame. I needed her to be someone I could want to be like, someone who would show me that it was good to be a woman. But I could see only danger. At that moment I wanted to disown her. I hated her, and I hated everything about her.

I looked at her body, fouled with vomit and shit, and felt a self-disgust that translated itself into years of confused and angry feelings about my own female body. The more my body became like hers, the more I fought any identification with her. I retreated into rigid rationality and undermined my physical attractiveness in order to strangle my sexual feelings, which threatened me with loss of control and a female's fate.

It was brutal, growing into adulthood while trying to fight my womanhood at the same time. I am still discovering what my efforts to exorcise my mother cost me. I am still learning to inhabit and enjoy my female body. Sexuality is now more about connection than about violation, although I am still frightened by sexually aggressive men. I am still learning that appetite does not have to be addiction. I have been lucky. I have found other mothers, women who have been mentors and friends to me and who have helped me deal with the social sexism that also diminishes all women's lives.

I now know that my mother's disease is alcoholism, not gender, and that I can be a woman without being alcoholic. Today I can identify with my mother's body and sense the similarities and the differences. Her body speaks to me now of our mortality, but with tones of poignancy rather than disgust.

When I was about twenty, I stood in the hallway and watched a scene between my parents that typified how they behaved toward each other. Dad was sitting in his favorite chair, reading, and Mom was standing in front of him, yelling about something. He ignored her, calmly turning the pages of his book. She became so enraged that her voice escalated into a screech and she began to jump up and down like Rumplestiltskin in the fairy tale. I began to laugh, filled with contempt for her and proud of my father's disdain of her childishness. She heard me, turned, and ran toward me, tears streaming down her cheeks. She hit me hard across the face. We began fighting with each other, hurling insults until she ran upstairs and I slammed out the front door. My father never stopped reading.

It took me years to discover the fury I harbor toward my father. He was always the rock I huddled against in order to escape Mom's stormy presence. I mistook his indifference for calm. I modeled myself after him as a way to avoid Mom's scary craziness. I tried to be like him and thought that we had a relationship.

It was my husband who first got angry about Dad. I remember my surprise the first time he asked why my father hadn't protected us from her. It had never entered my head that he could protect us. Mom was like a natural disaster, a hurricane, whose outbursts we all tried to live through. I was just grateful that his detachment balanced her ragings. I didn't notice his lack of input because it was such a relief that he wasn't contributing to the destructiveness. I didn't think about whether or not there was anything he could do to make things different. I didn't know it could be any different. My father did not grow up in an alcoholic home, yet he made no effort either to confront his wife about her drinking, or to protect his children from her random violence.

When I look back, I feel incredible compassion for this woman who was so abandoned by her spouse. Nothing Mom did could penetrate his calm. She must have felt his contempt for her, his sense of moral superiority and self-sufficiency. My father, a well-known lawyer in a university town, was married to his work, and Mom was married to her bottle. I think that Dad reacted to Mom's drinking by retreating from her, looking on her as a weak and distasteful person. I think Mom believed that husbands were supposed to work hard to achieve money and acclaim, but then felt abandoned by Dad's preoccupation with his career. She did not have a husband, and we didn't have a father. Somehow, this marriage of workaholism and alcoholism has survived for thirty-five years.

Once I invited Dad to go to Al-Anon with me, but he said

he was too busy. When my angry sister accused him of allowing us to be abused by Mom and challenged him to accept some responsibility, he told her that many children are abused and survive to live healthy, useful lives. So he knew and was, typically, concerned only that we not try to hold him accountable for our personal failures. I still can't believe that he didn't say he was sorry.

I feel ashamed now of laughing at my mother and of sharing my father's contempt for her. Today I have a better understanding of her unhappiness, and I know that she was ill, not bad. My mother came from a long line of alcoholics, so she might have become addicted in the happiest of relationships. But I sometimes think that if my father had confronted her, had taken more responsibility for the well-being of his children, we might have been in treatment many years ago.

Each of us has reacted differently to the past. One brother still speaks of our childhood like something out of the children's stories he wants to write. Having created a fantasy of the past, he lives in one in the present. I watch how he drinks. He abuses alcohol now, and I fear he is heading for alcoholism. I hate talking to him. It makes me feel scared and sad and helpless.

One sister is furious, holding on to her anger through years of therapy and Al-Anon. She goes home frequently, then storms out when she does not find what she wants there, leaving my parents bewildered and defensive. They talk periodically about hospitalizing her.

Another sister detached herself from Mom in her early teens and began her addiction to men. She has just broken off a relationship with her third alcoholic lover. She earns a lot of money and makes everyone around her laugh. I don't think anyone in the world knows who she is.

Another brother is a sexy womanizer with a cocaine habit. He works at a boring job for fast money and has no plans for the future. He was the most affectionate one of us as a child. I remember him crying for hours after he had tried to kiss Mom and she'd pushed him away. It sounds trite, but I think that in his promiscuity he is looking for the love and reassurance he never got. Underneath the macho bullshit, I see that little boy.

And the youngest, my little brother, is a determined go-getter who wants to have a lot of money so that he doesn't have to be dependent on anybody. He kicked cocaine because he didn't like needing anything. He is upset that he becomes periodically impotent when he falls in love with a woman. He is twenty-five and still lives with my parents, waiting until he has enough money to move out. Sounds like a soap opera.

The hardest part about getting to know my sibs has been finding out about their pain and their compromises with life. Except for my brother's drinking, we all look reasonably good on the surface. But, beneath the surface, I see the same self-hatred, self-abuse, anger, incapacity for love, and lack of trust inextricably mingled with the desperate hope for redemption yet fear of life that I know so well within myself. We look very different from each other, but we are truly brothers and sisters under the skin.

It's been hard for me to look at what I learned about myself and the world by being the daughter of an alcoholic mother. Thinking over my memories of her, I can uncover several themes operating within myself these past thirty-four years.

The first is about trust. I learned that people cannot be trusted, that professions of love are wonderful but fleeting moments that feel good but aren't real. I love people easily; I trust very few. It was a revelation when I slowly discovered another kind of love with the man who is my husband, a love that can be tested, that continues even as I hesitantly reveal myself. My first, very positive experience with therapy helped me get to the point where I could recognize the uniqueness and reality of this man's caring for me. There are now several more people whom I love and trust. It is still very hard for me to ask for help as I am still afraid of being a burden, of asking for too much, of being rejected. But so far I've been lucky in my choice of intimates and have not been harmed by them. They have taught me that I don't have to be perfect to be loved.

I also have trouble trusting myself and my ability to influence something in a positive way. I can be very ingratiating, so I struggle to learn a healthy assertiveness. I am more often aware of what another person wants than I am of my own requirements. I am learning to identify what I want and how to try to create it in a positive way. I want to stop feeling so impotent, so convinced that I will always make a fool of myself or that my impertinence will spread disaster. I need to know that I am not destructive, nor will I be destroyed.

I am preoccupied with death. If my husband is late coming home from work, I'm sure he has been in an accident. I am afraid of cars, and when I buy one my first concern is how it will survive an accident. An early morning phone ringing means a death. Life feels tenuous to me. I am sure that the world is a dangerous place, with disaster waiting in the wings to catch the unwary. I worry myself sick. It is a form of control. I still do not trust the universe.

My mother's moods ran my life for years, and I found it extraordinarily difficult to separate from her. I lived at home until I was twenty-five, locked in a battle to force her to love me and to force her to stop drinking. They seemed somehow connected. When I finally left, at the urging of my therapist, I felt as though I was abandoning her to increasingly worse bouts of drinking. And I thought I was giving up any chance for love. Her drinking has progressed over the years to the point where it's hard to believe that her body still functions. But it does, without me. And I found love instead of losing it when I left.

I hated her drinking, but I worshiped her. Only through therapy and learning about alcoholism was I finally able to put those two sides of Mom together. Having to accept the fact that my perfect mother did not exist initiated a lengthy mourning process in which I began to know who she really was and what she could never be for me. It's been a coming to terms with her limitations and knowing that she was incapable of giving the unconditional love I longed for. It was letting go of the angel and the witch, and allowing her to be an imperfect human being. That helps me accept my own humanity and makes me more able to love.

My mother's love was scary when she was drunk. I felt—and she sometimes acted—as though she was out of control. We children were afraid of physical attack. Even now when someone gets angry with me I can still feel inside me a cowering three-year-old child who is scared to death. I am afraid of my own anger, too, afraid that it will kill or provoke an attack. When she was angry, Mom said she wanted to kill us. Sometimes anger still feels as though it can kill.

Anger is still a problem. My husband and I sometimes do

fight. We talk in angry voices but never yell. A couple of friends help me by being willing to be reassuring even as they risk being angry and risk my being angry. It's slowly getting better, but I doubt I'll ever be at ease about it.

I almost have my body back. By learning how to relax and how to breathe, I'm recovering from years of physical tension, from the tensed shoulders holding fear, the constricted throat stopping words, and the old, old anger that is locked away somewhere, invisible—almost. I used to shrivel up, to make myself small so that Mom would not notice me, so I would not offend her. My body carries the guilty conviction that I harmed her, ruined her life. By shutting myself down, I tried to apologize for being alive.

The saddest part for her daughters is what my mother taught us about being a woman. When she was sober, she lived and preached a life of selfless devotion to others—the worst thing she could call us was selfish. I was taught that I was supposed to marry a man I adored, have his children, and feel fulfilled and happy being a wife and mother. That would provide me with peace and satisfaction. When Mom was drunk, I saw her loneliness, anger, boredom, guilt, and self-hatred. It came pouring out, the alcohol giving voice to what was otherwise denied. I learned about dutiful sex and unwanted pregnancies. I heard that she made herself always available, yet saw herself as a doormat that the world could walk on—and did. I saw, hidden within the rage, the things she longed for but had forbidden herself: companionship and respect, her own money, the freedom to say no, to put herself first sometimes.

Like many women of her generation, Mom believed in an image of womanhood that strangled who she was as a person. All the "bad" parts of herself that she could not otherwise acknowledge came out when she was drunk. Some of the things she said were the secret, horrible truths of women's lives. And some were the alcoholic's lies.

In joining the women's movement, I learned about the lives of other women and placed my mother among them. I believe her unhappiness is real. I know how trapped she was. For years I refused to consider marriage and children, I was so afraid of following in her footsteps. But in pulling apart the sexism and the alcoholism, I discovered what I can truly and effectively fight and what I must let go. I work to help make women's lives better. I do not try to cure Mom's alcoholism.

I do not drink, but that doesn't matter. Alcohol has affected every area of my life. This is true of every ACOA whose parent's or parents' most important relationship was with the contents of a bottle.

AFTERWORD

This might take a lifetime. Last year was frightening. My husband got very drunk at several parties, and I had to admit to myself that something was wrong. He was drinking alcoholically. He told me I was being oversensitive and exaggerating because of my history. In couples counseling to deal with another issue, he finally did admit to the therapist that he knew he was abusing alcohol and had a potential drinking problem. As relieved as I was that he recognized that, after his admission I was on an emotional roller coaster for days. I was frightened, furious; I felt trapped. All my sibs had either developed a personal problem with drugs and alcohol, or been involved with lovers who were addicts. I had felt blessed that I had somehow managed to escape. But when I looked into my dear husband's slack face and watched his personality change, I knew I hadn't escaped.

We have agreements now. He has only three drinks at any party. When we go out, I have the car keys and he carries money for a taxi. I don't want to be a policeman, so if I get uncomfortable with his drinking and he does not want to leave, I can go home knowing he will get home safely.

Several months ago he got very sick in the middle of the night after drinking, and I made myself go downstairs and sleep on the couch while he cleaned up after himself. It took a lot of self-control not to take care of him. I will not participate; I will not be a coalcoholic. Maybe that will help us both. He has been fine lately, I think shaken by what he saw inside himself. But I don't relax around alcohol with him the way I used to. There is a part of me that watches, that is scared.

Last year we decided to move to the West Coast. Soon after the announcement my family went into action. My parents decided to redecorate their house, and the turmoil has given Mom the excuse for a lengthy binge. One of my brothers had a serious accident while driving drunk. One sister thought she was pregnant by her alcoholic ex-boyfriend. The other sister terminated a lengthy therapy and became suicidal. One brother is dealing cocaine to support his habit. Only the youngest and my ever-unflappable father were able to tell me that they would miss me. The others were all busy with their crises. This whole mess shows me both how woven I am into this family and how we hold together through crises and guilt. I felt like a traitor, abandoning them by refusing to help.

Al-Anon has taught me about detachment. What a hard concept to understand as humane. I have had to learn to lovingly detach not only from my parents, but also from the siblings who try to pull me into their lives to fix them. I was supposed to sympathize with my brother because he was "tired" when he had an automobile accident. The pact in the family was that his exhaustion, not drunkenness, was the cause. At first I went along with the game; it made us feel close. Then I began to confront the denial. That was fine, but I took a further, fatal step. I thought it was my responsibility to make each one of them see what was happening. I drained myself trying to change them. I have had to learn not to do that anymore. I listen. I am interested. I confront. But I no longer make it my task to change them. The hardest part for me in being a part of an alcoholic family is this helpless loving, the heartbreaking realization that I cannot stop their denial, cannot live their lives. I wish I could.

This year I have learned that I must monitor the relationship I have with my brothers and sisters just as I do with my parents. We are closer than we used to be, but I have discovered with sadness that our interactions are also governed by denial. I know them better—for that I'm grateful. I cannot be as real with them as I can with my friends—for that I grieve.

This process of understanding and healing seems like an archaeological dig: I keep going down through layers, each discovery a piece of healing in itself. I rest for a while, then I begin to dig again, not because I enjoy it, but because something new and upsetting has just thrust up through the surface.

I don't know where this will end, but I've made a commitment to go as far as I can with it. I have recently begun thinking seriously about having a child, which brings up in a new way my mother and her mothering. And I know that more than anything else in the world I want my daughter to have a mother who can love her. I want to spare her the grief of the daughters in my family.

MY STEPFATHER IS AN ALCOHOLIC

Cynthia Stevens

Some days I think I am an alcoholic. Other days I am equally convinced that I just like to drink because it relaxes me and because life is so difficult. Anyway, why the hell shouldn't I drink? We're all going to die soon in a nuclear blast, so why should I care what I do for the next few years?

So far as I know, there has been no alcoholism in my biological family. If I am an alcoholic today, it is not because I was genetically predisposed to the condition. I do have an alcoholic stepfather, though.

Some family history is appropriate here. I have only general memories of my early years, so I make assumptions based on what I've been told and what I've pieced together in years of therapy and self-analysis. When I was about five, my father left my mother, me, and my three-year-old brother, and although he came back a few times after that, he was really gone forever. He and I had been extremely close, and I worshiped him. He was handsome, charming, and witty—a warm person. I had no idea why my mother didn't feel about him the way I did. Perhaps I was also convinced that I had driven him away.

In the next several years my mother occasionally brought home a man friend to meet us or arranged for us to go on outings with him. None lasted for more than a few months. Was she also drawn to men who were like my father? I suspect so. I know that for many years I had destructive relationships with boys and later with men who reminded me of my father. Only recently have I been able to seek a different type of man to love, and I feel very good about that.

When I was ten, my mother began to tell us about her interest in a married man she was working for. She seemed intent on having him and became involved with him while he was in the process of leaving his wife and three children. It was only after he came to live with us that I began to realize that my mother's new man had a severe problem. He was a binge drinker, the sort of person who goes days, weeks, months, even (once or twice) years without a drink and then gets upset over something or happy over something or bored or agitated and begins drinking. Then he drinks every waking moment, passing out when he is very drunk and eventually becoming so sick that he must taper off in order to function at all. I had never seen a person totally out of control before. Not even my father or mother at their worst could have approached that insanity.

Often he drank for ten days or more without slowing down, and then became so violently ill that he had to stop for a while. My mother's role frequently consisted of driving him to a detoxification center or mental hospital for professional help.

Life at home was often a horror! After a couple of drinks, my stepfather might be amusing and fun; a few more made him droopy and weepy, then depressed. As he continued to drink, he went from miserably begging for attention to extreme anger, berating whoever was near for bad behavior toward him or for not loving him or for all wrongs, real or imagined. And sometimes he seemed violent. He is a small man, and since he never used a weapon, he was not really dangerous, but he had strong hands and could grab my mother enough to hurt and frighten her.

I remember that as I became more aware of sex, I feared he would try to grab me. In fact he never did, and it was probably my own fantasy or fascination that scared me. His behavior was always very proper and fatherly. Whenever he wanted a hug or kiss, I was intimidated, and he often demanded affection when he was extremely drunk, but he was very cool and undemonstrative when sober. I didn't like him or love him most of the time. Rather,

I feared and loathed him. Sometimes I gave him the hug or kiss because I was afraid he would stand at the bottom of the stairs to our attic bedrooms and scream my name until I did. Sometimes that was enough to mollify him for a time, so I could escape to my room and hide for the rest of the evening.

At his worst my stepfather was out of control when he was drunk. Once he chased my teenage brother around the house with a pair of scissors in hand, threatening to cut his long hair until finally he had hold of his arm and swung the scissors at him, breaking one blade against the wall.

I have to mention that I respected my stepfather's intellect, generally agreed with his liberal politics, and sometimes enjoyed his company when he was sober. However, I always thought him overly stern and strict, and generally I rebelled against his rules. Even sober, he had a nasty temper, particularly in the first days after drying out from a binge, when my mother would say he was still drunk.

Sober, my stepfather was a total believer in the importance of a good education. My brother was not cooperative; he was frequently suspended from school for wearing the wrong kind of clothes or for having long hair. And he refused to knuckle under to school or to my stepfather. My mother and my stepfather had frequent and severe arguments about him, as she was very protective of her son.

When I was fifteen, my older stepsister moved in and started attending the same school I did, one grade higher than I did. She was a superachiever, a dedicated student, a good daughter to her father. Sometimes this took the heat off me, for which I was grateful. Unlike me, she was willing to sit with him for hours and talk out his rages and fears. She was not disgusted by him. I could not understand that, but it was a relief.

I had always been a good student, but from age sixteen to eighteen my academic interest waned and my studies went to hell. My stepsister studied intently and was accepted to college a full year early. I suspect that I stopped studying partly as a reaction to her success.

My brother and I were excellent grist for my stepfather's mad mill. My mother made him furious, too. It seemed that all of us were guilty of driving him to drink, all the time. He really got worse when I was in my midteens. He was rarely sober and his binges became almost one long, grueling episode. Later he did get sober for as much as six months at a time, and he really tried hard to stay sober. Thus he was able to keep a very responsible position for many years and sometimes even be a good father.

Often he was suicidal, and several times he disappeared for days, leaving my mother afraid that he would turn up dead. She became a genius at finding him in hotel rooms, in or out of the area, by piecing together information he left behind, hints he made, and places he had been to before. Twice she did find him after he'd taken overdoses of pills. Later he claimed the overdoses were accidental.

When my brother was fifteen the tension at home was so bad that he, my stepfather, and my mother decided it would be better for him to live with our maternal grandparents, where he stayed until he went out on his own. My mother was both relieved and disappointed by this arrangement. He went to several high schools but never did complete his education.

I could not wait to grow up and get out. In fact, my mother drove me crazy, too, with her meddling and insulting manner, although her bugging me was nothing compared to how my stepfather behaved. I would come home from school and go to my room to daydream or listen to music. If he was drinking downstairs, I would only come out if my mother arrived or if dinner was ready. I was reclusive and depressed. I considered suicide.

Eventually, I began hanging around with other kids. I discovered that boys were at last interested in me. My first outward behavior was centered around boys and sex. After I lost my virginity at age seventeen, I just couldn't seem to stop. I was obsessed with having the attention of boys. And I knew how to get it. This obsession led me to deeper depression, for I developed a stunningly bad reputation appropriate to a time well before the late 1960s. Had I been born ten years later, I'd have been just one of the kids. As it was, most of my contemporaries thought me the biggest tramp that ever hit our high school.

Ultimately, along with self-hatred, I began to hate my enemies. This drove me further from my peers and toward a different kind of society that was beginning to form in Harvard Square in 1965. Inexorably, I was drawn to the "hip" society, driven there by my unkind schoolmates and my increasing doubts about the world and the values of "straight" people.

I understand now that having casual sex was both a heady escape from drab reality and a terrific way to curse my parents and the rest of the world. I still think that my friends and I blazed trails of liberation and awareness in the 1960s, but I did so at a high cost. Sex could have been lovely, it could have been fun, but most of the time it was a desperate grab for love. It didn't work that way. I had steady boyfriends, and each of those several relationships had a special meaning for me, but they were obsessive and ultimately very sad.

At age seventeen I was so depressed that I wanted to leave school and just be with my boyfriend all the time. My parents urged me to see a psychotherapist. Misery made me agree with them for once. My stepfather had been working with a psychologist who ran a group for alcoholics at a local hospital. The therapist also had a private practice and a school for therapists in his home. I went to see him. He was a powerful person with an imposing manner who seemed very helpful and fatherly. Unfortunately he lived so far from my home that the trip became prohibitive. So my parents had me check in with the Massachusetts Mental Health Association, where I was assigned to group therapy. I remained in therapy for about another year, but dropped out shortly after leaving home. I never could decide whether psychotherapy did me any good at the time. I suspect that it did, and certainly it did me no harm.

I turned eighteen in 1966, a year of marijuana and LSD extravaganzas. We hippies, as we came to be called, were determined that alcohol was the drink of our dumb, duplicitous, and stodgy elders, the drug of the Establishment, the brew that smoothed the way for everything we despised about business and politics. I was certain I would never be interested in drinking booze the way they did. I recall my stepfather warning me that this phase would pass and I too would indulge in liquor because it was the only intoxicant that was legal and available at a reasonable cost. I didn't believe him.

The summer after I graduated from high school, I was allowed to leave home and do what I wanted within reason. If only I had been reasonable. I found some young people in Harvard Square who let me stay with them, and I discovered that there were lots of other sensitive, bright young people who were running from unhappy adolescence and trying to find a different way to live. By and large we found that way through rebellion, music, and drugs. At first I used only the two most popular mind expanders: marijuana and LSD. A year or two later, I went on to syringes of methamphetamine hydrochloride (speed) and heroin. I also got hold of several lesser-known drugs and a couple of poisons. I could have died numerous times in the next several years while having my fun, using heroin but fortunately not becoming addicted.

I did become very sick at about age twenty-one. It was never clear whether I had hepatitis or poisoning from something with which the heroin was laced. After that I stopped using anything that had to be injected.

I believe even now that I learned a great deal from my psychedelic drug trips. I also saw how easy it was to sink into depravity on hard drugs. But I might still be taking psychedelics and other drugs now if I hadn't learned so much about their potential side effects and dangers. Also, my current lover has never taken drugs and would not be happy if I did, and I am pleased that he cares about my mind and my health, so I find it easy not to do drugs. Besides, I think that a few hundred trips probably taught me all that I could glean from those substances, and I haven't enjoyed smoking pot for years.

Until my early twenties, I swore that my stepfather's horrendous behavior under the influence of alcohol would prevent me from ever drinking. I first tasted wine when I was seven years old, at a traditional Jewish ceremony where sips of wine are given to all. It was so acrid and unpleasant that I thought I would never enjoy the stuff. I still have a strong taste memory of it! My first beer, drunk when I was about fifteen and had decided to down one quickly to find out how it felt, was also unpleasant. I immediately upchucked most of it. My next experience was my first grown-up party, where I drank a cheap Italian wine and passed out on a mattress on the floor, awakening the next morning with a terrible hangover and with my brother and stepbrother groaning nearby.

My real drinking began when a couple of older men I worked with asked me to go out for Friday evening cocktails. I resisted for weeks, but finally agreed. When I explained that I wasn't a drinker, they told me to try a daiquiri. It tasted good. Later, a couple of friends got their first blender and began making delicious frozen daiquiris and other sweet fruity combinations. "Try this," they'd say. And it was yummy! So we'd have some more and some more. It felt good and we laughed a lot and I liked it. It was just as good as getting stoned!

This happened at the end of a dangerous time when I had stopped using hard drugs, particularly with needles. I thought nothing could ever be that dangerous again, and perhaps I was right. I was now ready for the more peaceful combination of marijuana and alcohol. And what a combination it was! It was giddy and great. It made me fall right to sleep if I was nervous or upset. It made me fall asleep if I wasn't nervous, too. Ultimately, it just made me fall asleep. Alcohol alone was acceptable now, both to my generation and to my elders, and I was of age.

I quickly forgot all the warning bells and barriers I'd set up when I lived with my stepfather. Drinking made me feel lively, funny, and unafraid of people. It cured my shyness just as drugs had done before. And what harm could it do? I knew enough about alcoholism to believe I was safe from it. After all, it was my stepfather, not any blood relative, who had been the drunk. I could not have a genetic predisposition toward alcoholism. So I could drink indefinitely and yet stop whenever I wanted.

For the next few years I was mostly a moderate social drinker. I don't recall feeling any strong compulsion to drink; it was just something I did with friends and family to relax and have a good time. And I had finally met a good man. We married when I was twenty-two, had our son when I was almost twenty-four, and settled down in the suburbs. It looked like the American dream. But with bills piling up and little money coming in, and with fantasies of a better life to keep us going, it soon became the American nightmare. I was bored as a housewife and tremendously burdened as a mother. My pregnancy had been hard and somehow I never developed a strong attachment to my son. I had expected to love having a child. Instead, I hated it!

I had few friends and nothing stimulating to do. I disliked my husband's family even more than I did my own. A family party soon became an occasion to get drunk just to relax. Besides, they did it and it made them seem so much pleasanter when I joined in.

That was the first time I can recall purposely and determinedly drinking to excess.

Our marriage deteriorated. I had a brief but torrid affair with a mutual friend and my husband caught me. But the deeper problem was that we were not mature enough to raise a child in difficult circumstances and had begun to drive each other crazy. I became more desperate and drank more frequently. I still drank generally only on weekends with friends, but I really looked forward to those escapes more and more. I continued to smoke moderate amounts of pot as well. The combined effect of these two drugs was potent and yet seemed benign.

The first time I ran away from our home was to escape my husband. He was showing his despair by studying the Bible every night and refusing to socialize with friends when I badly needed to get out. I went to a downtown Boston rock 'n' roll bar for singles. I was twenty-nine years old and about to embark on the serious partying stage of my drinking odyssey.

My husband and I had tried working with a marriage counselor in the last year or so of our relationship. We were even told that we seemed to be doing better. But my husband could never forget the betrayal he felt because of my affair. It always came up in every disagreement we had, causing terribly ugly arguments. At his insistence, I got a job working at a college for musicians, so we wouldn't be struggling all the time. It was rather fun, and I began to feel more independent than I had in years. Apparently this was very threatening to him. He demanded good home cooking every night, even after he had lost his own full-time job and I was the only one working. I resented that kind of behavior. The one useful thing he did for the last few months of our relationship was take care of our young son. He also was sure that I was seeing other men, especially when there was an office party and I came home late—despite my having his permission in advance.

When he said that he was leaving, I was tremendously relieved. I never again felt a strong desire to be with him, and I never longed for the past. Today, we are barely even friends and only stay in touch because of our son.

After the separation, I took advantage of the times my mother agreed to baby-sit my son. I either partied with my best friend and her husband on a weekend night or went to a club to hear music and to drink. Sometimes a friend would go clubbing with me, but increasingly I went alone. This seemed risky, but the risk was part of the attraction. I too was "looking for Mr. Goodbar." I was never totally sure of myself, but a couple of drinks would cure my inhibitions. And a couple more might be even better. Sometimes a man would buy me drinks. I always liked that. I liked it even better if he was attractive and good company. Always the man expected something in return and sometimes he got it. I was still obsessed with sex and believed it would find me love. Perhaps I was also becoming addicted to booze.

Still, I was certain that I was not a problem drinker, certainly not an alcoholic. Sometimes I thought I drank too much, but I was OK because I never had a blackout. In fact my memory was stunningly sharp, as it always had been. Sometimes I wished that booze could make me forget my life, but it didn't. My drinking, once largely confined to weekends, was now running over into the occasional weeknight and a very occasional noontime with a friend who liked to have a drink or two with lunch. I always felt particularly cocky coming back to work after having a drink at lunch—both naughty and good. But I really didn't like working when I felt that way, so I didn't do it often.

A year after my marriage broke up, I found a young man who said he loved me and whom I loved. I remember trying to stop him from drinking sometimes. Although he probably wasn't an alcoholic, he would drink when he was upset and it would have a terrible effect on him. I had met him at a bar, and we both drank a bit more than moderately. During the months we had together before he went out west forever, I drank less and less. I was happy and life burned brightly without alcohol. In fact, I wanted to be as alert as possible so I could enjoy his company.

When he left me, I thought I would die of misery. I must have gotten drunk sometimes, but this does not stand out in my memory of grinding, destructive unhappiness. Mostly, I dragged myself through days of work, then home to my apartment to sulk and cry. I knew that I would never love another man the way I loved him. I mourned for six months.

Meanwhile, by keeping the pressure on me for several months, my ex-husband had talked me into giving him custody of our son. He used unfair tactics, such as calling me at work on my new job and upsetting me so much with his demands that I would cry and could not regain control. By then I was seeing a woman therapist who had been recommended to me by my original therapist. She was the only person who could calm me when I thought I would lose my mind with grief.

I also joined a group with my original therapist, so I had two hours of therapy a week. Group therapy was not a comforting experience. It was meant to be tough and confrontational, and it was. I confided everything to my therapists, especially my strong temptation to give my son to my ex-husband and my equally strong feeling that it was wrong for a mother to do that. Eventually, the therapists recommended that I give up custody for a time. Despite great protests from my mother and stepfather, I let my son go. I had even asked him what he wanted to do, as I felt he was old enough to have a say. Reluctantly, he admitted that he would rather live in a nice house with his father and grandparents.

I was sad, but I was free to come and go as I pleased for the first time in seven years. I would see my son on the weekends, so I took to finding my social life on weeknights. I found lots of other young people who loved to drink and party. When I couldn't find friends to drink with, I would go to clubs and drink with strangers. I took chances. I was lucky. I was never hurt physically. But my mind was hurting. I felt degraded and unloved. Booze soothed the pain.

And then the pain became physical. About seven years ago, when I was in my early thirties, I developed a chronic pain in my neck, shoulders, and upper back. I was sure at first that I had a simple stiff neck, but it didn't get any better. I went to my doctor; he couldn't diagnose it, but he gave me a painkiller, Percocet. Now I was drinking two to four times a week, although it could have been a bit more. I was also taking the Percocet, which killed most of the pain and made me feel pretty merry. It also slowed me down and made my thinking sluggish. I didn't really notice how bad its effects were until after I stopped taking it three months later and my mind switched back on. Unfortunately, I had become addicted to Percocet. A friend had convinced me to stop taking it, and I am still grateful. I had thought I couldn't become addicted because I hadn't taken it every day. But I was wrong. I noticed unpleasant symptoms for a couple of days after I quit: chills, shakes, hot flashes. Now I began a series of experiments in which my doctor prescribed nonaddictive pain relievers and antispasmodic drugs. All they generally did was dry my mouth and upset my stomach.

Only drinking killed the pain a bit and made me feel happier. In the next few years, slowly, inexorably, I increased my drinking to every day and virtually always had a drink or two at lunch just to break even for the afternoon of work. The pain was wearing me down. I did not give up looking for alternative solutions, but acupuncture, chiropractics, and deep massage never worked as well as drinking. I went from doctor to doctor, looking for a new approach, but I was always disappointed. Besides, they all thought I should stop drinking, and I did not want to.

About two and a half years ago a doctor prescribed Valium for my pain, and it worked like a dream. Initially I did not take it every day, so again I thought myself safe from addiction. I started with five milligrams a day, moved up to ten, and after about a year and a half it took at least twenty to thirty milligrams to relax my mind and body sufficiently. I was playing suicide roulette. I thought that if I drank a little and took a bit of Valium I would not die—that happens only to other people.

Eventually, I chose my HMO's only holistic practitioner, thinking that he would take a fresh approach to my pain problem. He said he would see me only if I stopped drinking and taking Valium. Just before our first appointment, I stopped both. I have not had a Valium since then, and I am pleased about that. But after about five months of working with him, I became disillusioned, both by the lack of progress with my pain and by the fact that several times he made early morning appointments for me and failed to show up.

After not drinking for a few months, I began to have a drink now and then. Now I am again drinking every day. The only difference is that I very rarely get drunk. I rarely have even a beer at lunch, although on my latest job it is possible to have one at a nearby pub.

I am still trying to convince myself that I am an alcoholic and not just a situational problem drinker. Writing this has made me aware of how compulsive my drinking is. I am disturbed by that. I also noticed that the first few times I drank after quitting were not pleasant. However, I do find the level I'm at right now fairly comfortable. Sometimes I feel somewhat ill, and if I have more than three drinks, I suffer. Does this make me a maintenance alcoholic? I cannot say.

When he was thirteen, my son begged to leave his father and grandparents and asked if he could live with me. I had long since become used to having an adult roommate and was not a bit sure of my ability to relate to my son as a full-fledged mother. We compromised. My mother and stepfather had been divorced, and she was now living in the apartment next to mine in Cambridge. My son went to live with her. The three of us have been fighting out nasty problems ever since. One of them is my son's education. He has never done well in school, and after making a concerted effort for one quarter of his sophomore year in high school, he flunked everything the next quarter. None of us seems to have a solution to that.

Toward the end of 1986, I asked him to live with me, but the following summer he began "visiting" his grandmother frequently. Then he wanted to keep his computer hooked up to the TV, and she permitted that. In the early fall she subscribed to cable TV with movie stations, and I had not. Soon he was staying there almost every night, primarily to watch TV and run his computer. That and spending time outdoors with his friends are his only consistent activities. Our relationship has never healed since the early days, and I do not quite know what to do about it. Ultimately it became official that he live with his grandmother again because I could not convince him to leave. It was nearly impossible to impose any discipline on him as long as he was with her.

I do not take drugs anymore, and I wouldn't recommend them to anyone else. I think that pot is almost certainly less dangerous than alcohol or cigarettes, and when my sixteen-year-old son told me he'd been using pot for some time, I condoned it. I know people who started to use it in their early teens and I cannot see they were terribly harmed by it. I was rather shocked to be told that he had been smoking cigarettes for several years and would like to see him quit, as I have. I have been a laissez-faire parent and do not see fit to get heavy-handed now. I am afraid it is too late to change our relationship.

As far as I can tell, he does not drink. He has seen what booze can do by observing his grandfather, and by observing me in my earlier phases. However, he used to hate cigarettes and lecture people about smoking them, so I cannot say he will always be dry. I can only say there are worse things he could be doing today, and I am relieved that he is somewhat sensible.

In the last fifteen years I have developed a friendship with my stepfather that quite transcends what happened when I was young. He has been sober the last several years. Sometimes he makes me angry as hell when he's critical of my life-style, but I am glad that we have lived through the worst of our relationship. I cannot tell precisely what effect his drinking had on mine, but I know there is a lot there. I might have started earlier or become worse had I not had his negative example before me. Or perhaps my revulsion against booze became fascination.

He has been understanding of my drinking, never insisting that I join AA or that I quit drinking, but certainly suggesting that I consider those options. I suspect that it suits him to believe I am an alcoholic because both he and my mother tend to identify heavy, steady drinking with alcoholism. It would be tough to admit now that I cannot continue drinking moderately or occasionally, so I like to believe that I can. I never could think "one day at a time" as proposed by AA. I'm not a good AA candidate because I hate dogma, have no religious beliefs, and have never been a joiner. I believe in life and people and do want to have a good life.

Liquor is available everywhere, and ads tell me that I'll be glamorous and sexy if I just drink the right stuff; it's a tough world in which to be sober. I really do love the relaxation and the escape afforded by a few drinks. But I fear the long-range consequences of my dependent personality. I used to think that drinking was one pleasure I could live without. I wish it were as easy to say that now as it was when I was growing up.

WAYWARD GIRL

Ruth Hayes
(as told to Mitzi Chandler)

There was a little girl
Who had a little curl
Right in the middle of her forehead.
When she was good
She was very very good
And when she was bad she was horrid!

Scenes of my early childhood are banked in fog. A shadowy place, where memory is more impression than clear image. For a moment the fog lifts and I see my father, proud, puffed-up, his eyes twinkling. Someone is saying, "My, what a beautiful child you have." His hand strokes my hair, his fingers curl around mine. He loves me. Me alone. My knight in shining armor will protect and love me until the end of time. From the look in his eyes I can see that I am the center of his world. I will spend centuries searching for that same look in someone's eyes.

I see glimpses of my pretty mother, always busy cleaning, cooking. I see her braiding my hair, pulling up my socks, buckling patent leather shoes. On holidays I wear new dresses. She plays with me when Daddy is at work, is nervous when he is home. Sometimes she drinks and plays poker with Daddy and his friends. When she drinks she is not so pretty, not so sweet.

Other images blur through the fog. Daddy hurls angry words at my mother, hurls his fist in her face. Police. They take away the fear. Then silence, squirming silence. And I wait. I wait for that look to return to my father's eyes.

"Promise you won't hit Mommy anymore?"

"I promise."

"Promise you won't drink whiskey anymore?"

"I promise."

And I believe that I have made Daddy change back into Prince Charming. And I believe that everything will be beautiful for ever and ever.

At about age eight the fog begins to lift. Violent fights between my parents. Both parents beat us with a belt, switch, or brush handle for small infractions. The ground rules change from day to day, from minute to minute. The battle plan jells: I am Daddy's little girl, and my sister is Momma's right arm. My brother is protector of my mother. Punishments and retaliations are doled out accordingly. A fragile truce is called from Monday until Thursday afternoon—payday.

Up until now, my brother, aged fifteen, has tried to run interference, holding Daddy back, getting between them. On the day he leaves home for good, he lets out the rage and hurt he feels. His fists flail in clumsy fury. Blood spatters the walls of the hallway until my father lies in a heap. I run, hide in the closet, my hands over my ears. My mother snatches me from my hiding place and we run to a neighbor's. Soon there is pounding on the wall from our duplex, a pleading: "Ruthie, Ruthie, come help me. For Christ's sake, come help me!"

Daddy is sitting on the couch, his head in his hands, matted blood in his black hair. "Bring me a washrag and a beer," he says in a soft voice. When he looks up, his face is that of a monster from my dreams. I feel pity. I feel love. I feel afraid.

I escape from the fear and confusion in the woods near our home. I know each twist and turn in the trail, each bump formed by a tree root, each rock jutting from the sandy path. I have a favorite spot to sit, a magic tree to climb. Unlike my home, there is order and quiet here. I know what is around the bend. The sounds are those of wrens, chittering squirrels, babbling water. Not the snarls and cries that pierce the walls in my home.

When I am eight, a new and welcome cry comes to our home when a baby brother is born. I play pat-a-cake and peekaboo with him. I make him laugh, help him learn to walk and talk. I love loving him. It takes away some of my hurt.

By now, my prince has turned into a dragon. He abandons me, rejects and betrays me, spits fire at me. I feel fear, deep fear of him. Yet I pray that I will see that look of his that makes me feel loved. I still clutch at hope, still believe in fairy tales. And sometimes they almost come true.

"Be a good girl and Daddy will give you a birthday party." A saint could not be a better girl. I clean my room, help my mother, do my homework, and say my prayers. On my birthday I invite three friends to my party. There will be balloons, a chocolate cake, presents—maybe my ballet slippers!

Anticipating, giggling, we open the door to the tenement apartment. There are no balloons, no cake, no presents. Instead, on the linoleum lies my dead-drunk prince. Naked, his limp penis in full view of my friends. We back out the door and run down the steps. I mumble an apology. Fog rolls back over the memory of my ninth birthday.

Some dream, some hope dies in that fog. In my nine-year-old way I decide that if being good doesn't get you love, maybe being bad—whatever that is—will.

Other homes, other people begin to shape my life. I am invited to stay at a beach cottage with a family. The man works with, drinks with, my father. He says that I'm beautiful, that I'm like a daughter to him. Daddy says that the man's wife is dim-witted.

At the cottage I sleep on a screened-in porch, alone. Late on the first night I see the man standing in the doorway, looking at me. He is wearing only a T-shirt. My heart begins to pound in my head. I pretend to sleep. He kneels by the bed, fondles my breasts, puts his hand in my panties, rubs . . . pokes. . . . Can't he tell that I am awake by the thumping of my heart! Can't he see that I am paralyzed by fear!

Out of control, I trip through the dimly lit cottage, yank on the overhead light of their bedroom, scream, "I was awake! I was awake! You take me home, now! I'll tell my father what you did to me!" His wife blinks in disbelief. She makes him leave the room, tucks me into bed with her and holds me while I cry. She promises that he will not bother me again, that I will sleep with her.

I stay for a few more days. He informs me, coldly, that if I tell my father what happened, he will deny it. And he will tell my parents that he caught me smoking. I do not tell my dad, or anyone. Inside, the blush and hope of girlhood turns to shame and anger.

I begin to pick on a small girl at school. I taunt her, back her against the fence with a stick. I like having power over her, like making her cry. I don't know why I torment her. I feel bad about it, but I do it again the next day. I turn a stone ear to the scolding from my teacher.

I purposely cause trouble at home. It gets me attention. A belt or switch whacks across my back, my legs. "Promise me you'll never do this or that again," he or she demands. I promise not to sneak out again, not smoke again, not sass again, or whatever it is I've done. And I break that promise the first chance I get. I'd like to have a nickel for every time I defy the command: "Don't you cut your eyes at me like that."

Not only do I learn to "cut my eyes," I learn to cut myself a wide swath from getting tangled in their fights. "Where's your no-good mother," my father slurs when he comes home looking for trouble. I say she's out drinking, my sister says she doesn't know. He likes my answer better. My sister gets the beating. I learn to play my mother against my father the way they do to us kids. I know when Momma will say no and Daddy will say yes and vice versa. I know that I will do what I want anyway, and they will have another excuse to get drunk and fight to their hearts' content. I am their scapegoat. A black sheep.

My sister is a saint. By the time I am thirteen and she is sixteen, the contrast between us is glaring. I look eighteen, sexy, hard. She looks soft, sweet. Ever since we were little girls people compared us: "Ruth is the pretty one; Mitzi is the nice one." I love her. I resent her. She hangs around with nice kids. My friends have wandered from the flock the way I have. We are looking for a place to belong. I am searching for that look that was once in my daddy's eyes.

Wayward Girl

I begin skipping school with my friend Pam. We walk around in downtown D.C., window-shop, strut our stuff, giggle when men whistle, honk horns. Sometimes my pretty friend and I go to a bar in the red-light district. We gyrate to the beat of Fats Domino's "Blueberry Hill" and Elvis Presley's "Jailhouse Rock." Men at the bar offer beer, sex. I accept neither. I dance myself happy, bask in the glow of male eyes.

Skipping school becomes a daily affair. A truant officer is assigned to pick Pam and me up and take us to school. We walk in one door and out the other. We are not part of the crinoline crowd, the girls who get good grades and sing in the glee club, the girls whose parents kiss them good-bye in the morning. The girls we would like to be.

We find ways to be. We feel cool driving around in a red Ford convertible, hanging out with guys in ducktail haircuts, guys who wear black leather jackets, Camels tucked in the rolled-up sleeve of their T-shirts. Our Maybelline eyebrows point up in defiance. Red smirks replace smiles. And our dreams and our innocence disappear in smoke rings.

A woman in a veiled hat, black gloves held in one hand, approaches my sister and me on a street corner. She looks me up and down, her eyes narrowed to hate. "You are the most disgusting thing I've ever seen," she hisses. My heart folds into itself.

At fourteen I fall in love with Hank, Pam's seventeen-year-old brother. His home is a battleground like mine. He understands, holds me when I cry, strokes my hair, curls his fingers around mine. I see love shining in his eyes. I have found my prince! I have saved myself for this moment. I lose my virginity on a lopsided couch, but I feel like the most beloved princess in the land.

My parents don't like Hank, don't like any of my friends. They forbid me to see him, restrict me to the house. I pit them against each other, sneak off to be with Hank as they battle it out.

Besides wanting to be with Hank, I have to get away from the bedlam in that home. Away from the love I feel for my little brother and two baby sisters. It hurts to see the fear in their eyes, the tentative smiles on their lips. And I know that when my mother is drinking, she wants me gone. Perhaps a poison apple...a hunter's dagger...

My parents separate and reunite frequently now. Sometimes

he moves out, sometimes he kicks us out. I begin to run away. Overnight at first. I stay at a friend's house, go home when I feel like it. Take my licks, then do it again when I can't stand it at home anymore.

One day two boys drop me off at home. Inside, I hear Momma screaming, Daddy cussing. "Make him stop beating her," I tell them. My friends bolt through the screen door, drag my father outside, stomp on his stomach, kick him in the head, two mad dogs raging at a bloody rag doll. I fear they will kill him. My mother and I beg them to stop. When they do, we take him inside, clean him up, and put him to bed.

More fog. Somewhere in the mist Daddy leaves for good. He works for his brother in a drug store when he is sober. Money from his ailing mother keeps him in booze and rundown rooming houses. After she dies, he is on the streets. He sleeps in the woods, begs, sits on a bench sipping muscatel or whatever else he can get by hook or crook. He is dead to me. My heart switches off.

So has Momma's heart. Years of beatings, poverty, lost hopes, and drinking have worn her down. Different boyfriends come into our lives. Trash cans of beer sit in the kitchen. Her face is puffy, her eyes heavy lidded much of the time. My sister takes care of the kids and I take care to get home as little as possible.

I run away often and for longer periods of time. Pam and I spend a week in a barn. A friend brings us food. We feel free, have a good time hanging out. We are walking down a country lane when a police car drives up. "Where are you girls going?" The officer smiles. We give him phony names, think we have fooled him with our charm. "How about a ride?" he offers. We hop in and he informs me that he knows who I am, and that my mother is looking for me.

My mother staggers into the police station with my uncle. It is decided that I will go to the Good Shepherd, a home for wayward girls. I beg and plead not to be put in the home. My uncle promises that I won't be there long. I am hurt that Momma came to the station drunk.

The policeman who picked us up takes me to Good Shepherd. We walk up a long flight of stairs toward a huge wooden door. A nun unbolts the latch and takes me inside. When I look around at the man who brought me here, I see a look of compassion in his eyes that tells me he understands why I run away. That look engraves itself into my heart, and I hold onto it for dear life.

Good Shepherd houses "bad" girls, orphans, and sickly old women. Nuns rule with an iron hand, a few with compassion. The place is rigid, structured. We are herded from mass to mess hall, to laundry room, to classes, and to bed. I brag, "I'll be out of here in a week." I stay a year. My mother has put me in this place for a year! I have only two visitors during this time, an aunt and my sister. It is a grim year. A lonely year. I am a princess locked up in a tower, put there by a witch who does not love me. There is no one to rescue me.

On a Christmas outing from the home, I beg the bus driver to go a few blocks out of the way and let me visit my brother and sisters. It is against the rules to do this, but I promise him that I won't run away. The Christmas spirit overpowers his hesitation and he allows me fifteen minutes.

Tree lights twinkle and so do the kids' eyes when they see me. I hug them, cry, ask what Santa is bringing them. Momma does not speak to me; she stays in the kitchen. She looks afraid. Of me? Of getting into trouble with the home? Of feeling? I want so much for her to be happy to see me, to hold me. But I am a bad girl. A bad girl with a huge ache in the middle.

I return to Good Shepherd feeling hopeless. I don't care anymore. I plod through days and try to stay out of reach of the fighting and the homosexual activity at night. A few months before my release from the home, one of the teachers looks at me and says, "Ruth, you are going to make it." Does she know that she saved my life? Does she know that I'll never forget her? The look of pride in her eyes warmed the inside of me and a thimbleful of hope trickled out from that ache in the middle.

When I am released from the home I go to live with my brother and his wife. It doesn't work from the start. One night I pass by him and he hits my leg, hard. He is drinking. I should know better, but I smack him back. With that he leaps up, shoves me against the wall, punches my stomach and face. I get free, throw an ashtray at him. Before it's over I am cut, bruised, swollen, and minus hunks of hair. I call my mother, tell her what happened, and beg to come home. Reluctantly, she lets me.

The one person who has always loved me, my older sister, has moved out. I am sixteen. Momma and I have a standoffish relationship. There are moments of caring between us, but I am too confused to know what to do with them, and she is too beaten down, too much in need of booze and men to bother.

While I was in the home, Hank, my former boyfriend, married. We run into each other and fall in love all over again. Sweet Hank. He is not a bright guy, but he has a good heart and gentle manner. And he loves me. I am his life; he is mine. Hank separates from his wife and asks me to be his bride.

Eight months later and eight months into my pregnancy, Hank and I marry. A Baptist minister agrees to perform the ceremony in the church Sunday school room. Crayoned pictures of the manger scene and snowflakes decorate the walls, and an overhead fluorescent light glares down at my wedding. I am wearing an ugly black coat. I button it closed, hoping the minister won't notice how pregnant I am. Momma, my sister, and her boyfriend are the only guests. Hank has divorce papers in one pocket, a marriage license in the other.

Until the moment the minister says, "I now pronounce you man and wife," I feel lower than a snake. And then, like magic, I turn into a lovely princess. My prince by my side, a beautiful child on the way. Now I will live happily ever after. The wedding party goes to the Dixie Pig for barbecued pork sandwiches and root beer.

A few weeks into the marriage, our son is born. He is instant love, a blessing, a gift from God. All my prayers have come true.

But I have an insatiable need for Hank. I am love starved, cannot get enough verbal or physical attention. Three months later, I discover I am pregnant again. I begin to doubt Hank's love, try to control him, demand to know where he is every minute. One night I insist that he get the diapers from the clothesline. He says, "No, you've been home all day and I've been working my butt off. I'm tired." I hound him until in a fit of frustration he puts his fist through each pane of glass in a French door. A main artery gushes open. Hank is dizzy, incoherent, drops to the floor. I call an ambulance and he is rushed to the hospital. I am flooded with guilt and shame.

I try to make amends. Try to make happily-ever-after happen for the three of us and the child on the way. But I don't have any idea how to be a wife. After another argument Hank storms out the door, saying something about his ex-wife. I wait up all night for him to come home. By morning I am a maniac. When he returns, I demand, "Did you spend the night with her?" The next thing I hear is myself screaming, "No! No! No!" And then I'm in a hospital. I have flipped out. Memory is vague. I am behind a wall of rejection. Rejection by my father, my mother, my brother, and now the man who was to make up for all those losses, the second man who promised to love me until the end of time.

We try to patch it up, but neither of us knows what a healthy relationship is. We both love our son and hope that our next baby will make our marriage right. I begin having problems with the pregnancy. My second son is born breach. He is brain damaged. He lives just two days. We do not know how to deal with the grief and guilt. Hank blames himself. I blame myself.

We continue to try for the sake of our child. But Hank stays away often, and I am glad he does. I want to forgive him for sleeping with his ex-wife, but I can't. Hate seethes in me. Two years into the marriage I leave. Now I am not looking for happily-ever-after; I am looking for the maturity to raise my son the way he deserves.

Instead I meet Danny, who sweeps me off my feet with his charm and good looks. He courts me with roses and candy and stuffed toys for my son. He is intelligent, worldly. For about six months I feel happy. At times his behavior is bizarre, secretive. I attribute it to excessive drinking.

Driving home one night from a party, I complain about his friends, say that I don't like them. With that, Danny begins beating me with one hand. We weave over the road until he pulls off at an isolated construction site. He straddles me and for an eternity bashes my face and chokes me until I am gasping for breath. I am fighting for my life. My short life, my son's face, pass before me. I see a newspaper headline: TEENAGER MURDERED ON CONSTRUCTION SITE. I go limp, black out.

At home, I look in the mirror. Like Daddy's face, I look like a monster from my dreams. My legs are gouged where my high heels dug in while I was trying to fight Danny off.

When Danny calls, he apologizes, says he doesn't know what got into him. He tells me he loves me and will never hurt me again. I refuse to see him. About two months later he knocks at the door late one night. I won't let him in. I live on the top floor of an apartment, and somehow he works his way to the area over my ceiling. I hear him sawing something. I hide my son in a closet, tell him not to make a sound, then call the police. A guy yells to Danny that the cops are coming. By time the police arrive at my door, Danny is gone. He had sawed through my ceiling. I learn from the police that Danny is a psychopath and a drug dealer, and that he has a long criminal record and has been in and out of mental institutions.

Hank and I get back together briefly after I fall and badly sprain an ankle. He helps with our son, takes me to work, holds me. And I discover I am pregnant again. I have a baby girl three months early. She is beautiful. She lives two days.

When I reach twenty, a light goes on in my head and I realize that I've been diving at life like a blind bat. Slowly, I emerge from the debris I have left behind. I pray for faith—whatever that is. And slowly I find a pattern of life that keeps me sane and provides some stability for my son. In time, I reach out and accept the love that my sister offers me. I begin to believe that God loves me. I join the Catholic Church and hold on with all the faith I can manage. I date men who treat me like a lady. I get a marriage proposal from a wonderful man, but I see that he is jealous of my son and possessive of me. My son and I are a package deal, and I see the potential for problems in this relationship. This insight is a new and welcome twist in my growth. It is a beginning, but only a beginning.

At twenty-three I meet Mike, a man from a small Nebraska town. There is something solid about him, something different from the other men who had been in my life. On our first date he tells me that he is going to marry me. He treats me like a queen, tells me that he will be there for me always. Somehow I know that I can trust this man, can believe in what he says. He and my son click right away, and Mike's parents are swept off their feet by my blue-eyed charmer. We could have a good life with him.

We marry. I settle into being a good wife, mother, citizen, church supporter, grateful daughter-in-law, the epitome of what I thought a woman is supposed to be.

Mike and I have a son. I call him Sunshine. He is doted on by parents and grandparents, surrounded by friends. Cub Scouts, Little League, rodeo days, parades, picnics. A Norman Rockwell boyhood. My first son thrives in this stable environment. We succeed in giving the boys a life better than my own. They grow into fine young men. I do not know that beneath this picture-book world that I have created is still a sad, angry little girl who has been shoved aside so that I could survive.

In 1978 I travel to Washington to visit my mother and sisters. My father is dying of cancer of the mouth and throat. He is living in an attic room my uncle has provided. My sister and I go to see him, go to clean up the hovel he is living in. Trash, rotting food, wine bottles are piled along one wall of the steamy room. He sits in a rocker, wiping drool from his mouth. Little more than bones, he wears a shirt, pants, sweater; a dirty towel drapes around his shoulders. Some coherence seeps through his wet brain.

I clip and clean his curled fingernails. As a child, I loved watching his hands—graceful, soft, shaky. Yet in a blink those hands could turn to talons, tear my heart to shreds. As I hold his limp hands, I am aware that they are a reflection of how he was as a father.

I practice over and over what I want to say. I tell him that I love him, that I forgive him for not being there for me. I tell him that I am sorry that I had not been there for him when he was in the streets. I feel like a grown woman doing the right thing, expecting nothing in return. But, oh how I long to see a glimmer of love in his eyes. All I see is the bleak stare of a dying man.

In the car I sob, tell my sister, "I think Daddy said 'I love you Ruthie.'" I don't know that he said it. I have to think that he did. Surely he would have. After all, I had been Daddy's little girl. . . .

After my sons are grown and out of the home I begin to have deep depressions. The problems that have cropped up and been skirted over in our marriage begin to glare at us. We have both tried to control one another through verbal push and shove. We have both given and withheld nurturing and loving according to our vulnerabilities. I withdraw into myself, Mike into work.

Deep inside me a rusty door creaks open and the ghosts of my past begin to haunt me. I pull away from people, from commitments. I spend hours staring at walls, crying, then feeling numb. I feel that I am losing my mind. At church, at work, I wear my mask, leave it on the front door when I come home. I cannot pretend any longer that I am this person I have created, cannot pretend to be happily married, cannot pretend to be happy. I have no idea who I am. Like a chameleon, I can change, blend into any scene, be anything others want me to be. I have wonderful friends, good women who care about me. But I feel that if they really knew me they would reject me the way I have rejected myself.

By now there is a national movement afoot that offers hope and healing for people who have been hurt by the behavior of alcoholic parents. With the encouragement of my sister, who went through therapy many years ago, I call a priest in our community who I'm told is good at counseling people from alcoholic homes.

For months we talk. I am matter-of-fact about any topic we discuss except my father. Any mention of him and I am reduced to a quivering little girl. I confess that I don't understand these tears, that I have resolved my feelings about my father. I resist the priest's suggestions that children from alcoholic homes feel responsible for their parents' drinking, feel guilt, shame. I get irritated when he insists on focusing on this. I tell him that my problem is in the here and now, that my marriage is the problem. I am at a standstill in understanding what is wrong with me until a trip to Alaska to visit my older brother makes it painfully clear what the problem is.

Bud greets me and my sister with open arms. He is sober, eager about the art studio he is opening in Juneau. We love him, but he is a hard man to like. His personality has been distorted by having been abused as a child and by his own drinking problem. But now he is on the wagon, has found religion, is out to make millions, conquer the world, walk on water, show all those sons of bitches. My sister and I are skilled at walking on eggshells, and for a week things go fairly smoothly between us and our volatile brother, a man who has followed in the footsteps of his father.

On our last day in Juneau, he begins drinking in the morning. We get sloppy kisses on the cheek, excessive praise, true confessions, and he gets another beer. By evening the little studio is a powder keg. His female business partner tells him he shouldn't be sleeping with the young girl who works for them. With that, all hell breaks loose and we are transported back in time. He is my father standing there and I am a small girl. Vile, vengeful words slide from his mouth like a blade. This man, who hours before had showered me with love, now is cutting me apart. My sister grabs me to leave, but I can't go. I have to face the fury in myself. I want to show him, to show Daddy that they can't hurt me anymore.

Oh, am I wrong! I have taken on a giant. The sickness in him, the power of him, takes away any semblance of sanity that I have. His vicious words stab me again and again, and I cannot fight them off. He convinces me that my sister has jumped in the river, attempts to run over me with his car when I try to find her. I am totally caught in the madness of his inner world. And of mine. Two hours later when my sister returns, I am a whimpering child. From this night on I cannot deny that the giant called alcoholism is the cause of my pain.

I crawl back into therapy, ready to accept help for my deep wounds. With the wise and loving guidance of this priest, I learn that even though the adult in me has resigned itself to my losses, the little child in me has not grieved the loss of my father, of my childhood, has not felt the full sting of his and my mother's rejection. I have not accepted that I am a worthy human being, and I am still trying to make amends for being a wayward girl.

With the support of my family and friends I am now finding my way back to myself. I am learning to understand that defiant girl who made desperate choices in order to survive. I have made peace with my mother, and I am gaining the courage to feel the pain of the loss of my father. I believe that before alcoholism took him away, my daddy really did love me.

Most important, I am at long last learning to love myself.

PHOTOS FROM HOME

Marie Sorensen

Sometimes when I'm home for a holiday, I look through the family photo album that my older sister keeps. It's mostly filled with standard-issue pictures of the two of us playing in the backyard, school portraits, and Christmas trees over the years. There's one photo, taken when I was five years old, that I always stare at. My father is seated at the kitchen table, and I am standing beside him, holding his arm and resting my head on his shoulder. I am looking up at him. My face pleads for his attention. He is staring directly into the camera. His face expresses irritation and disgust. That photo captures the tone of my relationship with my father. My never-ending attempts to win his affection were met at best with boredom, at worst with abuse.

My father is a biomedical researcher at a large state university. My mother is a social worker. My sister and I were born while he was completing his Ph.D. My mother was a full-time parent until I was seven, when my father settled into the research position he still holds. She then went back to school to complete undergraduate work she had begun in her hometown before she and my father married. She then went on for graduate degrees in psychology and education. She finished her schooling when I was a junior in college.

I don't remember a time when both of my parents didn't drink heavily. Dinner was often delayed because my father had stopped at his local bar on the way home from work. My mother would have a few beers while we waited. A screaming fight would begin as we finally all sat down over the spoiled food: my mother would rail at my father for being late and ruining the meal; he would respond that if she were a good cook and a pleasant person, he'd be home on time. Since dinner was our family hour, my sister and I were forced to sit through the meal until we had eaten enough that we could beg to be excused. Most often, my father did not limit his verbal assaults to my mother but would direct attacks toward my sister and myself.

I frequently left the table in tears halfway through the meal and hid in my bedroom. Unfortunately, my bedroom was over the kitchen, and I could hear the fight continue—my mother would be yelling at my father because he had tortured me again. Later she would come up to my room and explain to me that he had had a very hard day and that he really loved me. I was supposed to pity him and understand that he was troubled. My father never apologized or made any effort to explain himself.

Fights and violence were not confined to the dinner table. Many nights I awoke to hear my parents screaming at each other. I would lie awake, too terrified to cry or go into my sister's room for comfort. Over and over I would hear my father yell, "You can just pack your bags and go anytime you want to." Frequent themes of the fights were money or in-laws. I was too young to follow their specific meaning.

For the most part, the fights were not physically violent, but one night at about three A.M. I heard my mother burst out of their bedroom screaming, "You hit me! I'm bleeding!" She ran into the bathroom. I heard my father chase after her and hit her more. She escaped from the bathroom, ran downstairs, and called the police. I didn't get back to sleep that night until after four A.M., with the red police light flashing through my window onto the wall. There was still blood on the bathroom floor the next morning. My mother never pressed charges.

Luckily for my sister and me, most of the violence in our family was directed at our pets. We almost always had a dog of one sort or another. One barked too much. My parents bought a device that strapped onto the dog's neck and delivered a painful electric shock triggered by the vocal vibrations. The poor dog would bark, yelp, and continue yelping because his cries triggered shock after shock. Our dogs were brutally punished when they misbehaved. I watched my father throw a dog down a flight of stairs because it had chewed the hem out of the drapes. The dog suffered a broken leg. I watched my mother beat a dog with a kitchen chair that it had chewed the foam seat out of. I would later be amazed when my parents acted contrite to the dogs and claimed to love them.

I learned that abuse was love, and that those who loved you best abused you the most. I learned that pity and tolerance were a return of love. I learned that my opinions, feelings, and problems were a potential source for an excuse to abuse me. I learned to keep quiet.

Much of my time as a child was spent in my bedroom, reading, writing, and doing my homework. Books and school gave me the first clues that other people didn't live the way we did. In novels, I found fathers who loved their daughters. In school I learned that I could be a good girl and receive praise, attention, and high grades from my teachers. These were the positive things in my childhood.

Socializing as a child was almost impossible. I was not allowed to bring playmates home from school because my father spent many drunken afternoons away from his research lab, sitting in his underwear in the living room, watching cartoons on television. I had a few friends whose houses I would visit, but I was not allowed too many visits and was never allowed to take trips with them—my parents did not want to incur obligations that could not be returned. I was not allowed to participate in after-school clubs or activities because my mother did not want to have to come pick me up later in the afternoon when she'd had a few beers. Ironically, she complained that I was too much of a bookworm and made me feel guilty for spending time alone in my room.

As soon as I was old enough, I started to get around on my own with my bicycle. I learned to rely on myself alone, to stay away from home as much as possible, and to divert my attention from family problems to my friendships.

Sex and sexuality were an area where my parents' alcoholism caused our family to be extremely dysfunctional. My mother professed to be sexually liberal and was very frank with us about sex. I was so young when I learned the physical aspect of lovemaking that I don't remember not knowing where babies came from. When I was eight or nine, she confessed to me she had had numerous affairs while my father was in graduate school. She said that sexual experimentation was important, but that I should be sure to get that out of my system before marriage. I believe she recommended that because she felt guilty for having committed adultery. She implied that she had fooled around all she wanted and was now quite sexually satisfied with my father.

Later, when I was nine, I awoke in the middle of the night and got up to go to the bathroom. It was quite late, but the lights were on downstairs. I heard my mother in the living room, making love to my father's best friend—I could tell who it was by his voice as he moaned. I did not know where my father was. I stood at the top of the stairs and screamed, "Mommy, Mommy, Mommy!" as loud as I could. She came to the foot of the stairs, dressed in her bathrobe. I told her I was afraid someone was hurting her. She replied that everything was fine and told me to go back to bed. Although I knew what had been going on, I denied it for years, believing what I wanted to hear—that everything was fine. Finally, when I was in high school, my sister told me that our mother confessed to her that she had in fact carried on an affair with this man for five years. I was shattered. I understood needing to experiment while you were young, but I intensely wanted to believe that love meant fidelity and trust. I had no role model from whom to learn this.

Alcoholism is frequently linked to incest. I first noticed my father's incestuous attention toward my sister when she began to develop breasts. He would compliment her on how nicely her "fried eggs" were coming along and would squeeze her bottom affectionately. I was quite jealous of all the extra attention my sister was getting. I couldn't wait to grow up and receive compliments on my breasts, too. My sister developed very full breasts; I never did. My father never paid that kind of attention to me. As we got older, my sister started to complain to my mother and me that the attention was more sexually overt when she and my father were alone together. My mother accused her of lying to make her jealous and denied the existence of a problem.

A few weeks before I left home for college, my father took

my sister and me camping at the beach in our 18-foot travel trailer. It was supposed to be fun, the final weekend for Dad and the girls before I went away. I was sleeping in the trailer's upper bunk, my father had the lower bunk, and my sister got the kitchen table, which converted into a bed. I woke up in the middle of the night to find my father in my sister's bed. "I won't hurt you," he was saying. "I promise I'll be gentle." He was stroking her breasts. "No, Dad, I don't want to," she replied. I was too afraid to speak or move. Finally, my father gave up.

When my sister and I told my mother what had happened, she could no longer deny the problem. She moved my sister out of the house into an apartment in town. Years later, I was amazed by a TV movie on incest in which a social worker intervened and removed the father from the house! My mother, a true codependent, was willing to sacrifice her daughter in order to protect her husband.

At home, I learned that sexual attention, not fidelity or expression and acceptance of feelings, meant love. I learned that a woman should do anything to keep a man.

I left home to go to college when I was seventeen. I chose art as a career because my hometown university had a poor program for art students, which necessitated my attending an out-of-state school. At last I could leave home for good. I studied hard for four years, then came to New York City to pursue a career as a designer. I have been successful, possibly because of good luck, possibly because I'm good at what I do, but mostly because I find work a fairly unemotional environment where effort and hard labor are generally rewarded with increased pay and responsibility.

Shortly after I moved to New York, I met a man through mutual friends. We fell immediately into a serious relationship—within a month we were spending almost every night together. We moved in together after a year and married after another year. My husband reminded me a great deal of my father, with one exception: he seemed to love me. He was addicted to sex and wanted it constantly. After years of being passed over by my father's preference for my sister, my husband's incessant sexual demands seemed like the love I'd always craved. It took several years for me to realize that his need for sex had nothing to do with feelings of affection for me.

Like my father, he sent very mixed messages: sometimes he

could be unbelievably sweet and considerate; other times he would be cruel and ignore me completely. The latter usually happened after he had been drinking. We had an understanding that we wouldn't chat when we'd both arrived home from work until he'd had a few beers to relax. I fell for the biggest manipulation of all: he told me he was cruel because he loved me, because I was the person closest to him, with whom he could truly be himself. I wanted the love; I tolerated the abuse to get it.

We were married for three and a half years. We talked about having children, but decided to wait. During our last year together, I fell into a deep depression. I was convinced that all the problems in our marriage were my fault. I had completely lost interest in sex: I was convinced that something—I wasn't sure what—was wrong with me. He continually complained about his high-stress job as an advertising art director. I felt I was at fault if I got depressed about my job because he'd told me he needed me to be happy to cheer him up. I felt guilty for wanting to share my troubles with him.

Finally, I had an affair with another man that lasted nine months. I was relieved to find out that I did like sex, but I felt extraordinarily guilty that I was an adultress, just like my mother. The affair ended. I became completely numb emotionally. I still believed that if I were just good enough, I could make my husband happy, but I couldn't shake the severe depression to do it. We decided to enter couples counseling. At the same time, my husband joined AA and quit drinking. We had occasionally discussed the possibility that he drank too much, but our denial prevented us from admitting his alcoholism.

Our therapist immediately suggested a trial separation, and after two months of counseling, I was able to decide to divorce my husband. Counseling ended.

Initially, I was quite happy after my marriage ended. I'd learned that I had a right to ask for what I wanted, and I thought that was all I needed to get along. I started dating right away. I dated losers. I dated another alcoholic and a manic-depressive concurrently, and finally a psychologically abusive recovering drug addict/alcoholic. About six months after my marriage ended, I realized that I was repeating a pattern, and that I was getting much worse. I did not feel worthy of love, and I deliberately chose men who were incapable of giving me love. I fell into another depression. Suicide seemed the rational alternative to continuing my self-destructive pattern. I'd been suicidal once before, but the thought of how much my mother would be hurt by my suicide had stopped me. This time, I didn't care about her pain. I believed that my pain was greater than hers would be. I now see that the beginning of recovery was in that thought; for the first time in my life, I wanted to attend to myself before someone else.

I did not commit suicide because I found the strength to call myself a coward. Suicide was not the only alternative. I could change. I was afraid to change because I knew it would be hard. I decided to get help.

Through therapy I have begun the slow, painful process of picking apart what I learned as a child and trying to learn ways of thinking as an adult. I am in individual therapy, I attend meetings of Adult Children of Alcoholics (ACOA), and I recently started group therapy. Individual therapy has been useful in helping me to name emotions and understand them. Ten months ago, my ten-year-old cat died. I cried for two days. I was able to identify grief for the first time and to correlate it with other times when I had felt grief and not known what it was, such as the last day I lived with my husband. I have also been able to examine the messages hidden behind my parents' behavior. For example, when I was eleven, my mother told me that my conception was an accident. So intensely had she not wanted me that she had spent hours running up and down the stairs, hoping she would fall and miscarry. I started to cry as she told me this. She asked me why I was crying, said she loved me now and was glad she had me. I couldn't explain then why I was upset. In therapy, I have learned that the message in that situation was "I love you because I have to, not because you're a lovable person."

ACOA meetings have been helpful because they let me listen to how others have learned and grown. However, I find it almost impossible to speak of my feelings in front of such a large group and I wind up feeling isolated. For that reason, I have entered group therapy. I believe it is important for me to learn that I can say what I feel and not be considered a bad person for feeling any particular way. I feel unbelievably vulnerable in group. I am beginning to be able to allow myself to feel the pain from all the years I was deprived of love.

In the process of learning to identify and express my feelings, I have begun to gather up scraps of self I never knew existed. I have about a handful now, and that's enough so that I finally know my parents' disease had nothing to do with me: I am not responsible for their pain—now or when I was a child.

My parents tell me they love me, and I know they mean it. I was recently home for a weekend, and I told my father that I didn't like seeing him persecute my mother for her drinking, smoking, and constant coughing. He told me he picked on her because he loved her; if he didn't care he wouldn't say anything. I realized then that my parents and I no longer define love the same way.

I still have a long way to go, but now I have something that I never had before. Recently, my sister gave me a photograph that was taken when I was two years old. I am an adorable little blond girl in the photo, and I am clapping my hands and grinning at the camera. I can look at the photo and see very clearly: I was a lovable little girl.

I am a lovable adult.

THERE'S
ALWAYS HOPE

Bobby Truesdale

The wind is blowing hard tonight. The building is shaking, the windows rattling, and I am alone. I am twenty-eight years old, and I have lived in this apartment by the ocean two years now. When I moved in, I had no idea how much better things would get. I finally had to look at myself. Slowly, carefully, and with the help of others, I am now piecing together the puzzle of my road to recovery. I am convinced that every step has been exactly as it should be, that nothing has happened by mistake. The difference today is that I don't have to keep repeating my destructive behavior, that I can break family patterns and move on.

It's amazing that my parents fell in love and married. They seemed complete opposites. He was outgoing, athletic, always quick to tell a story, the life of the party. My mom was extremely intelligent, fluent in three languages, bookish, and not socially adept.

When we were growing up, my dad was a stickler for always having one or both parents there when we got home from school. I realized later that his need stemmed from the inconsistent environment he had grown up in. His mother was an alcoholic, and he never knew when he got home whether she'd be sober.

I loved my grandparents, especially my maternal grand-mother. We were always sewing or painting or dressing up in Hal-loween costumes that she made. She was an artist and very creative. Everything about her was flamboyant and gay. I think my mother shrank in self-worth next to her. Grammy encouraged me to draw, and from age five I knew that I wanted to be an artist.

When I turned six, we moved to a house on the other side of town. It was the first time I had the feeling of being on the outside looking in. In the strange neighborhood, we were the new kids, and I felt alone. It was an easy environment for my mother to hide in. She said, almost in a snobbish way, that we were different and special. This attitude set us apart from the other children and made it difficult for us to join in. My sister became my closest friend. Only a year apart in age, we grew up together and experienced the same inconsistencies at home.

Physical affection was never shown. My parents rarely touched or hugged us. They kissed only to say hello and never touched or hugged each other. I never knew them to go to a movie or to dinner together. Mom had trouble going out in public. Later I realized that my father's drinking embarrassed her. In time, she stopped going out socially with my father. All through my high school years, my mother put her hair in curlers and was in bed no later than eight o'clock.

My father insisted we attend church every Sunday. He was always grouchy Sundays, and some of the biggest and loudest fights we had were over what my sister and I were wearing. He would shout, "Don't you have shoes to wear! God damn it! I'll give you the money to get shoes!"

Appearance and money were big issues for him. He had grown up the son of a wealthy doctor, and no matter how much money he earned it would never compare to his father's income. It was very important how we looked because we were "a reflection on your mother and me." Most of my clothes were ordered from the Sears catalog. My mother hated to shop for anything that was "nice," especially for herself. We never went shopping together. When she did go out by herself, she'd get us stuff only from dis-count stores.

For my father only the top of the line was good enough. He loved to buy expensive clothes. I can remember him throwing out one Brooks Brothers shirt after another because the collar was frayed. In reality, he was very insecure about the money he was earning. He was a furniture salesman working on commission, so his hours were his own. He had an office in the house, and many days he didn't go out on the road at all. My mother countered by cleaning the house obsessively, from top to bottom, every day. Now I know that it was her way of trying to control an increasingly uncontrollable environment.

My mother was very rigid; everything had to be perfect, in its place. We never had a chance to pick up after ourselves because my mother was right there to do it for us. If I ever did try to help her by making my own bed or picking up my own clothes, my mother would redo the task her way. That sent a strong message to me early on. Why should I bother to be responsible for myself when someone else will swoop in and clean up my messes for me? And when I did try to be responsible, I could never do it perfectly. Why try at all?

My mother hated to cook. We were served the same meals week in and week out. It was almost as if she were trying to punish my father because he was a pig when he ate and drank. She retaliated with stale bread, brown lettuce for the salads, and spaghetti with bottled sauce.

At dinner we always sat in the same seats. My sister or I always did the dishes, and my brother or father was responsible for the garbage. My mother gradually took over the dishes and the garbage herself, along with cutting the lawn, paying the bills, and doing painting or maintenance work around the house, while my father slowly relinquished all household responsibility.

School was my salvation. There was always a special teacher in my life to guide me. In junior high I had my first opportunity to try out for organized sports. I played on the field hockey, basketball, and lacrosse teams. I pushed myself hard to succeed.

I learned early to say, "I am strong. I can handle this. I don't need your help." I intimidated people with my intelligence, looks, and talents. The more I excelled, the easier it was to isolate myself, to push people away, to feel apart, to feel different.

My father, the alcoholic in my life, went out of his way to make me feel inadequate. If I got all A's except for one B, he would berate me about the B. No matter what I did, it was never enough. I thought that he and my mother would love me more if I became the perfect child, but the more I tried, the more disappointed I became because I couldn't please them. I still wasn't getting the attention and love I desperately craved.

It wasn't until high school that my father's drinking became a noticeable problem to me. It had been a problem for him all along, but the progression didn't really dawn on me until I was a senior in high school. Growing up I never actually saw a lot of drinking and there was never any violence. My father would yell, my mother would vacuum, and we three kids would defy and rebel. Physically the disease wasn't much evident. But mentally and emotionally it was insidious. My father's self-hatred and his insecurities and my mother's increasing withdrawal and isolation were great markers of the disease. To the outside world we were a model family. But inside things were just not right.

Sports were very important to my father. Since my brother did not live up to my father's expectations in athletics, I became the "son" my father never had. I bent over backward to excel in sports, but again there was no pleasing him. His expectations were ridiculously high. I pushed myself even when I wasn't enjoying it, just so my father might say, "Yes, isn't Bobby a great athlete!" But he never said that.

My father's disease began to be apparent in public. He would humiliate me publicly. He came to every game that I played, home or away, for three years. He would yell at me from the stands to do better.

My senior year became a nightmare. I was under constant scrutiny for every move I made on the basketball court, and the minute I got home after a game I was greeted by my father, the drunken color commentator.

My mother's progression into the disease of dysfunction paralleled my father's. Her humiliation was great. She had attempted to come to my games, but my father embarrassed and disgusted her. If she came at all, she would drive her own car and stand back as far from the action as she could. She would catch my eye and wave wanly and then leave as quickly as she had come. Inwardly I hated her for not yelling at my father for embarrassing me in front of my friends and teammates.

At home, mother had quietly instilled in me a love for literature, language, and the arts, and she encouraged me to read anything and everything. She always corrected my writing and nurtured my love for art.

I scored high on my college boards and, unlike my brother who enrolled in a state school, I tried for scholarships at large universities and private colleges. My father pulled out his bank books one night and, beer in hand, yelled: "Do you see this?" He forced me to look at his savings accounts. "This is all I have for your college education. There is nothing for you, Bobby, nothing. If you don't get a scholarship, you will never leave this town!" He berated me until I wept at his feet.

It ws never a question of whether or not I was going to college. The question was which one. I wanted to move as far away from home as I could. And all along I had this secret dream of becoming an artist. Art meant to me a world and a place where no one could touch me or tell me what to do.

Father pushed real hard for me to attend a small liberal arts college where I would get a well-rounded education and have fun and party all the time, just the way he had.

Swarthmore College, near Philadelphia, offered me a full ride —room, board, tuition, everything for four years. It was a very prestigious scholarship offered to only one student. The scholarship almost required participation in a sport, for it might lead to a Rhodes scholarship. This was the college that my father wanted me to attend, and the pressure to accept was almost overwhelming.

Meanwhile, the admissions director at Syracuse University, in upstate New York, called to tell me I had won a scholarship. Syracuse had an excellent arts program and opportunities for study abroad. I chose Syracuse. In doing so I chose myself, chose to keep my dream of becoming an artist alive. My dad was upset by my decision.

I had accomplished what my mother had shrunk from all those years: confrontation with my father. My mother could not believe that I had actually picked Syracuse. I think that secretly she envied me because I was going to get away.

That summer I worked as a lifeguard at a local swim club and attended a five-week summer workshop at the Philadelphia College of Art. I learned early about burning myself out. I had had great lessons watching my mother manage the entire household herself.

Now I became a workaholic, pushing myself to the limit and not taking breaks and not scheduling anything just for fun!

That was the summer I met Charlie. He walked into my brother's birthday party, and I saw no one but him from then on. I had had little experience with sex; I had never even had a boyfriend. In fact, I'd hardly dated at all. So Charlie was my first real experience with men. He was tall, dark, and handsome, and a bundle of problems. I was going to solve them. I spent every day . and night with him for two weeks until I went off to college. It was easy for me to get that involved because I knew I was leaving. There was never the threat of his really getting to know me or establishing trust or a solid foundation for a relationship. I had never realized that a relationship is not just physical, but an intellectual, emotional, and spiritual process that grows and evolves. I didn't know that it takes time to get to know someone and that it isn't totally up to the boyfriend to make one happy. That responsibility was up to me.

I left for college and hoped to leave all my anxieties behind. Unfortunately, distance wasn't the cure; I still had to contend with myself. I began college and immediately realized what a sheltered life I had led in Pennsylvania. Because I had never had any close girl friends, I was completely inept about makeup and fashion and the opposite sex. Most of my classmates in college were from the New York City area. They had money, experience, and flair, and I felt totally inadequate.

The second day on campus, I was sent to the bursar's office because there was a discrepancy in my bill. Supposedly my parents hadn't paid the balance and I still owed a thousand dollars. I wasn't permitted to register until it was cleared up. I handed them a cashier's check for all my savings from the summer as a lifeguard— just one thousand dollars. I remember bursting into tears. Now I didn't have money for books or supplies.

That was the first time I remember thinking, "You can't wait for them to follow through, Bobby. You've got to get off your butt to survive. You've got to pull yourself together." So that year, on weekend mornings, I mopped floors at six A.M. in the dorm beer-and-sandwich hangout. What a great lesson in humility!

I drank a lot freshman year. Millers and shots of tequila were the norm for Thursday and Friday nights. And I would dance and dance, as if I couldn't get the rage and frustration out fast enough. School was difficult to adjust to, and this was a release that I knew and could easily relate to.

I buried myself in artwork. I had always loved to stay up late, but I now became obsessed about working into the early hours of the morning on art projects. I pushed myself much too hard. If I was inadequate in my appearance and in my knowledge of men, maybe I could make up for it in my artwork.

Martin, my resident advisor freshman year, was the first of many special people that, as I look back now, were put in my path. He was one of the main reasons I was able to continue at Syracuse. He gave me the attention that I so desperately wanted. He made me feel that I mattered. Our kidding with each other was a great bonding factor that often helped me put things in their proper perspective.

I knew that I was going to have only one shot at a good education and wanted to make the most of it. I applied for the abroad program in London. My scholarship could be used toward the program. This would prove to be the second biggest decision in my life. My father's attitude was, "No child of mine is going to Europe before I do!"

That summer, I got a job as a waitress in Ocean City, New Jersey, at a restaurant owned by a friend's parents. My father could not believe I had taken the job in Ocean City. "Where will you live? How will you get around? What will you do at night when you are alone?"

I rented a room in a large rooming house, two blocks from the ocean. It was very hard at first. I didn't know how to cook or pay rent or basically how to take care of myself. But I knew that if I was going to live in London for a year, I'd better get used to fending for myself.

It was both wonderful and terribly lonely. I loved being right on the ocean and being able to go to the beach every day. But the nights were hard. I had only a bicycle to get around with, so I walked and walked every night on the boardwalk. After that summer, I would live with my folks only for short periods. I was on my own!

London was one of the best things that ever happened to me. The moment I arrived I felt at home and happy. For the first time in my life, I was Bobby. I was free! My father couldn't hound me or call me or judge me or tell me what to do. And I had made it happen!

Going to school in England was incredible. Our teachers showed us slides of paintings on Mondays; on Thursdays we would go to see the actual painting. Several teachers, one in art history and one in drawing, had a profound influence on the way I draw and the way I view art even today.

My education outside the classroom was even better. Every weekend I traveled—to Scotland, to Paris, to Holland, a different adventure each time.

Also, for the first time I felt beautiful and special. I felt like an artist. I never forgot that feeling of self-worth, and that memory has always kept my spirit from dying.

Meanwhile, my family continued to disintegrate. My dad was drinking much more heavily. My sister was experimenting with drugs. My mother was getting sicker and sicker with her disease of codependency. I had always been the shoulder, the enabler that everyone relied on. With me gone, the focus had to be placed elsewhere.

By the time I returned to the United States, my sister really hated me. She was drunk at her graduation from junior college. My parents had convinced her that she was not as intelligent as I, and that she should settle for a two-year business degree. She now informed me that I had abandoned her, had left her to fend for herself alone with my parents.

My senior year was very difficult. I was disoriented, I hated the prospect of having to go out into the real world. The fear grew daily, and I became extremely anxious and unhappy. I was now a maniac, staying up all night two or three times a week to work on art projects. Because I had seemingly just played around in Europe, I felt the need to catch up with my peers. I also had to take a work-study job as advisor at a resident house of forty-four students, with no backup to help me. This was the perfect setup for someone with my obsessive personality. I'd leave my studio at two A.M. and come home to my job. Again everything became work, nothing was fun.

I gained about forty pounds that year. Meals were the only time I allowed myself to take a break. The longer I spent eating, the more time I had to relax.

Eating also was a wonderful substitute for having someone to sleep with or to hold me. I had had a lot of affairs that year. Many of those nights and many of those men have been completely erased from memory. It all seemed like the same guy. All I cared about was feeling that I belonged.

I also acquired an almost martyrlike attitude. I had to work all those long hours. Poor me! I had to be responsible for the students in my house. Poor me! While everyone else was enjoying college, I set myself apart and trudged on alone. Secretly I felt I was better than all of them. I'd show them!

In one year I had gone from feeling beautiful and vital and alive to being overweight, depressed, and ugly. I hated how I looked and I couldn't understand why I wasn't in a steady relationship with some guy.

I was searching for something or someone to fill me up. The affairs left me feeling alone or more empty than ever. It never dawned on me that no one could feel all the time the way I had in London. The answer I needed did not lie in being with a man or eating another slice of cherry pie. The answer was in me, in my spirit.

Graduation was a nightmare. I hated my appearance and I was completely burnt out. My brother and father showed up with a van to move me home. I felt as if I were being returned to prison. They were drunk from the minute they arrived to the minute they left. I felt as if I were the parent at their graduation.

My mother could not make it to my graduation. She had finally cracked and told my father she needed professional help. He told me quite casually that she wasn't coming and then said firmly, "I don't want you to say anything about it." I understood why my mother had chosen to skip this party, yet I was angry that once again she had left me to deal with my father's drunken behavior.

I had graduated cum laude with a degree in illustration. I had gone to Europe on scholarship, worked my way through school, and studied hard at a major university. I should have felt proud of my accomplishments. Instead, I focused on the fact that my mother skipped my graduation and had never once visited me in college.

All of us lived at home that summer. I was overweight and unemployed, with no idea of what to do with myself. My father's drinking and his unhappiness with himself had increased while I was away. He was a binge drinker; he could control it for a while and then be drunk three or four nights in a row. My sister and brother and I sometimes brought him home from local bars. It was embarrassing for us to get him out of a bar; he was a big man and difficult to maneuver. I can remember begging a bartender to cut him off so we could get him out to the car. And when we convinced him to come home with us, he'd trick us by pretending to go to bed and instead head for the kitchen to eat and drink. One of the most vivid memories I have is seeing him at the kitchen table, passing out, his head slowly falling into his food. I screamed at him, "You're drunk! You're going to end up just like your mother." But I realized that he couldn't hear me and that he couldn't control himself.

Almost immediately after graduation I started getting free-lance art assignments from the local daily newspaper. My father hovered over every job I did. To get away, I spent several weeks pounding the pavement in Boston so I could move away from home. But I knew that first I had to lose weight and get back on track.

I traveled a lot that summer. I stayed anywhere I was invited —Syracuse, Boston, Martha's Vineyard. I was grateful just to be out of the house. Finally, I took a job waitressing on the campus of the University of Pennsylvania and moved to a damp efficiency apartment across town. I remember talking to so-called successful friends from college who had ventured to New York to pursue their careers. Here I was stuck in a dive studio apartment, waitressing and going nowhere. Although I was still getting a fair amount of free-lance work for local publications, that did not compare to what my friends did in New York. I just couldn't be grateful for what I had.

I hung out at the restaurant bar and through the group of friends I established there, I met Dave. I had already slept with his best friend, so sleeping with Dave seemed a logical progression. Our relationship was very physical. I needed Dave to fill the void left by my self-doubt.

Dave's sister caught me having sex with him and immediately told his mother. Before I knew it, I was history. I had lost my physical fix, and I was devastated. I packed my car and for three weeks just drove up through New England to get away from the rejection and pain.

When I returned, I was fired from my job. I packed my VW Beetle, picked up a friend, and drove to New York City. I had a hundred dollars to my name. Emotionally I was riding a roller coaster: crying, then feeling fine, crying, then fine again. In two days of sheer guts and determination, I landed a job waiting tables and an apartment with a dancer on the Lower East Side. It was all I could do to keep myself together. I spent most of the money I had left to buy myself a uniform for the job.

The following weekend I drove home to close the apartment and officially move to New York. What a weekend! Everything was so strained at my parents' house that at first I thought they were angry at my making such a drastic move. But that wasn't what was wrong. On Sunday afternoon, my parents called me out to the backyard. "Your mother and I have something to tell you. We have decided to separate." I burst into tears instantly. "Don't you love each other anymore?" "Well, we do and we don't," was the reply. The worst thing about it was that it became clearer and clearer they were resigning as my parents. It had never dawned on me until then that they had lives and problems separate from my own. Another rug had been pulled out from under me, and I was emotionally devastated.

I moved to New York and took another full-time job as waitress on the day shift at a restaurant in the heart of the fashion district. I saved my money for nearly a year before I got a job at O'Neal's in Times Square.

O'Neal's was better money and hours at a much better place. The people there made a real difference. We had actors who had just come from filming on location or from closed Broadway plays. We had singers who worked professionally in cabarets. We had dancers, comedians, and artists, each with a different personality and style, each uniquely interesting. Not since London had I felt so challenged, so alive. O'Neal's became sort of a graduate school for me. While I was there I majored in life.

I moved into a two-bedroom tenement apartment in the Chelsea section of Manhattan and lived with a guy (platonically). I didn't like living with him but the rent was cheap and I had my own bedroom. I saved enough money to rent a studio in Union Square with three other artists. It was within walking distance of the apartment.

One of my professors in illustration had his studio right around the corner from mine. Ivan befriended me. He'd show up when I was waitressing and take me to lunch. He taught me how to act in public, how to dress, what to order. He really saw the spirit in me, "the force" as he liked to call it. New York was a beautiful and wonderful place when I saw it through his eyes. We talked a lot about art and life, and he used to say that living in New York meant walking a fine line between genius and insanity, between good and evil. I felt that edge he was describing every day. It was an exciting, exhilarating, chaotic, gut-wrenching, and horrible ride all at the same time. I once asked Ivan why it had to hurt so much. He replied, "Ah, but that is what makes your artwork so great."

I started doing posters and brochures for off-off-Broadway theaters. Slowly I built up a clientele, but unlike the other three illustrators in the studio, who had fairly established careers, I had trouble following through with my work. In the meantime, my roommate and I were not getting along. My attitude was that he was jealous of me because I had started to be published and had my own studio. In fact, however, I was very domineering and judgmental, commenting about his lack of responsibility for household duties. Finally, I told him that I was going to move out. He was as relieved as I was.

I had had enough of New York City for a while—the dirt, the people, the heat. And I was tired of men coming and going in my life, tired of the late hours of waitressing, tired of the loneliness. I was ready for someone to take me away from all that.

I spent a weekend on Martha's Vineyard and there met Nick in a nightclub. We recognized each other immediately. I went home with him that night.

The stage was set. I slowly pushed away everything I had cared for in New York—my friends, the artwork, the studio, the theater. Now I would concentrate on making money so that I could commute to Boston to be with Nick on the weekends. I had found a new god.

At first the weekends were exciting and fun—an intense whirlwind of sex, drinking, drugs, and then the race to catch the train to New York. Nick drank heavily and did drugs. His parents were divorced. He told me the night I met him that his father was an alcoholic and a bum and that no one in the family wanted anything to do with him. After seeing the house and family together and the Boston house they shared as one happy unit, I was convinced that Nick was the one for me and nothing else mattered.

Yet everything went down hill after that. I moved into the hotel above O'Neal's—one room with an adjoining bath and no kitchen. My life revolved around Nick's calls and our weekends together. Work meant only train fare for another trip north. I was obsessed with him. He was going to take me away from all this madness, fill that void in me that had been empty so long.

The more I focused on Nick and let go of my obsession with art, the better my free-lance business became. The *Village Voice* and the *New York Times* both started to use my work. I was thrilled, but inside I felt like a fraud. I couldn't really be that good; this must be a fluke. I also pushed the people in my studio away. I had started to cop an attitude that said loud and clear: "I don't need you, so leave me alone." And that's exactly what they did.

Nick broke his arm and was out of work for almost two months. I suggested he stay with me for several days so I would take care of him and of course help him out financially. He would sit at the bar while I waited on tables. One day, R. J., the bartender who had served Nick the night before, said, "Hey, Bobby, let's go for coffee." We went to a small place around the corner. R. J. looked me right in the face and said, "Bobby, your boyfriend is an alcoholic." I said in complete denial, "No he isn't. He just drinks a lot." R. J. then said, "Bobby, I know this because I've been sober for ten years. You know, you can do something about this." I hemmed and hawed, and he finally said, "Bobby, when are you going to commit to yourself?"

R. J. gave me some pamphlets from Al-Anon. Even though I was living alone, I hid them in my apartment. I started thinking about Nick's behavior, how on our first night he had been drunk and slapped me. How he had repeatedly pushed me around, and the endless party it had become every weekend. But most importantly, his uncontrollable anger!

One sentence in the Al-Anon literature really hit home: "The woman stands alone." Family and friends can't help you if you are involved with someone who is an alcoholic. I gathered up all the courage I could muster and went to a midday Al-Anon meeting in Union Square. I shook and cried through the entire metting. I blurted out: "Nick was drunk and angry at me the entire weekend." The people at the meeting were very kind and understanding. I knew deep down that they and R. J. were right. But I still needed to believe that I was to blame, that I was the bad, inadequate person. I wasn't ready to cut through the years of denial. I never went back again, but the seeds of recovery had been planted.

Emotionally, my life in New York slid even further downward. Almost daily I would sit in the corner of my bathroom and sob hysterically. I ripped every piece of art off my studio walls. It was as if I really wanted to hurt myself by denying myself the pleasure of my studio.

My parents were divorced during this time. The telephone rang every morning with a different member of the family telling me his or her side of the story. My father, after four months of being separated from my mother, had started seeing a cousin of his, also separated. They decided to marry. My father bought a huge house two towns from where my mother lived.

I was stuck in the middle of this mess with nowhere to turn. I grew desperate, called Nick almost every day, and started to smother him with my neediness. I begged my sister and brother to come and get me. I really wanted to get off the merry-go-round and seriously thought about killing myself.

That same month, O'Neal's and the building where I lived were sold. Not only did I lose my job but my apartment as well. I continued to work my shifts as if nothing had happened. It was the only way I could cope. I felt cornered, trapped, and utterly alone. I dreamed up an elaborate scheme to work on Martha's Vineyard so that I could be closer to Nick. He was my only hope. Nick will take care of me, I thought. He'll make this all better.

I went to Martha's Vineyard to escape my madness. On Memorial Day weekend Nick was supposed to pick me up at the ferry in Woods Hole so we could spend the rest of the weekend together. He never showed. Finally, I boarded the ferry and returned to the island. I spent the entire weekend crying and feeling that this was the ultimate betrayal. I had no way to get back to Boston. That Monday I stood pitifully in a phone booth, sobbing to an old boyfriend in Boston to come and get me. He had to work, but said reassuringly, "Bobby, just get here." That was enough for me. I hitched a ride to my friend's apartment. As he let me in he said,

"It's okay, Bobby, you can cry now." I fell apart, sobbing uncontrollably until he convinced me to try to sleep. All my support systems had been removed. The *New York Times* had called to give me some work and I had turned them down. I knew that I was not capable of doing an illustration. I was not even responsible enough to take care of myself.

I went back to New York and moved in temporarily with a girl on the Upper West Side. I was a mess. Nick called as if nothing had ever happened, saying he had just been too drunk to come and get me. It was over, everything was over, and I knew it. I broke my lease for the studio. I borrowed money from anyone and everyone who would give it to me. Nightmares came more and more frequently, and mornings were spent in crippling fear. There was nothing to keep trying for.

I left New York and moved in with my father. This was the summer before he was to be remarried and he was in the new house alone. My mother refused to let me come to her house because she said she couldn't handle it. My father's house was almost empty—the only furnishings were a kitchen table and chairs and two beds, one in each room. I have never experienced such constant fear as I felt there. My dad would leave for work very early in the morning. I would wake up alone in that empty house. I slept a lot during the day because I got so little sleep at night.

Every time I talked to my father, I cried. I was convinced that my heart was broken. I couldn't eat. I had no idea where I would work or live.

But slowly I began to draw again. I knew that the spirit inside was still alive and that I could still create. Clients from New York called with free-lance assignments. I always seemed to get a project exactly when I needed it. My friends and family thought I was crazy. I knew I needed help but felt incapable of asking for it. To my family, it was a sign of weakness that I couldn't handle my own problems. And I knew that I couldn't stay with my father much longer. His new wife would be moving in and the last thing she would want would be to start her new life with me there. I had nowhere to turn. I was running out of people to help me.

One morning in July I woke up with the most crippling emotional fear I had yet felt. It was then that I started to pray for help. I didn't think I had the strength to carry on alone. Then the phone rang. A friend from Boston had heard I'd left New York. He had an apartment to rent downstairs from his. Would I want it? I immediately said yes. I still had no idea what I'd be doing and the fear was still overwhelming, but now I had a place to go. So I moved into the two-family house in a suburb of Boston. Three friends from college owned the house and lived upstairs. I had about two hundred dollars and I slept on a porch couch until I found a job and a roommate. The money ran out quickly. I was still very shaky emotionally. Fear would come over me in waves, and my life still seemed unmanageable. But I did find a job doing production work for a Boston weekly newspaper, and a roommate through an agency.

Nick and I got back together. He had called me before I moved to Boston, and we decided to take a trip to my grandparents' cabin in Canada to see if we could salvage anything from our relationship. My parents and friends could not believe I was willing even to see him again.

On our trip to Canada, Nick introduced me to cocaine. I wanted to stop the merry-go-round. I was willing to do anything to keep him, and I hated to drink. Cocaine seemed the logical solution. I snorted coke and smoked pot for the first time in my life. It was thrilling and exciting to feel like I belonged at the party that weekend. Coke became another dimension of my weekends with him. Nick's rationalization was that he worked hard all week so he deserved to party equally hard.

The minute I made up my mind to live with Nick, I instinctively knew it was the wrong decision. He had found a three-bedroom apartment for us south of Boston. I would be breaking the lease with my friends, leaving my roommate with nobody to replace me in the middle of winter, moving to a town where I knew no one and from which I would have to commute an hour by bus to a $165-a-week job in Boston. I soon quit the job because Nick said it was an inferior position. Nick got high every single day I lived with him. Mornings were the only time I saw him straight. Weekends were always the same: Friday night if he was home, he'd be high when I got there. Or he would hurry home, shower, and leave alone to party with his friends. Saturdays he would work all day, then drive over to his family's house to drink or do coke with his brothers and friends. At first, I accompanied him; we spent almost all of our free time there. There was no commitment to our own place.

I seemed always to be waiting—waiting to be noticed, waiting to go home, waiting to be talked to, waiting to be acknowledged sexually and emotionally. It was like living with my father all over again. I was never enough for Nick. No matter how I cooked or cleaned or made love, he always found fault. And if I got upset when he came home late or drunk—or didn't come home at all—he would twist it around to appear I was to blame. I was so shaky emotionally that I believed I was the cause of his rages and indulgences.

I stopped going to parties with him. I could never keep up with his drinking and drugging, and I got tired of waiting for him to throw me a tidbit of affection. He began to stay out all night and do coke more frequently. I never slept those Saturday nights, waiting for him to come stumbling home. Sundays I spent crying from fatigue, anger, and worry, while he spent the day hung over, with all the shades drawn.

Then Nick left to build a house on Nantucket. Despite his drinking he had developed a lucrative construction business. He said he would be gone for several months. I started a new job as a designer at a local newspaper the day he left. I thought that I would die without him. It was worse than any physical withdrawal I could ever have felt. But I had experienced losing him before. With a new job to concentrate on, I went ahead with my life.

For New Year's Eve Nick had come home and we went to a family party. It was all cocaine. Everyone, myself included, had lines spread over the glass tabletops. Someone snorting next to me said, "I was at a party last night and all they had was pot! Can you imagine? How boring!" I looked around the room and realized that these were the people I had chosen as my friends. As high as I was, something good clicked inside me that night.

Nick left for the island the next day. I went into the bathroom to take a good hard look at myself. I appeared twenty years older than I really was. I was tired and overweight. I said out loud to the mirror, "What happened to you Bobby? What happened to that good person inside of you?" And then R. J.'s words came back to me clear as a bell: "Bobby, when are you going to commit to yourself?" I called the local chapter of Al-Anon. I had lost enough, and I thoroughly hated my life and what I had become. The woman who answered sounded genuinely concerned. Though originally I wanted only to find out where the meetings were, I wound up telling her about my problems. She said that Tuesday nights there was a meeting right up the street from me.

It was time to focus on myself and get on a road to recovery. I stopped doing drugs and went to my meeting every Tuesday. Three months later, Nick moved back home. He had become an animal, drinking a case of beer a night with his crew. I could now easily see the disease. I was afraid of him, but I was more afraid of losing my sanity and myself, so I continued to go to meetings.

The more I changed in those next several weeks, the more Nick punished me verbally, sexually, and emotionally. He refused to sleep with me and gave me the silent treatment. I had a tough time detaching from him. I started to attend two meetings a week and signed up for speaking commitments.

Eventually I got the strength to move out. I was still going to meetings to get him sober. I truly thought I could help him with his problems. One woman said that by leaving him I might save his life. That helped me to gather courage to finally get off the destructive merry-go-round I had been on for years. I began to blame him for everything. I still didn't see alcoholism as a disease. I thought that if he wanted to, he could stop drinking and doing drugs. I beat on myself for loving a man who was so charming, handsome, and sensitive when he was sober, but who became angry, ugly, and cruel when he was drunk.

Nick immediately started sleeping with another woman. Even though I had left him, I was still addicted to him. I thought we could date and start fresh. But I had almost ruined his drinking for him, and he needed to replace me with another enabler right away. I remember being alone in my present apartment when I hung up the phone after talking to him that last time. I realized that I could never go back. I couldn't call him anymore, or drive by his place, or drop by unexpectedly. It was over and I had to move on.

It was terribly painful at first. A woman at work said to me that as bad as I felt, God was not going to leave me without a life preserver. I clung to the idea that things just had to get better. Recovery is a slow process. They say that as far as you walked into the woods, that's how far you have to walk out. I had been affected by alcoholism my entire life. I had a lot of catching up to do, and I dove headfirst into the program. No matter how bad I felt, there was always a meeting I could go to.

At work I was promoted to full-time graphic designer. This time I shifted my focus from Nick to my job, working up to fifty hours a week for little money and few benefits. As my self-esteem slowly grew and I realized I deserved better, I applied for other jobs. I took a much higher paying one in charge of the art department of a large daily paper.

I really worked at building my self-worth. One problem was my appearance. No matter what I put on, I hated how I looked. So every morning, I would look in the mirror and say out loud: "You're looking great!" At first I laughed at myself, but slowly I came to believe it.

A guy at one of the Al-Anon meetings said that every morning before he left for work, he read the sign he had put over his door: "What kind of day do you want to have today?" Now, no one is going to answer "Terrible!" So every morning I set out trying to have a good day. It didn't always work, but I started noticing trees and birds that I had not seen before. Looking for beauty every day, particularly during my ten-minute beach walk, was especially helpful that first year.

I also had to confront that I had not been very good at taking care of myself or my finances. I finally learned to pay bills as they came in rather than being overwhelmed by them once a month. I had always neglected cleaning house, probably in defiance of my mother's obsession. I would let laundry and garbage pile up for weeks. Now I followed through one task at a time so that by the weekend the cleaning became more manageable. Today, one measure of self-worth is my coming home and knowing there are no dirty dishes in the sink and that my bed is made.

It would have been easy for me to jump headfirst into another relationship and not face up to myself and my shortcomings. My sponsor in Al-Anon suggested that I wait a year before becoming involved romantically. As lonely as life was, that was probably the best advice I got. I spent the weekends going to meetings or helping out by sponsoring Alateen kids. I practiced being sociable by having one friend at a time come over for tea and conversation. I started to draw again and returned to some of the other activities I had forgotten I liked.

Asking for help was the hardest obstacle. I had been taught to be strong and to solve problems on my own. Now I have learned to ask for help. It can be as simple as picking up the telephone. Letting others get to know my true self and trusting they won't hurt me takes a lot of faith. But each time I have the courage to ask for help today, it works out. My faith grows and grows. And I find that the more connected I am to my Higher Power, the easier it is to ask for help and to know that all the help I need is already right there.

Today I don't wait until I'm in the middle of a crisis to ask for help. I pick up the phone or go to a meeting when things are even a little bit off. This is *acting* instead of reacting to life. For too long the alcoholics were the Higher Power in my life. I listened and waited for them to act, and then I would react accordingly. Today I am responsible for my own happiness. I didn't know who I was and what I liked and disliked when I moved into this apartment three summers ago. I knew I had choices, but there were so many that they seemed overwhelming. It seemed so much easier to run to the loving arms of a caretaker—a boyfriend or my parents. I wanted to participate in life, but life was a fearful thing.

Now I know that what is right for me today is what I feel comfortable with. And I know that I do have a caretaker, my Higher Power, who will help me to accomplish every goal that is set in this stage of my life.

Things aren't as frantic and chaotic as they used to be. My expectations of myself and of others are a lot less demanding than before. I have serenity in my life. Every morning I read my Al-Anon literature. Then I get down on my hands and knees and ask for help from my Higher Power. I ask for courage to act on His will. And at night I focus on what I'm grateful for.

Today I also have a new relationship with each of my parents. I have accepted them for what they are and have begun to realize that they did the best they could to cope with this insidious disease.

I also have a new relationship with myself. I trust and like myself today. I like to spend time alone. I know that I can take care of myself. Because of this I am a lot easier to get along with and a lot more accessible to other people. I am attracting healthy and interesting people into my life, people who genuinely like me for myself. My boyfriend, Max, who is a recovering alcoholic, and I have a good relationship. I can look directly into his eyes and believe that he will not hurt me and that he is honest in his caring for me. As he sees beauty, humor, and life in me, so I see fine qualities in him. When we focus on each other's good qualities, they seem to grow and grow. That is focusing on the answer and not the problem, and I can apply this axiom to everything I do today.

I am able to follow through. Recently I hung my first art show in a gallery. I prepared for it by working on completing one picture at a time, one day at a time. The bills are paid today. I can take care of, nurture, and be good to myself. I have finally faced myself.

I am the only member of my immediate family in recovery. It is very difficult to break through the walls of denial and to share the family secret as I have in these pages. I had a great fear that I would be punished for letting others know my shame. It takes courage to let people see the pain, but it's worth it. I feel like I'm a walking miracle because I dared to ask for help. I was very willing and ready to commit to myself. I am convinced that my spirit—that wonderful, beautiful quality that we all have inside of us—never died. The flame flickered and often looked as if it would go out completely. But there was always hope. All I have to do is have faith in my Higher Power and realize that things will get better. They alway do. My life today is wonderful.

If you are living with an alcoholic or grew up in an alcoholic home, there is hope for you, too. Help is all around. Pick up the phone. Get going. My life is getting better and better a day at a time. And yours can too.

LIFE AS
A CHALLENGE

Tamela Beth

The greater the difficulty, the greater the glory.
Cicero

Adult children of alcoholics—
that phrase has very recently become both part of our popular psychology and public property. Dozens of books and long lists of specialty counselors and therapy groups are all shouting, "You need help! Let us help you!" And many seem to be buying the words, sympathetic ears and therapy sessions—buying into the popular modern myth that says if we can understand and name a problem, it is no longer a problem; buying into the assumption that because we grew up in alcoholic homes, we are automatically in need of psychological help. Self-pity rears its ugly head here; it's lovely for some to get the attention, to be sure—and it's long overdue attention at that—but it all leaves a very sour taste in my mouth. It's just too hard to assume and generalize where human beings and their emotions are concerned, especially since there will always be at least one person who adamantly refuses to run with the pack or follow the popular or easier path. That person absolutely will not be a victim of her own life and circumstances.

I'll take hard-won integrity over cheap self-pity every time. No contest!

Yes, my mother is an alcoholic. Yes, it is nearly certain that both my father and stepfather are undiagnosed alcoholics. Yes, things were certainly difficult growing up. One might assume I would be dissatisfied with my childhood and upbringing. On the contrary. I'm actually rather pleased. Although my childhood was certainly not pretty or conventional, it was a challenge, and I am a firm believer in the positive power of challenging situations.

I am the eldest of four children, the others being a half brother and two half sisters. During my childhood I was often involved in caring for them, whether I was willing or not. But children are great teachers of responsibility if one chooses to learn the lessons. Being the eldest, I was exhorted by my parents to set a good example for my younger siblings. In reality, I did more than that. At various times, I acted as caretaker, advisor, shelter from the neighborhood bullies and the creature under the bed, even the port in the storm. This meant that I learned to deal with my own fears privately, a capability that has certainly come in handy.

The faith my younger brother and sisters invested in me was particularly clear during several stressful situations. One was a blizzard—not a small one, but a major whiteout. We were living on a remote ranch in Colorado. For three days, the two youngest children were stranded with me, alone, miles from the nearest help. The children were calm and trusting, and even seemed disappointed when the rest of the family made it home.

Several months later, when our stepfather, William, made an insane but fake attempt at suicide, their faith in me really paid off. Not only did it help them through the crisis, but it was rather like a reward for me—it made me feel that the years of care had been well invested, and it reinforced my ability to be calm in a crisis.

William was feeling sorry for himself because my mother had finally decided to divorce him. One sunny afternoon he claimed he was upset enough to kill himself. Just the two of us and his three children were there that day, isolated on that ranch in the middle of nowhere. Drunk and full of self-pity, he declared he was going to end it all then and there. I tried to talk him out of it, told him he had a responsibility to his children that he couldn't just disregard, but I was unable to dissuade him. His bedroom had a balcony, and he walked out onto it and told me he was going to jump. I was disgusted with him by this point, and I didn't think he had even enough courage to commit the cowardly act of suicide, so I said, "Do what you want to do."

I then hurried downstairs to comfort my brother and sisters, who were understandably confused. We looked out the window of the family room together; we could see William on the balcony. Then we watched in astonishment as he climbed carefully (he was drunk) down the post and laid himself on the ground so his children would think he was dead. Feeling nothing but contempt for him now, I gathered his children to me and reassured them that everything would be all right somehow, and then we walked outside together so I could inform him that we'd seen him climb down and knew he wasn't injured. The fool continued to play dead, however, and after a few minutes I took his children back inside with me, made them some dinner, and life went on. That was another very important lesson: life goes on.

Other indirect benefits of my childhood were the development of comfort in solitude and a passion for reading. They grew simultaneously, as I was housebound caring for my siblings much of the time. I became a voracious reader, consuming book after book — even reading through our encyclopedias. I read for escape, for entertainment and adventure, for the sheer pleasure of learning, and for the information I could glean from the volumes, especially about how others experienced life. I wanted perspectives other than my own, views I could never get from where I stood. Reading became my one compulsion, a comparatively harmless one, really, and one that has given me immeasurable rewards: knowledge of myself through reflection and introspection, knowledge of the world around and beyond me, and introduction to flights of fancy and imagination that gave license to my own.

My sense of reality is yet another advantage. I'll never try to change the world through wishful thinking, since I already know quite well that that simply doesn't work. Reality is what is, not what we want or wish it to be. When one is realistic enough to depend primarily on oneself and to see one's own conscience as the ultimate authority, one is never without guidance or courage, no matter the various hazards of life. I believe self-sufficiency is good for people, especially for women. All too often we are taught to rely on others as the focus and purpose of our lives; of course, this is unfair to the people around us as well as to ourselves. It is undoubtedly from watching my mother display the extremes of dependency that I have made myself as independent as I am: she is utterly convinced that she cannot make it, cannot be a whole person, without a man. Fortunately for me, I have seen where belief like hers can lead. I can only trust others to a certain extent, probably because of my untrustworthy alcoholic parents, but at least I will never lay myself down, body and soul, at another's feet and expect them to take responsibility from my hands and do what must be done.

Obviously, during my childhood there were exceptionally ugly experiences directly or indirectly attributable to alcoholism. My mother was involved in two of the most memorable, not because she was necessarily my worst parent, but because I simply spent more time with her.

The first was relatively minor: she unexpectedly showed up at an elementary-school field day. It would have been fine, enjoyable even, except that she was a mess: unflattering old clothes, no stockings, wild hair, no makeup, and she seemed to be staggering. My teachers were politely horrified, and my classmates giggled. This was one of the very few times in my life that I was socially sensitive. I quit the various games and contests and dragged her to the top of the hill overlooking the field. For the next few days I was aware of pitying looks and gossip about the incident, but it was also my first conscious experience with hardening against the opinions of others.

The other episode was much worse. My mother and stepfather had separated by this point, and she had an apartment of her own. I was staying with her for the summer, and I got my first experience of the sordidness both of severe alcoholism and of a woman, my mother, entirely wrapped up in a sick relationship with a heartless married man I'll call Robert. She would wait by the front window of the apartment on nights he was expected, watching for him with a bottle of tequila in her hand, all night long. Some mornings when I awakened she would still be out in the living room, asleep or passed out, awaiting her faithless lover with a now-empty bottle in hand.

Her lover had a good friend, also married, whom I'll call

Andy. My mother claimed Andy was her best friend, although like many drinking buddies, all they ever did together was drink or sometimes smoke dope and take downers or painkillers. There were occasional trips to country-western bars and the like, but since Robert and Andy were, after all, married men, they didn't have much discretionary time.

I had turned fifteen that spring; an experienced and cynical fifteen, to be sure, but fifteen just the same. My mother and Andy decided to party one evening. It started with margaritas and beer and progressed to downers and dope smoking. Eventually my mother passed out on her bed. I suspected Andy had intended for this to happen as he'd brought the drugs and booze and encouraged my mother to "loosen up and have a good time."

At any rate, as soon as she was out of it, I wanted Andy to leave. I'd never liked or trusted him. Although I'd tolerated him for the sake of my mother's dubious friendship with him, I always felt very uneasy around him and had always taken care never to be alone with him. I walked to the front door to let Andy out, but when I turned around he was still back in the living room. "You know, I've always been attracted to you," he said, grinning, obviously not intending to go anywhere.

My heart sank. "I need to get some sleep," I replied, unable to keep the nervous fear from my voice. "Mom and I are going to Cheyenne tomorrow for the rodeo, and I'm pretty tired, and—"

"Aw, come on baby doll, don't make excuses. You want me, I can feel it." With that he grabbed me and kissed me hard, grinding his rough beard into my face.

"Oh, no, please don't, please," I cried again and again, but he wouldn't stop, and wouldn't stop, and wouldn't stop. . . .

It was useless to scream; my mother was beyond hearing my screams, drugged to unconsciousness in the next room. I had never felt so alone, so beyond help, so dirty and used, so degraded.

And I never looked at men the same way again.

My point is not to cause shock or to evoke pity with ugly stories. I could tell several more, and most people could probably tell at least a few. There are indeed ugly things in the world like rape, abuse, incest, and neglect. They happen to real people like you and me, which is what makes them so horrible. After all, how many of us come from truly ideal homes? For that matter, what is an ideal home? No parent or home can be perfect, and children from a perfect home, if such a place and such parents could exist, would hardly be prepared to deal with the real world of occasional failure, heartache, and certain death. Everyone has a sad story to tell—the important thing is what we do with our experiences, our feelings, and ourselves. No experience, no matter how humiliating, painful, or devastating, can be entirely negative if we learn something from it. And that in turn, makes it easier to say to the world, "Go ahead. Take your best shot!"

Such an attitude gives a certain set to the shoulders, a special jauntiness to the walk. It creates a rock-solid self-confidence that has been through flame and acid tests until one can be sure that not only is it indestructible, it is unalterably and undeniably one's own. An identity and security that are not at all mysterious because one has literally given them birth and nurtured them through years of despair to final triumph. A soul that one is well acquainted with because it is self-made and cherished.

Of course, social structure can make an individual identity difficult to create and keep. Social norms are like cookie cutters in that their products are all the same shape, but to carry the analogy further, is a cookie any less a cookie because it's a star rather than a circle like the rest? Is a human being any less valuable, any less a person, if she refuses to be the same as everyone who's declared normal? What is normal, anyway? Who decides? Even psychologists can't seem to agree, and definitions of normal vary widely between cultures and eras. I know that I wouldn't feel unique or an individual if I wasted my life trying to be just like everyone else. Society encourages us to play follow the leader, to preserve the status quo. Is it worth the sacrifice of self?

Naturally, it's easier to do what everyone else does. One always knows just what to do, what the proper reaction is, what the proper goal is, and one can bask in the complacent and easy comfort of conformity and general, impersonal social approval. But true freedom is taking responsibility for oneself and telling the Mr. and Mrs. Grundys of the world to go fly the famous kite. Once that freedom has been tasted and savored, going back to the status quo seems insane. It looks like walking into a prison voluntarily, locking the door behind oneself, and handing the key to an anonymous authority figure.

In the difficulty of individualism lies the challenge, and therefore the attraction, for those of us not satisfied with the average, the normal, the easy, the known. Of course, it takes courage, but courage is the complement to fear and the use of fear, not the absence of it. Like anything else one wishes to master, it also takes desire and practice.

The wildest scenery is off the beaten track. It demands courage to strike off on one's own to find it and glory in its very wildness. In its very wildness lies its haunting beauty. It is like the difference between a caged, semitame lion at the zoo and an utterly wild lion roaming the savanna, free and proud, living as it was meant to live. The same animal, yet not the same animal at all.

None of these attitudes and beliefs would probably have occurred to me, much less become an intrinsic part of me, had I not been raised in an alcoholic home. My life has always been a challenge. I chose to take the challenge rather than buckle under in weakness and self-pity. The choice, like all choices, was mine alone. I continue to challenge myself. I am a single mother by choice; I'm also putting myself through college, self-supporting, independent, and a radical feminist. I'm convinced that life would be boring and unrewarding if it were too easy.

And what an exhilarating challenge my life is! I'll never settle for the easy answer or the easy way out, and I continually test myself, my strengths and weaknesses, and thus expand and improve my abilities. I'm quite outspoken, highly curious, and very self-confident. My upbringing and its difficulties have taught me many valuable lessons. The most important were to trust and respect myself. I'm proud of my abilities, my attitudes, my courage in the face of adversity, and my calm during crises, for I know I build my better qualities alone. Certainly there are disadvantages, including, in all honesty, a seeming aloofness, a lack of trust in others, and occasional recklessness. But to me the benefits of my personality far outweigh the few drawbacks. After all, nobody is perfect, including myself.

My life has made me strong and reliable, honest and individual, and I don't regreat a minute of it. The alcoholism of my parents stole my childhood, my trust and innocence. But I don't blame my parents for being alcoholics—victims of a disease that robbed them of as much as it robbed me. Neither do I blame myself. At my first and last session with an Al-Anon counselor, I was told that I was at least partially responsible for my mother's alcoholism because I was an enabler. To the contrary, I did what had to be done and found myself in the process. I don't wish it had been different, for it was as it was, and I rather like the way things turned out.

I wouldn't change a thing.

A FAIRY TALE

Angela Thomas

My room. Dark now except for the faint glow of light from the hall, creeping in from under the door. I couldn't sleep. My mind was consumed with the joyful anticipation of returning to college the following day, an event I had impatiently awaited since the first day I stepped into my mother's house for summer break. Summers at home for me are not happy retreats from the pressures of college life, as they are for my peers. Tearstained memories prevent me from feeling anything but anxiety at the thought of returning home. Home for me is not a haven from stress, or a loving refuge, or a supplier of welcome-home feasts. My home is the antithesis of safety and love. It is the home of an alcoholic.

The atmosphere of my home is best described by the word *thud*. That is what I feel through every inch of my body when I cross the threshold. *Thud*, as if someone had just closed the lid of a coffin over my prostrate body. Lack of communication and under-standing thickens the air between me and my mother.

Apart from the rest of the house, however, is my room, my private domain, my own little paradise because it is safe. It is best described as fluffy—fluffy pillows, fluffy toys, a thick carpet, and frilly draperies. I am not trying to express my femininity, but to create an insulated fortress against the emotional harshness of the house. I have decorated my walls with posters of unicorns and enchanted forests, and on my bookshelf lies a library of fantasy novels. I escape into such books as frequently as I can. Despite the lack of caring in my house, I like to believe that fairy tales always have happy endings and that someday, I too will live happily ever after.

My room is still not totally invulnerable to the insanity of the house. Little reminders are scattered about: toys and stuffed animals my mother gave me to soothe her guilt after a night of beating me; a desk drawer filled with report cards that she had torn to shreds because I had received an occasional B instead of straight A's; and a picture of me as a two-year-old in my mother's arms. Where, I now wonder, has that innocent little child gone? We all at times long to be again in our mother's arms, to be comforted and cuddled. I learned long ago, however, that once I was old enough to take care of myself, I could never return to my mother for comfort. She has no comfort to give.

My transition from childhood to puberty was not just difficult, it was tragic. It meant not only asserting my independence, as many thirteen- and fourteen-year-olds do, but fortifying myself against physical and mental abuse. It meant analyzing my relationship with my mother and choosing whether I would continue to live with her for financial security or pack my bags and risk life on my own. I did not cope well with decision making. Not only the many problems of puberty, but also those of my parents were too great for a maladjusted teenager to deal with. I developed some rather poor coping mechanisms that eventually led to bulimia, several suicide attempts, and—like mother, like daughter—alcoholism and drug abuse.

Had I been a "normal" kid-next-door with loving parents, I might have chosen more healthful ways of dealing with my adolescent dilemma. My family, however, was quite abnormal, even though we managed to maintain a fairly respectable public facade. In fact, that facade worked very well for me for many years. It hid my loneliness. Having little to compare my family to, I thought that it was normal for families to fight and argue constantly. Dad, when he wasn't away on business, spent most of his time in front of the TV or out with various grisly-looking buddies. Mom slept late, until two or three in the afternoon, unless she had decided to get me up for school. When I heard her get out of bed, that was my signal to go outside and play. I knew if I got in her way as she stumbled to the coffeepot or the liquor cabinet, I would be stepped on forcibly. I didn't have any siblings with whom I could play. My only brother is ten years my elder, and he moved out when I was three. I had nothing that I felt normal children should have: no dog, no brothers or sisters, no pigtails. Mother had cut my hair off almost completely because she was too drunk to realize how much she was taking off. Looking like a little boy who had paid a visit to a blind barber didn't do anything for my already rather unattractive appearance.

In kindergarten I would get lost in crowds because I was so small. I had to sit inside during recess because I was anemic and too weak to play in the sandbox with the healthy children. I now wonder if my premature birth, low birth weight, and anemia were not symptoms of a mild form of fetal alcohol syndrome. When not physically separated from my peers, I was separated by a pervasive lack of self-confidence. The tiniest blink of an eyelash from another kindergartener was enough to send me whimpering into a corner.

By the first grade I had acquired a small circle of acquaintances, mostly oddballs like myself. Where I had been ignored in kindergarten, I was now actively picked on in elementary school. I always wore shorts under my skirts after some hyperactive boy pulled my skirt and underwear down to expose my naked rear to the entire first grade. I was teased unmercifully for having a derriere that resembled the skin of an orange—I had puncture wounds from having been spanked with the bristle side of a hairbrush. I was teased for my boyish haircut, my skinny legs, my missing baby teeth, and most of all, my shyness.

At home I led what I considered to be a typical existence for a little kid. I spent few afternoons with friends, preferring to sit in front of the TV until dinner, which occurred anywhere between six and twelve-thirty, depending upon my mother's level of intoxication. I usually spent weekends at a nearby beach, collecting seashells and building sand castles. Without the structure of the workweek, Saturday and Sunday offered a prime opportunity for my parents to argue and eventually to fight physically. Walking home, I would pray that I would not intrude upon yet another conflict between them. It so broke my heart to see them fight that I would involuntarily throw myself between them, often getting bruised in the midst of the fray. I was never informed about the nature of these fights, nor could I deduce it for myself. I did not take sides, either. I simply wanted my parents to stay together because I knew that was the way it was supposed to be. I saw the chronic threat of divorce as the only problem in our family. I was too blinded by that fear to examine its causes.

I did everything I could to force my parents to stay together—a big task for a little girl. By junior high I was as perfect as I could be. I had perfect grades, a spotless room, numerous athletic awards, perfect manners, and a perfect outlook. I was a model twelve-year-old, the perfect result of a perfect household. Unfortunately, my facade was nothing more than a perfect lie, and it did nothing for me except to foster the great interest I have in acting.

After about a year of continual pretending, I became exhausted and heartily disillusioned. I was failing at my ruses and was certain that my parents would break up and abandon me. I still had only a few friends. Being perfect doesn't allow a lot of time to create friendships. My growing fear of aloneness plagued me more and more. Rather than reaching out for help, however, I became more and more withdrawn. I had few social skills, and what I had learned as the member of an alcoholic household was that to get love you had to be a people pleaser and that to keep it you had to be a manipulator. I found myself continually questioning the sincerity of others and asking myself what the other person really wanted from me. I lacked trust, I lacked confidence. And I lacked sympathy for the pain of others because I refused to believe that anybody else's problems were worse than my own.

I was terrified by an invitation to the eighth-grade graduation dance by an attractive member of the soccer team. I had grown out of my preteen awkwardness, gained weight, and developed some curves in the proper places. Yet I still hated my appearance. My mother had teased me about having "thunder thighs," and I honestly thought that I looked like a pear: skinny on top and plump below. No one else shared my feelings, least of all my escort, who eventually told me that he had always thought I was one of the prettiest girls in the school. Poor, blind boy, I thought.

That dance was epochal. It represented the culmination of disillusionment with my family, school, and friends. I decided to change. I had enough for one childhood and now it was my turn to fight back. I was going to make friends, I was going to be popular, I was going to have fun, and I was going to enjoy my adolescence as much as possible.

This change began symbolically with my first alcoholic drink, at the dance. I did not feel guilty or shameful, but pleased with myself for exhibiting enough backbone to rebel. For the first time, I allowed myself to relax and to act like a normal kid who didn't worry about perfect standards all the time. The effects of alcohol, of course, increased my enjoyment and my sense of well-being, while at the same time lowering my inhibitions and making it far easier to socialize. I suddenly became friendly and talkative. Social grace mysteriously appeared as I blossomed into the world's largest social butterfly. My first experience with alcohol led me to regard it as some sort of savior, a guardian angel that would transform me from a wallflower into a homecoming queen. With alcohol in my system I could release the pressure of perfection I had created for myself and become a sparkling, charming, attractive young girl who could bounce through the rest of her school days as Miss Popularity.

Surprisingly, I did not get drunk. At that point I was content to drink just enough for relaxation. My parents were not at all suspicious. In fact, they were pleased that I seemed to be spending more nights with my peers. I was finally growing up, they said. However, the importance that I attached to the alcohol as the key to what I thought would be a happy life detracted from my own sense of self-worth and would greatly contribute to my later problems with drugs and alcohol.

My drinking continued to be light until my worst fear was realized: my father was planning to leave. Instantly, my fear of abandonment returned like a slap in the face. I was terrified of being left alone with my mother and disgusted that, despite my painful efforts to the contrary, we would no longer be a family. Out of a sense of guilt, my father finally told me his plans, face to face. Without even asking me to sit down, he said blankly that he could no longer live with my mother because she was an alcoholic and refused to go for treatment. He added that it would be best for me to remain with her until I finished high school, since I suddenly seemed to be doing so well and had so many friends. He finished by telling me that he was moving to Colorado and he would write, and asking would I like a Kleenex for the tears that were beginning to stream down my face.

My father packed his belongings and left three days later. My mother wasn't even home to say good-bye. I stood in the driveway as I watched him drive away. I was shocked and outraged. How could he leave? That bastard! I had spent all my life in constant fear of this and had thrown energy I didn't have into preventing it, and here he was doing it anyway. On top of that, he was leaving me with my mother, a woman I hardly knew because she spent much of her time in bed. Living with her meant living with the loneliness and abandonment I so much feared. She might as well have been a ghost.

I knew I was going to have to do something to lessen the burden of living alone with her, but I had no plan of action. The problem was that I was fed up with coping. I didn't want to cope any longer. I wanted to turn off the world. I began to view my life as a sick joke, an attitude that caused me to see my problems as insurmountable and to lose all hope. Positive turned to negative, light to dark. My self-esteem was shattered. Deciding first that I was tremendously obese and gruesomely ugly, I broke every mirror in the house and went on a crash diet, eating only two apples and one slice of bread each day. After three months I had gone from a sleek 115 pounds to a skinny 90 pounds. My mother didn't even notice until one day she spied me dashing naked across the hall and into the bathroom shower. Seeing how thin I had become, she yanked me out, shivering and screaming, and told me I could either eat or she would beat me until I did. Outraged, I told her that since she never bothered to concern herself with any of my other problems, she could damn well stay out of this one. To my surprise, she let me loose and walked downstairs to the liquor cabinet. Eyeing me fiercely as she poured herself a vodka, she said, "I know what you're trying to do, you little bitch. You can die of starvation for all I care, but you'll never change me, never." I had lost again.

Having nothing else to try, I returned to drinking with gusto. More and more, I seemed to be the life of the party. After about a month of serious partying, I had gained back all the weight I had lost. Everyone was amazed at my incredible capacity for booze, a tolerance that I now attribute to heredity. Despite my burgeoning fame as a party animal, I managed to keep my grades steady and to present a good front to anyone who might question my "extracurricular" activities. My life at home, however, steadily worsened. Mother was a periodic alcoholic, alternating between heavy and moderate drinking, so that no steady escalation of her problem could be noticed. This cyclical nature of her disease prevented me from attributing her behavior to alcohol. Every time I considered that she had a drinking problem, she would stop for a while. Her heavier bouts with alcohol were usually precipitated by stress, and my father's departure was certainly stressful. However, it was difficult to estimate exactly how she felt at the time because she refused to discuss it with me, despite my frequent overtures toward communication. I was witness to her actions, however, and interpreted them to mean that she was just as much destroyed over the breakup of our family as I was. She returned to drinking alcoholically to the point of blatant drunkenness and frequent stumbling.

Until then, I had been accustomed to the less severe characteristics of Mother's behavior: her mood swings, her authoritarian inconsistencies, and her often childish actions. Rarely had I been exposed to the more stereotypical stumbling, vomiting, and passing out. Some alcoholics, including my mother at this stage, have a remarkable capacity for controlling their behavior when they are intoxicated. The body learns to compensate for the deluge of booze so well that it is often difficult to tell whether or not someone is drunk. Women, especially, learn to adapt their behavior to high levels of alcohol. The foolish behavior often ignored by society when the drunkard is a man is openly condemned when the drunkard is a woman. Oh, just think what she's doing to her family! Think of the children!"

I vividly remember my first Al-Anon meeting, which a friend took me to. I had told her that I just wanted to check it out, not the truth that my mother was an alcoholic. I was not yet ready to admit to my friend that my mother had a problem. I recall looking around the meeting room, desperately trying somehow to x-ray through the clothes of the people to see if they had whiplash marks. I was sure that everyone there who was the son or daughter of an alcoholic would be bruised up one side and down the other, or would be mentally retarded from having been locked in a closet for several months. Or maybe I had even seen them on "Donahue" or on the nightly news, talking about child abuse. To my sick disappointment, however, I found nothing unusual about their dress, manner, or speech; they were frighteningly normal. I listened intently to a speaker who told her story without shame or embarrassment. As others spoke, I found myself understanding what they were talking about and I began to want to share something of myself. But I quickly caught myself before my hand went up. No! I thought. I cannot air my feelings here. I sat with my head bowed in mortification and guilt. My mother was not the problem. I was! It was my own fault that I drank so much. I shouldn't blame my problems on my mother because I was too weak to admit my own.

I suddenly realized that someone else in the room had been crying desperately as she shared her experience with the group, and I had trouble trying to comprehend her words as she babbled through her tears. Finally, I managed to understand that she had been severely abused by her alcoholic father. See, I thought, these people are really crazy! My mother only hits me when I deserve it.

Then the woman said something about an attic where she had hidden to escape from her abusive father. Wait a minute, I thought, hadn't I hidden in the closet to escape from my mother? Revelation! Yes, I had, more than once. Yes, I did feel unloved. Yes, I felt that everything was my fault and that if only I had been a better person, Mother would have stopped drinking long ago. Yes, I probably did belong in that meeting. And I stayed.

The support I gained through the members of Al-Anon was indispensable to me as Mother's drinking worsened. I learned first of all what alcoholism really is and that I have no control over my mother's drinking, no matter how hard I try to manipulate her into quitting. I found this to be both a relief and a frustration. On the one hand, I was sick and tired of constantly trying to improve the situation; on the other hand, since I had previously devoted so much of my time to doing just that, I was afraid that I would now lose all reason to exist. I realized that in a sense my fear was valid; my only purpose in my family had been to try to keep it together. After my father left, my purpose vanished. My fairy-tale image of family was shattered. It was and always had been a fallacy. Why couldn't I just let go?

A Fairy Tale

The disintegration of my image of the perfect family was painful at first, but as it dissolved, so did its tenacious hold over me. A new independent me began to emerge. I finally realized that my existence was unique and separate from my family and that I had rights and could assert them. Unfortunately, however, rather than using my newfound assertiveness to better my relationship with my mother, I used it to aggravate her. If Mother acted aggressively toward me, I assumed that having rights meant the right to hit back. Gradually, years and years of unleashed hostility began to arise in me. I became increasingly more hostile to Mother, twisting Al-Anon philosophy to justify my revenge.

I also assumed that independence offered me a free ticket to drink. My perception of independence was pitiful: no concern for maturity, for personal pride, for a true sense of responsibility. Besides, I was in Al-Anon, and that would prevent me from developing a drinking problem of my own. This attitude actually kept my drinking reasonable for many months, until the changes alcohol caused in my life-style became apparent to me. I began again to feel grateful to the booze for the magic it worked. I did not lead the life of the typical high school kid. I had temporarily moved out of my house to live with my boyfriend, a gentleman by my standards, who opened doors for me and took me to all the best parties, not some sloppy football player who couldn't afford to take me to dinner and chewed with his mouth open. We went to all the best Miami bars, not the little dives for teenagers. All my friends were older, and successful, I thought, because they were on their own and worked hard and had fast cars.

As this new life became more and more precious to me, I began to fear that it would be taken away, just as my fairy-tale family had disappeared. This fear created an awkward sense of haste. I began to burn with life. I had to live fast, fast, fast—before it all disappeared. I had to stay out later. I had to go to all the best clubs, wear all the latest fashions, drive the best car, spend the most money. Most of all, I had to party the hardest and drink the most. I associated everything good in my life with the amount of alcohol I drank. Alcohol had saved me from depression and loneliness in junior high. Look what it was doing for me now! I felt that I had to be seen, to be noticed. I thrived on my narcissism and began thinking the world revolved around me and that I was doing it a great favor by not jumping off. I was doing all the right things, going to all the right places, partying with all the right people.

Never before had I felt accepted by others. But whom exactly they were accepting, I'll never know, because I had no clue to my identity. Today I can hardly imagine what insanity caused me to act so foolishly. Most foolish was to try cocaine at a party in order to appease several friends. While I had smoked pot occasionally in high school, I didn't enjoy it because I hated to smoke and associated pot and LSD with hippiedom. In short, it wasn't chic. I wanted something chic, something in, something beyond the scope of my high school peers. I agreed to snort a line of coke after the offerer told me that I would make a good coke addict. I'm not certain what he meant by good, but if he was implying that I possessed all the characteristics of a stereotypical coke "whore," then, unfortunately, he was correct. I snorted my first line. My impression was that the stuff was mediocre; I was probably too drunk to notice its effect on me. But it was chic, everyone had applauded me, and that was all that mattered, wasn't it? I wasn't just accepted by these people, I thought; they loved me! I was *in*.

And I would soon be in trouble deeper than I could ever have imagined.

Drugs were fun because they were bad. My group of socially deviant friends expected me to do them, so I did. Drug use among my friends didn't make me a criminal, it made me a hero. I became exceedingly arrogant, sure that what I was doing was right. Nothing pleased me more than to overhear one of my former high school friends whispering about me, "Remember how quiet and ugly she used to be? Look at her now. Just look at all those wild people she hangs around with! I heard she's a drug addict." Whoever was speaking would soften her voice whenever she said the words "drug addict" and her voice would assume a real expression of apocalyptic tragedy. Frankly, I thought the melodrama on my behalf was rather neat. If people had started crossing themselves and throwing garlic on me, I would have thoroughly enjoyed it. Drugs were bad. I was bad. And for a while, I liked being bad.

I simply had no clue as to the consequences of my actions when I started out. I didn't realize what drugs would do to me until it was too late for me to stop using coke, pills, and booze without help. Too late was after I had hurt everyone I knew and after I had transformed a beautiful, healthy girl into a crazed invalid, crippled by the disease of addiction.

For quite a while my exciting life-style was far too attractive for me to admit to its negative aspects. But in time I could no longer ignore certain events. I was broke and in debt to everyone I knew. Cocaine is expensive and I used a lot of it. And I needed a lot of vodka to help me come down off the coke. I also needed a supply of day drugs, as I called them: speed and diet pills for energy and weight control, codeine as needed for various aches and pains, sleeping pills to take the edge off the speed, and of course a multivitamin supplement, just in case. This daily diet was all washed down with about four to eight glasses of beer before I could go out and really party at night. As this regimen became a habit, I found that I couldn't function without it. I was going broke and found myself compromising my values to get the drugs I wanted. What I was using was losing its potency. I needed more and more just to get the same effects. Terrified of running out, I would stock my liquor cabinet with pills of every color of the rainbow, only to wake up in the morning to find that I had taken everything.

Aside from the financial difficulties, I initially received few signals that my behavior was out of control. Then I began to feel alienated from my group of friends, the bottom rungs of society. To be rejected by them left me nowhere to go except under the ladder. What began to separate me from them was my growing reputation as a coke whore who would do anything for drugs. I was no one's friend because I had used them all and would again when I wanted more drugs. I stole, I lied, I slept around. I lost my coolness, and my friends didn't want to hang around me anymore. Bars and discos and steamy Miami nights seemed glamorous until I came to again and again bent over the toilet with my nose bleeding. I still wanted more. I knew I was beginning to hurt, but I couldn't stop.

I cowered in the face of addiction and gradually turned into a morose, self-pitying little crybaby. It is ironic how I held so much egoistic pride in my accomplishments until things went awry, when I felt that I had suddenly become the victim of some evil force or lax angel. Life, I was convinced, was God's sick joke. In my self-centered way, I truly thought that I was the most pitiful, destitute creature on Earth, singled out by God for punishment. I used to imagine that someday a tragic movie would be made about me: I would appear at sunset wearing a long, white flowing gown with flowers in my hair. The camera would zoom in on my Camillesque face. My tears would be illuminated by soft, fading sunbeams, and maybe I would gracefully drift into the sea and be swallowed up by Mother Earth or turned into a mermaid. Everyone in the audience would cry. I did. I cried for days. I cried because I genuinely hated myself. My fantasies of stardom may have been silly, but all those damn tears were real, very real. I had no place to turn. No friends. No family. And no mother, because she suffered from the same disease that was destroying me.

Still, the only way I knew to medicate my sorrow was to take more drugs. I want drugs, and I deserve them because my life is so awful. You have them. Gimme! That was my attitude. If you can't give me family, or friends, or love, then give me my goddamned cocaine. And I have no doubt that I would have continued to use until I killed myself if I hadn't almost killed my best friend. I had turned her on to coke, how to snort it and how to shoot it. One day I watched her being carried away from work on a stretcher because she had shot too much and was going into convulsions. As they put her into the ambulance, I began to cry. A coworker approached and callously informed me that he wished it had been me on that stretcher instead of our friend. Immediately, all my childhood guilt resurfaced. He was right. I was awful and had been since the day I was born. My mother drank because of me, and now my friends were beginning to die because of me. Life had always hurt, but now I was doing the hurting. Suddenly, I imagined that my friend was my daughter, looking at me through tears because I had hurt her. I had become a hurter. I had become my mother.

"I'll get help," I said, and walked away.

But the fact was that I was a raging addict, and although my sentiments about quitting were genuine, I could not. Breaking the denial of an addict is extremely difficult, like breaking the Washington monument into little pieces with an ice pick. Often, it is broken in just that way, one little bit at a time. A frightening experience here, a confrontation with a friend there, over and over again until just the right person says just the right thing at just the right time. After I had lost all my money, my apartment, my boyfriend, and now my girlfriend, a talk with an old friend from Al-Anon was enough to push me over the edge of surrender. I told him my plight and that I thought maybe I ought to stop. Recovering in AA himself, he looked at me with a grin and said, "I've heard that before."

"How do you know I won't stop, you bastard! Who are you to try to predict my life, you high and mighty AA person? I'm not just your average run-of-the-mill coke addict, you know. I can do anything. I have before."

"Then why don't you seriously quit?" he asked.

Invincible little me! Capable of changing everything and everybody except everything and everybody I had ever really tried to change. I was really a powerless little fake, incapable of changing my mother, and incapable of changing myself. At least incapable of changing without help.

"Hi, my name is Angela. I am eighteen years old, and I am a drug addict and alcoholic." This was my first AA meeting; I had joined the ranks of the high and mighty AA people that I had previously detested so much. I hated them because they could do something I couldn't: they knew how to smile. I joined them because I too wanted to learn how to smile again. At that meeting, I saw many faces I had seen before, people I had seen at Al-Anon meetings who were children of alcoholics. I was again nothing out of the ordinary, just another addict who was the daughter of an alcoholic. Being in the seat of the addict myself helped me tremendously in understanding my mother. I realized that my life had been something of an illusion. All those things that I thought had been missing from my life—love, acceptance, warmth—were there. They were just hidden by the stench of alcohol. And the woman I had grown up with was not my mother but an alcoholic pretending to be my mother. My mother loved me, deep down. She also loved alcohol. Now I could understand and even sympathize. Love does not have to be apparent to be there. I loved my friend and did not mean to hurt her. Yet I had.

With a new sense of understanding for my mother, I moved back into her house, without telling her I was in AA. She knew very little of my problem. In fact, she refused to discuss alcohol at all because it was an obviously painful subject for her. Despite my newfound understanding from the addict's point of view, I still had difficulty relating to her. As I became sober, I questioned why she couldn't do the same and began to consider her as weak and undeserving of my respect. I, at least, was trying to better myself. Communication between us was superficial at best: "How was your day?" (not that either of us cared) or "Terrible weather we're having, isn't it?"

After three months, I finally decided that I would move out for good, finish high school, and eventually go to college. I called a long-lost friend from freshman year of high school. Surprisingly, she was glad to hear from me and suggested that we go out to lunch. I spent the rest of the summer catching up and trying to make amends to the people I had hurt. I devoted more time in church-basement AA meetings, bleeding my heart out to other addicts, than I would have thought possible. I searched and searched for Angela, but never found her. What I did find was the most remarkable mixture of personalities I have ever known.

Defining me was like trying to define empty space—impossible! But I learned to accept myself for whoever it is that I am, and that acceptance is part of the magic of AA. One doesn't have to change, just to accept what's there and work with that. Nor should one try to change others. I vowed to welcome whatever comes down my road and to let my mother do as she pleased. Yet also I gently let her know that I was hurt by her actions and that I wished she would stop drinking. But I can't force her to do anything.

Mother never stopped. She slapped and kicked me when I told her that I wanted to move out again. I just reminded myself that her abuse was nothing new and that it had nothing to do with her love for me.

Nearly five years later, I am now in my final year of college and my fifth year of sobriety. AA and Al-Anon have guided me through these years. I had to learn to love others and to realize that I too am lovable. Yet I still blush when my boyfriend tells me he loves me. Something inside still tells me that I am no good and not worthy of his love. But I am learning to believe him. It still pains me tremendously to go home and find my mother drunk. I don't like home. It holds too many painful memories. Most of all, it houses a woman, my own shadow, too afraid to stop.

Friends often ask me what keeps me from giving up. Life, for one thing. An I'm hung-over-and-bent-over-the-toilet-again fear. Faith keeps me from giving up. A sense of ardent spirituality fills my life today where before it was empty. I believe there is someone watching over me. I am not alone. Most of all, I now believe it is possible to change if you choose a positive, realistic goal and ask the right people for help.

My life is my own example. From a destitute addict to a healthy, happy participant in life, I have found my Prince Charming, and maybe someday we'll even have a castle. It isn't always easy, but with support, I've at least gained the courage to try. Every fairy tale I ever read as a kid had a happy ending, and I'll be damned if mine doesn't too.

GRANDFATHER

Mary Louise

I learned a lot from my grandfather: that love is sometimes expressed gruffly, that work can be a source of pride and commitment, and that you can respect someone even if he or she is an alcoholic. My grandfather was a physician, the kind of man who is still remembered clearly seventeen years after his death, even by casual professional acquaintances. From him I gained my view of medicine, that sense of intimate attachment between patient and doctor.

But my earliest legacy was to feel, as a child, the freezing loneliness and isolation of alcoholism. From the time we children were very small, visiting Grandpa after dinner meant seeing him in his room. In the unlighted front hall a long wooden staircase spiraled upstairs. As we climbed through the dark on the bare stairs, we could see that the door at the top was pulled almost closed. Leaking around the door was enough light from the bedside lamp to find our way. But even then it seemed like such a long way away. He would sit in the room alone, on hot nights with a window air conditioner, on cold nights with a small portable heater, but every night with a bottle of scotch. He would drink there from the end of the evening meal until bedtime, although less, I suppose, on those nights when he was on call.

All this was mysterious. No one said anything about Grandpa drinking, but I knew, even before I was old enough to go to school, that he was in great pain. He was always so glad to see us, but there was little warmth in his life. Even the spark of greeting and love seemed insufficient to warm him. Only later did I realize that the secret closet in the dining room was filled with cases of scotch, first noticed because I thought the wooden boxes were very fine stuff and I wanted one to store all my childhood treasures in. My grandmother couldn't understand why I wanted one of those "nasty" things, and I couldn't understand then why she was so upset.

Away from the house, at his office, my grandfather was the opposite of an isolated, lonely man. In his work he was confident, very skilled, and much loved by his patients. As a child I enjoyed making rounds with him and learned, as children learn, indirectly and without perfect understanding, that he was happier there than anywhere else. His public life was filled with many rewards and professional honors. As my own medical career began, I was so proud to be his granddaughter and hear his peers remember him with affection and respect. I couldn't tell then if any of them knew that he drank every night. The drinking certainly didn't affect his work as far as they were concerned.

In the South where I grew up, children learn their social lessons from their elders in no uncertain terms. We were taught the right way to act, what things little girls do and don't do. But much of that was indirect and oblique. I recall asking my mother, not a southern woman, why Grandpa never came downstairs after dinner. She answered that he simply preferred to sit upstairs, and then sadly added that he and my grandmother weren't very happy together. As children do, I began to notice, out of the corner of my eye, things that would seem to support what she had said. My grandmother often had an angry, tight-lipped expression on her face. She never said anything much about our grandfather's drinking, though we heard in great detail the shame of it all that our great-uncle drank so much and was such a trial to his wife, my grandfather's sister.

My father, an only child, grew up caught between these two —my grandmother disapproving silently but destructively and my grandfather withdrawn and isolated. My father too became a physician, but not the general practitioner my grandfather was. Rather, he was a radiologist. In many matters, my father was a mixture of my grandfather's traits combined with characteristics he cultivated as a means of being as different as possible from his father. He chose a very intellectual branch of medicine, as opposed to the personally oriented style my grandfather had. My father never overtly seemed to struggle with alcohol but was addicted to cigarettes. This dependency, which he could not stop despite clear and strong warnings, eventually killed him. He died of lung and pancreatic cancer, this physician who did a chest X-ray on himself every year to look for trouble but still could not stop smoking.

In our own generation, this struggle continues amongst my brothers and sisters and myself. We grew up in a society that encouraged social drinking. If addiction is predisposition plus opportunity, then all of us presumably had both well before we were teenagers. We all knew of bars that would sell alcohol to any minor tall enough to see over the counter, no questions asked. In addition, any problem brought on by alcohol, like getting thrown into jail to cool off after a fight, was in some curious way a badge of honor rather than shame, at least for boys. Southern tradition is notoriously accepting of the "wild boy." In that context, it is often hard to say whether one is drinking too much or being hurt by drinking. Societal acceptance reinforces our own denial. Of my four siblings, one brother no longer drinks at all. One sister and one brother continue to drink regularly, but I can't tell how safely. My other sister and I have both at different times in our life had to confront ourselves painfully, honestly, and fearfully about our drinking. We know that in the right circumstances, without support or out of despair, we could become alcoholics. Instead, we struggle to learn to eat and drink in a way that is nurturing and not addictive.

What I carry from my past into my work with patients struggling with chemical dependencies is a clear sense that it could be me, or my father, or my grandfather, or my siblings. I don't have in the least a sense of being judgmental, of feeling distant from them in the way so many health-care providers are toward alcoholics. I am myself so human too. The pain and suffering caused by the disease of alcoholism are at times almost overwhelming. But I am so moved and rewarded when a patient comes back to show me his pin for one year of sobriety, or tells me how much he enjoys being in the same job for a year, or how grateful he is to have a second chance to redeem a marriage. My grandfather's addiction was used as a weapon or a punishment in our family. My father on his deathbed, jealous of the closeness I shared with my grandfather, turned to me, trying to break my illusions, and said, scornfully, "Well, you know your grandfather was an alcoholic." But he either forgot—or never learned—what my grandfather had taught me.

It didn't matter. I loved my grandfather and he loved me.

Acknowledgments

I am most indebted to the men and women who contributed their narratives to this book and who patiently bore my nagging and editing. Jeffrey Laign was very helpful, especially with the bibliography and list of associations. Friends and associates, among them Walter Berkov, James Carozza, Shelley Finn, Alexia K. Hayes, Jon Lehman, Shiela McHatton, Andrew Meacham, Joan Sandison, and John Caswell Smith, gave valuable advice and other assistance. Nicholas Basbanes and Ann Murray of the *Worcester Telegram* encouraged me from the beginning. And Michael Pietsch of Harmony Books has been a thoughtful and considerate editor.

Contributors to this book do not speak for AA, Al-Anon, Adult Children of Alcoholics, or any other organization or group.

Suggested Readings

Adult Children of Alcoholics. New York: Al-Anon Family Groups, 1979.

The Adult Children of Alcoholics Syndrome: From Discovery to Recovery by Wayne Kritsberg. Pompano Beach: Health Communications, 1985.

AL-ANON Family Groups. New York, Al-Anon Family Group Headquarters, 1984. Al-Anon's basic text, first published in 1966.

Adult Children of Alcoholics by Janet Geringer Woititz. Pompano Beach: Health Communications, 1983. A basic study of characteristics common among Adult Children of Alcoholics (ACOAs). Highly recommended.

AL-ANON Twelve Steps and Twelve Traditions. New York: Al-Anon Family Group Headquarters, 1981. The text of the AA book *Twelve Steps and Twelve Traditions*, appropriately rewritten for family, friends, and colleagues of alcoholics.

ALATEEN—Hope for Children of Alcoholics. New York: Al-Anon Family Group Headquarters, 1973.

Alcohol: Use and Abuse in America by Jack Mendelson and Nancy K. Mello. Boston: Little, Brown, 1985. A detailed study of alcohol in American life.

Alcoholics Anonymous. New York: Alcoholics Anonymous World Services, 1976. The "big book" of AA, first published in 1939.

Alcoholism: The Genetic Inheritance by Kathleen Whalen FitzGerald. New York: Doubleday, 1988. On alcoholism as a family disease, not a moral weakness, by a recovering alcoholic. Stresses that the whole family needs help.

Another Chance: Hope and Health for the Alcoholic Family by Sharon Wegscheider-Cruse. Palo Alto: Science and Behavior Books, 1981.

Bradshaw on the Family: A Revolutionary Way of Self-Discovery by John Bradshaw. Pompano Beach: Health Communications, 1987.

Becoming Your Own Parent: The Solution for Adult Children of Alcoholics and Other Dysfunctional Families by Dennis Wholly. New York: Doubleday, 1988. An ACOA and a recovering alcoholic, Wholly tells, through the words of fourteen participants in a self-help group, how the group becomes the new family of the dysfunctional. Highly recommended.

Changes. Pompano Beach: Health Communications. A self-help magazine for dysfunctional families, including alcoholic, published every other month.

Children of Alcoholics: A Guide for Parents, Educators and Therapists by Robert J. Ackerman. New York: Simon and Schuster, 1983.

Children of Alcoholics: A Bibliography and Resource Guide by Robert J. Ackerman. Pompano Beach: Health Communications, 1987.

Children of Alcoholism: A Survivor's Manual by Judith S. Seixas and Geraldine Youcha. New York: Harper and Row, 1985.

DATA: The Brown University Digest of Addiction Theory and Application. Published by Manisses Communications Group, P.O. Box 3357, Wayland Square, Providence, RI 02906-0357. Publishes summaries in lay language of recent articles in professional journals; under the supervision of the Brown University Center for Alcohol and Addiction Studies.

Family Secrets: Life Stories of Adult Children of Alcoholics by Rachel V. New York: Harper and Row, 1987.

Grandchildren of Alcoholics: Another Generation of Co-dependency by Ann W. Smith. Pompano Beach: Health Communications, 1988. Gives recognition to the problems of second-generation co-dependents affected by family alcoholism.

Growing in the Shadow: Children of Alcoholics edited by Robert J. Ackerman. Pompano Beach: Health Communications, 1986.

Healing a Broken Heart: 12 Steps of Recovery for Adult Children of Alcoholics by Kathleen W. Pompano Beach: Health Communications, 1988. Based on the program of AA modified for ACOAs.

Suggested Readings

Healing the Child Within: Discovery and Recovery for Adult Children of Dysfunctional Families by Charles Whitefield. Pompano Beach: Health Communications, 1987.

Home Before Dark by Susan Cheever. Boston: Houghton Mifflin, 1984. The novelist's frank but loving remembrance of her alcoholic, bisexual father, one of this country's foremost American writers of fiction. Highly recommended.

Hope: New Choices and Recovery Strategies for Adult Children of Alcoholics by Emily Marlin. New York: Harper and Row, 1987. On how the ACOA can reexamine the past, reform the present, and reaffirm the future, written by the president of the New York Association for Marriage and Family Counseling. Includes self-tests, sources of help, and bibliography. Highly recommended.

How to Stay Sober: Recovery Without Religion by James Christopher. Buffalo: Prometheus Books, 1988. Outlines an alternative to AA that has led to the founding of new self-help groups nationwide.

I'll Quit Tomorrow by Vernon E. Johnson. San Francisco: Harper and Row, 1980. Explains a program somewhat different from that of AA, especially in stressing the need for intervention by family, friends, and associates to lead the alcoholic to an awareness of his or her problem, and emphasizes the alcoholic's lack of self-will and self-esteem when hitting bottom. Highly recommended.

Intervention: How to Help Someone Who Doesn't Want Help by Vernon Johnson. Minneapolis: The Johnson Institute, 1988.

Keeping Secrets by Suzanne Somers. New York: Warner Books, 1987. The candidly told story of the secrets of the actress and her family as they lived with, coped with, and recovered from the alcoholism of her father and siblings.

A Life Worth Waiting For: Messages from a Survivor by Dwight Lee Wolter. Minneapolis: CompCare Publishers, 1989.

Natural History of Alcoholism: Causes, Patterns, and Paths to Recovery by George Vaillant. Cambridge: Harvard University Press, 1983. A major scientific study incorporating findings since World War II. Highly recommended.

Potato Chips for Breakfast by Cynthia Scales. Rockaway: Quotidian, 1986. A teenager on her material and emotional deprivations in an alcoholic home.

Recovery: A Guide for Adult Children of Alcoholics by Herbert L. Gravitz and Julie D. Bowden. New York: Simon and Schuster, 1985. Commonly asked questions and commonsense answers.

Twelve Steps and Twelve Traditions. New York: Alcoholics Anonymous World Services, 1980.

Whiskey's Song: An Explicit Story of Surviving in an Alcoholic Home by Mitzi Chandler. Pompano Beach: Health Communications, 1987. Powerful verses on the emotional effects of parental alcoholism.

A number of these and other books are now available on audiotapes from Health Communications, Enterprise Center, 3201 SW 15th Street, Deerfield Beach, Florida 33442 (formerly located at Pompano Beach, Florida).

Organizations Helpful to Alcoholics and ACOAs

AL-ANON FAMILY GROUP HEADQUARTERS, PO Box 862, Midtown Station, New York, NY 10018-0862. Provides information about self-help group meetings, modeled on AA, for family, friends, and associates of alcoholics. Distributes literature and videotapes.

ALATEEN, PO Box 862, Midtown Station, New York, NY 10018-0862. Sponsored by Al-Anon, provides information on group meetings for teenage children of alcoholics.

ALCOHOL AND DRUG PROBLEMS FOUNDATION, 444 North Capitol Street, NW, Suite 706, Hall of the States, Washington, DC 20001.

ALCOHOLICS ANONYMOUS, Box 459, Grand Central Station, New York, NY 10163. Provides information on self-help group meetings of alcoholics and distributes AA literature and other aids.

AMERICAN COUNCIL ON ALCOHOLISM, 8501 LaSalle Road, Suite 301, Towson, MD 21204.

CO-DEPENDENTS ANONYMOUS, PO Box 5508, Glendale, AZ 85304-5508.

HAZELDEN FOUNDATION, Box 11, Center City, MN 55012. Publishes literature and conducts programs paralleling the AA program.

NATIONAL ASSOCIATION FOR CHILDREN OF ALCOHOLICS, 31706 Coast Highway, Suite 201, South Laguna, CA 92677-3044. A clearinghouse for information.

NATIONAL ASSOCIATION OF NATIVE AMERICAN CHILDREN OF ALCOHOLICS, Seattle Indian Health Board, PO Box 3364, Seattle, WA 98104.

NATIONAL BLACK ALCOHOLISM COUNCIL, 417 South Dearborn Street, Suite 700, Chicago, IL 60605.

NATIONAL CLEARINGHOUSE FOR ALCOHOL AND DRUG INFORMATION, PO Box 234, Rockville, MD 20852. Prepares and distributes reference materials.

NATIONAL COUNCIL ON ALCOHOLISM, 12 West 21st Street, New York, NY 10010. Central office of nationwide affiliates; provides information.

NATIONAL INSTITUTE ON ALCOHOL ABUSE AND ALCOHOLISM, Parklawn Building, 5600 Fishers Lane, Rockville, MD 20852. Distributes materials on alcoholism and treatment programs.

SECULAR ORGANIZATION FOR SOBRIETY, Box 15781, North Hollywood, CA 91615-5781. Established by the author of *How To Stay Sober*.

The 12 Steps of AA

1. We admitted we were powerless over alcohol—that our lives had become unmanageable.

2. Came to believe that a Power greater than ourselves could restore us to sanity.

3. Made a decision to turn our will and our lives over to the care of God *as we understood Him*.

4. Made a searching and fearless moral inventory of ourselves.

5. Admitted to God, to ourselves, and to another human being the exact nature of our wrongs.

6. Were entirely ready to have God remove all these defects of character.

7. Humbly asked Him to remove our shortcomings.

8. Made a list of all persons we had harmed, and became willing to make amends to them all.

9. Made direct amends to such people wherever possible, except when to do so would injure them or others.

10. Continued to take personal inventory and when we were wrong promptly admitted it.

11. Sought through prayer and meditation to improve

our conscious contact with God *as we understood Him*, praying only for knowledge of His will for us and the power to carry that out.

12. Having had a spiritual awakening as the result of these steps, we tried to carry this message to alcoholics, and to practice these principles in all our affairs.

These 12 Steps have been adopted by Al-Anon with only the change "alcoholics" to "others" in Step 12. Reprinted here with permission of Alcoholics Anonymous World Services, Inc.